# *The Soviet Communist Party*

Also by Ronald J. Hill:
*Soviet Political Elites: The Case of Tiraspol* (1977)
*Soviet Politics, Political Science and Reform* (1980)
*The Soviet Union: Politics, Economics and Society:
    From Lenin to Gorbachev* (1985)

# The Soviet Communist Party

Third Edition

RONALD J. HILL
*Fellow of Trinity College, Dublin*

PETER FRANK
*Senior Lecturer in Government, University of Essex*

Boston
ALLEN & UNWIN, INC.
London        Sydney

**Allen & Unwin, Inc.,**
**8 Winchester Place, Winchester, MA 01890**

George Allen & Unwin (Publishers) Ltd,
40 Museum Street, London WC1A 1LU, UK

George Allen & Unwin (Publishers) Ltd,
Park Lane, Hemel Hempstead, Herts HP2 4TE, UK

George Allen & Unwin Australia Pty Ltd,
8 Napier Street, North Sydney, NSW 2060, Australia


First published in 1981
Second edition 1983
Third edition 1986

---

**Library of Congress Cataloging-in-Publication Data**

Hill, Ronald J.
    The Soviet Communist Party
Bibliography: P.
Includes index.
1. Kommunisticheskaia Partiia Sovetskogo Soiuza.
2. Soviet Union—Politics and Government—1953–1982.
I. Frank, Peter (Peter John), 1934-      . II. Title
JN6598.K7H53        1986        324.247'075        86–13993
ISBN 0–04–497024–2 (pbk)

---

**British Library Cataloguing in Publication Data**

Hill, Ronald J.
    The Soviet Communist Party—3rd ed.
1. Kommunisticheskaia partiia Sovetskogo
Soiuza
I. Title        II. Frank, Peter
324.247'075          JN6598.K7

ISBN 0–04–497024–2

---

Manufactured in the United States of America

# Contents

# Preface

In this book, we hope to provide the student of Soviet politics with an up-to-date picture of the Communist Party of the Soviet Union (CPSU) and its role in that country's political system. The approach reflects the change that has taken place in the study of communist politics in the past fifteen years, being essentially analytical and descriptive, rather than historical or legalistic. The book should thus be seen as a complement, rather than a competitor, to Leonard Schapiro's masterly 'biography' of the party, which indeed it would be pretentious to try to emulate. In this book, therefore, history is introduced only when it is needed for giving a perspective against which to judge recent phenomena.

It is in the nature of political systems to change—a law to which even the Soviet Union is not immune. Hence, inevitably, new statistics are likely to become available, new structures may be introduced, new personalities will probably come to prominence perhaps even by the time the book appears. And even though it is the fruit of many years' study of Soviet politics, there is a sense in which such a fruit can never be fully ripe, as our views and interpretations change along with circumstances. Ten years ago, different points would have been made: a decade hence, perhaps Soviet politics will again look somewhat different, although it is a safe guess that the CPSU will still be playing its central role in the system.

We wish to acknowledge our intellectual debt to many colleagues in numerous institutions, and to the staffs of libraries whose assistance over many years has been invaluable. We are thankful for the support of colleagues in our respective institutions, and Hill is particularly grateful to Trinity College, Dublin, and St. Antony's College, Oxford, for the benefit of a fruitful sabbatical term spent in the latter institution while working on this book.

Finally, we are proud to be able to dedicate the book to the memory of the late Alfred Dressler (1916–64), an inspiring teacher and friend in the University of Leeds, without whose guidance and encouragement in our undergraduate and graduate-student days neither of us might be where we are today, and this book might never have been written.

R.J.H.
P.F.

# Preface to the Second Edition

The authors have been highly gratified by the general warmth of their professional colleagues' response to the first edition of this textbook, and by the knowledge that students of Soviet politics, for whom the book was principally written, have found it useful.

The departure of Leonid Brezhnev from the Soviet political scene occurred with his death, on November 10, 1982, as this revised edition was being prepared for the press. That long-expected event, and the death in January 1982 of the powerful *éminence grise* Mikhail A. Suslov, emphasizes the validity of the disclaimer included in our original preface: new names may have appeared by the time the book is available in print. The situation remains fluid as Yuri Andropov attempts to consolidate his political authority, and this is but one reason a complete revision is not being undertaken at present.

In preparing this revised edition, we have updated statistics and references where possible, corrected factual and typographical inaccuracies that have come to our notice, and reformulated certain points in the light of recent publications and further deliberation. We are glad to acknowledge the value of the comments of reviewers and users of the book, and we have done our best to meet their criticisms. We, the authors, of course bear complete responsibility for what remains.

R.J.H.
P.F.

# Preface to the Third Edition

The accession to power of Mikhail Gorbachev in March 1985, in succession to Yuri Andropov and then Konstantin Chernenko, signaled the transfer of power to a new generation of Kremlin leaders, confirmed by the personnel changes introduced in subsequent months and at the Twenty-Seventh CPSU Congress in March 1986. It remains to be seen what significant changes, if any, this fifth leadership generation will make to the structures and functioning of the Soviet system as it approaches its eighth decade.

The time is not yet ripe for a fresh assessment of the party and its role; yet, there is a clear need to revise this book in the light of the substantial changes that have taken place since the spring of 1983. Statistical and personnel data have been updated where appropriate, references to the party program and rules have been amended in accordance with the 1986 version of those documents, further amendments have been made to the text, and the bibliography has been expanded to take recent research into account and to provide fresh material for the benefit of students.

Soviet politics appears to have entered a more dynamic and interesting phase of development; the authors hope this book will continue to be of help in attempting to understand what remains, after all, an alien and perplexing political system.

R.J.H.
P.F.

*The Soviet Communist Party*

# CHAPTER 1

# The Party in the Soviet System

The Communist Party of the Soviet Union (CPSU) is by far the most important political institution in that country. Indeed, it has strong claims for recognition as one of the most powerful political institutions in any country in the world. Founded in 1898 at the Minsk Congress (still referred to as the First Congress, even though after it the party existed more in the mind than in reality), the Russian Social Democratic Workers' Party split in 1903 into two wings: the Bolsheviks, led by Lenin, and the Mensheviks, under Martov. Although attempts were made in subsequent years to reunite the competing factions, notably in 1906, for all practical purposes they led separate existences, divided by clashes of personality and by more fundamental doctrinal differences over the appropriate road toward the socialist revolution, and over the time-scale on which a revolutionary Marxist party should operate. It was the more militant, more politically sensitive Lenin who propelled the Bolshevik wing into revolution in the autumn of 1917, seizing power from the Provisional Government in a virtually bloodless coup on 25 October (see Schapiro, 1970, chs. 1–9).

Thereupon, the Bolshevik wing of the party—which in March 1918 changed its name to the Russian Communist Party (and in 1952 to CPSU)—became the ruling party in Russia and took on the task of leading the society toward socialism and communism. Initially, power was shared with the leftists of the Socialist Revolutionary Party, but this lasted a mere three months, and no party organization apart from that of the Bolsheviks survived the Civil War. Since then, the CPSU has enjoyed a political monopoly.

The party today sees itself as the 'tried and tested militant vanguard of the Soviet people,' the 'leading and guiding force of Soviet society' (*Rules*, Prologue). Its role has developed to that of leader: it was referred to as the *vozhd'* (Leader, Duce, Führer) by Brezhnev and by some writers; also as *rukovoditel'* (leader), 'organizing and leading force,' 'the

1

leading and directing force in the state and in the whole society' (for these descriptions, see *XXIII s"ezd*, I, p. 84; Paskar', 1974, p. 78; Tikhomirov, 1975, p. 77; *XXV s"ezd*, I, p. 87; Shapko *et al.*, 1977, pp. 4, 5). Other concepts that express the same notion tell us a little more about precisely what this role is supposed to entail: 'co-ordinator,' 'catalyst,' 'accelerator,' 'organizer,' 'tutor' (see Babii *et al.*, 1976, pp. 421, 436; Chekharin, 1977a, p. 18); or even, in one sentence that conveys a number of images: 'The CPSU is the directing, inspiring, mobilizing, organizing and leading force in Soviet society' (Shabanov, 1969a, p. 27). But whatever word or phrase is used, the party's central position in society is implied. Indeed, the 1977 USSR Constitution (Article 6) acknowledges the party's position as the 'nucleus' of the political system. One Soviet writer has even referred to 'our party's monopoly in exercising the leading role in relation to the Soviet state' (Shabanov, 1969a, p. 33). It has, as numerous writers have stated, an effective monopoly of political decision-making in the Soviet Union, and its influence covers every aspect of a Soviet citizen's life, whether he is directly aware of it or not. So pervasive is the party's influence that the whole system has been characterized as a 'partocracy' (Avtorkhanov, 1966). In the words of one Soviet scholar, the leading role of the party is 'the beginning and the crowning point, the alpha and the omega' in the process of establishing and developing socialist democracy (Shabanov, 1969a, p. 6).

The CPSU possesses a number of characteristics that define its position in Soviet society.

### The Party's Uniqueness

As noted, the CPSU is the only political party in the Soviet Union. This is an elementary point, but it is for many writers the essential point. Quite obviously, it places the party in a very special position in the political system, different from that occupied by parties in competitive polities, and even somewhat different from the position of the Communist Party in countries like Poland, the German Democratic Republic, and Czechoslovakia, where other parties are involved in the process of government, alongside (rather than in opposition to) the communists (see Nagy, 1981).

This unique position means, most fundamentally, that the CPSU has no rivals for power. It is a permanently ruling party, its tenure of office limited only by the remote probability of accidents of history: revolution, military coup, overthrow by foreign intervention, or (possible, but unlikely) a deliberate 'abdication' of political monopoly, such as Dubček attempted in Czechoslovakia in 1968, and as was called for more recently in Poland (Wiatr, 1982).

In principle, this uniqueness can be of great benefit to a party, in radically influencing the type of policies that it can introduce. It does not have to justify its every action before an opposition, formally institutionalized in parliament and willing to take its place in power. It can, if it wishes, largely ignore public opinion, as indeed the CPSU has done over the years. It can pursue a constant policy, without the creation of 'political footballs' (such as nationalization and denationalization of industry, or private versus public education or hospitals), which occasionally happens in competitive systems. But it can also sharply switch policy, from one extreme to another, without the loss of face that a governing party in a pluralist system would suffer: the sudden pact between Hitler and Stalin in September 1939 is the most notorious example in Soviet history.

These features can greatly assist a single party like the CPSU in devising policies that will achieve its stated goals and promote its own self-preservation.

In fact, notwithstanding the horrifying social and political costs, the Soviet one-party system has impressive material achievements to its credit, most notably the social, economic, and industrial transformation that was initiated in the late 1920s with the Five Year Plans, and the heroic performance of the Soviet forces in the Second World War. The abolition of illiteracy and the spread of education, together with the universal provision of health care and other welfare services, also rank as major positive benefits brought about under that system. This experience suggests that such a political system may be a suitable instrument for policy-making in a relatively simple society with one or two overriding goals to which all else is subordinated: economic development, welfare provision, winning a war. Indeed, that is the assumption behind the assertion by many leaders of developing countries that democracy is a luxury that their society cannot afford (see Raymond Aron's comment in 'Can the party . . . ,' 1967, p. 171). It may also help to explain the attraction of one-party rule in developing states: the fact that the single-party system has flourished in the twentieth century is ample testimony to the benefits it can bring, at least as perceived by its leaders, and the CPSU leadership undoubtedly appreciates this. (However, the association with one-party rule of the military coup as a standard means of changing rulers in certain parts of the world points to a further weakness in such a system.)

What is by no means certain is that a single party is the ideal instrument for ensuring the all-round development and smooth running of a complex, modern, sophisticated, and educated society. If the task of the political system is to produce policies that permit and encourage the development of the country's potential and to resolve the conflicts inherent in the society, then it may be that a lively political debate is likely to produce a wider range of acceptable and effective policy options. On top of that, opposition and the threat of defeat may force governments to adopt policies that are acceptable to a broader mass of citizens than might otherwise be the case: hence, they lead to less disruption of the orderly functioning of society and are 'better' for that reason. For example, it might be argued that Stalin's collectivization of agriculture, with its creation of a catastrophic famine in 1931, could probably not be attempted in a liberal democracy because it would be unacceptable. Against that, however, one needs only to point to the fall of the British Conservative government in 1974, after the chaos caused by the three-day working week, or the dogged persistence of Margaret Thatcher's administration during its first years in office, for evidence that governing parties in pluralist systems do not always trim their sails and instead pursue what they perceive to be 'the national interest,' even though unpopular and 'unacceptable.'

In any case, the Soviet response is that bargaining and compromise in order to win acceptability masks the class essense of capitalist society and simply reflects the pragmatic approach of bourgeois liberalism, which allows society to drift aimlessly (Kerimov, 1979, pp. 119–22.) In the 1930s, certain things had to be done, and as quickly as possible, in order for the Soviet system to survive. Letting things drift according to whatever happens to be acceptable at a given time leads to chaos. 'Spontaneity,' said Khrushchev, 'is the deadliest enemy of all' (quoted in Brumberg, 1962, p. 626). The whole point about the Communist Party, they say, is that it has a goal for society: it aims to bring about communism, a society that will not develop spontaneously but 'arises as the result of the conscious and deliberate efforts of the working people' (Shevtsov, 1978, p. 45, quoting the 1961 party program). Communism is an ideal type of society defined in outline in the ideology. Here we have the second distinctive characteristic of the CPSU: it has a special relationship with Marxism-Leninism.

### The Party and the Ideology

The CPSU justifies its own existence in terms of its understanding of the ideology, whose nature has been identified by Soviet and Western writers alike as one of the most distinctive features of the political system. It was an element in the 'totalitarian model' of Soviet politics (see Friedrich and Brzezinski, 1966, p. 22 and ch. 7), and one writer went so far as to depict the system as 'an ideology in power' (Wolfe, 1969). The ideology is based on the voluminous writings of Marx, Engels, and Lenin, although it is more than simply their collected works (Lane, 1976, p. 28). Soviet writers, as one might expect, stress Lenin's contribution to the theory. 'Leninism,' according to a leading party scholar, 'is a new and higher stage of Marxism, its creative continuation in the changed historical conditions of imperialism and proletarian revolutions, of mankind's transition from capitalism to socialism and communism . . . Lenin's theory of the socialist revolution is a major contribution to scientific communism' (Chekharin, 1977b, pp. 31–2).

Marxism-Leninism is said to embody scientific truths about human society, laws of development that are true in the same sense as the laws of physics are true: they are universally applicable. Marxism-Leninism is described as 'a universal scientific theory, which is constantly developing and being enriched by the experience of the workers' struggle for socialism in the whole world' (Shakhnazarov, 1972, p. 95).

Moreover, the CPSU claims that it, and it alone, clearly and correctly understands those truths. This is an important point. Individuals, no matter how much they study the works that form the basis of the ideology, can at best attain a 'subjective' interpretation, which is liable to error: only the party as an entity can reach correct conclusions. This monopoly of ideological wisdom is a feature of the CPSU that again distinguishes it from parties in pluralist systems, which by and large reject the very notion of 'truth' in political philosophy and adopt instead a more pragmatic, relativist view of politics and ideas, as Soviet observers have correctly noted (Kerimov, 1979, pp. 117–22). This characteristic gives the CPSU the moral right to rule: 'It is precisely this quality, together with others, that permits and obliges the Communist Party to take upon itself the responsibility for the fate of the people' (Ukrainets, 1976, p. 13).

Thus, the party's special relationship with the ideology justifies its position and role in the system, which is to devise policies for developing society toward communism. Because of this special ideological insight, the party claims to devise policies imbued with scientific truth. In the authoritative words of the late Mikhail Suslov, for many years regarded as the ideologist of the Politburo (1978, p. 23):

> The policy of the CPSU is strictly scientific. It is built on a profound knowledge of the laws of social development, and it comprehensively takes into account the various conditions of the country's internal life, and also the whole system of international relations.

This understanding, as Brezhnev once expressed it, permits the party to predict trends, to work out the 'true' political course, and to avoid 'errors' and 'subjective decisions' (*XXIV s"ezd*, I, p. 127). It also follows, since these policies are 'scientifically true,' that they must be applied without question. Any alternative policies—be they bourgeois, dissident, nationalist, or based on religious views—are by definition 'false'; that is, deemed inappropriate for achieving communism; they must be opposed, by all the authority of the principle of democratic centralism (see Chapter 3), including subordination of the minority to the majority, and the binding nature of decisions taken centrally. However, the ideology contains no blueprint of the future communist society, whose features have to be identified as they appear (and the party, of course, has the responsibility for recognizing them), so the ideology and the assertions about it give the party a great deal of power in policy-making and implementation.

The relationship between Marxism-Leninism, the CPSU, and policy therefore reveals how powerful the ideology is as an instrument for legitimizing the party and its policies, whatever they may be. In its capacity to relate policies to the ideology, the CPSU has an impressive and valuable flexibility, which enables it continually to justify its policies and hence maintain its rule. Thus, Marxism-Leninism sustains rule by the CPSU.

The flexibility in policy that is permitted by the ideology is assisted by the fact that the ideological heritage of Marxism-Leninism is very broad in its compass and can be interpreted in more than one way. Or, to express it differently, there are writings in the Marxist-Leninist classics that can be used to support markedly different broad policy trends. So, if certain strands in Lenin's thought could be used by Stalin to justify repression, as Schapiro (1970, pp. 286–7) has argued, other strands can be used as a powerful tool by reformers and liberalizers in the Soviet Union (Hough and Fainsod, 1979, pp. 107–9, 560, 572). Indeed, it has been imperative for those engaged in leadership changes in the 1980s to appeal to Lenin in order to win their own legitimacy, so important is the ideological heritage in supporting the whole system. However, its very complexity and flexibility, not to say ambiguity, render it an ideal tool for being used in that way.

A further vital element in the nature of the ideology strengthens its significance for the party and the whole system: it is itself not constant but is subject to change and development, by such devices as reinterpreting existing concepts and introducing fresh ones. Thus, by defining 'socialism' as consisting, in essence, of state ownership of the means of production, distribution and exchange, the Soviet Union has been able to claim that what it has is indeed socialism—'real socialism' or 'existing socialism,' as it came to be called in the late 1970s (Ponomarëv, 1979a, 1979b). In 1961 Khrushchev introduced the new concept of the 'state of the whole people' or 'all-people's state,' reflecting an attempt to adapt the ideology to changing conditions, as Soviet society moved beyond the stage of the dictatorship of the proletariat further along the road toward communism (see Kanet, 1968). More recently, under Brezhnev, the major innovation was the concept of 'developed' or 'mature' socialism, which is still being explored and expounded at length, in the writings of scholars and politicians. The point here, as explained by Soviet commentators, is that Marx, Engels, and Lenin could not possibly predict the precise stages though which society would have to travel before communism was reached, in particular because they could not foresee the forms and levels of technology that would be available. Hence, each new generation has to recognize and interpret new developments as they take place: the ideology needs to be updated to account for new trends. Nevertheless, its basic truths about the materialist nature of human society are said to remain perpetually valid. This power to reinterpret the ideology gives further adaptive capacity and legitimizing power to the party.

### The Party and the Revolutionary Heritage

In addition to fulfilling its self-appointed role as interpreter of the ideology, the party acts as defender of the revolutionary heritage, which further serves to legitimize the system. This role is reflected in Soviet historiography, particularly in histories of Russia and the Soviet Union, which are extremely stylized in their presentation and interpretation of historical facts. In this version, history pivots around the year 1917, in which the Bolsheviks seized power. Before the Great October Socialist Revolution, the worker and peasant masses suffered oppression and deprivation at the hands of the autocracy, abetted by the landed gentry and supported by the Orthodox Church; after October 1917, the Soviet people, under the leadership and guidance of the party, have transformed their existence and become citizen-proprietors in a superpower. All this was made possible by the revolutionary transfer of political and economic power to the working people, in a revolution masterminded by the founder of the Bolshevik Party, the political genius Vladimir Il'ich Lenin.

There is, of course, an important element of accuracy in this official presentation, as there is in any great mythology, and it is always put forward in such a way that the Communist Party wins the credit for the positive achievements since 1917 (which are indeed substantial) while managing to blame the weaknesses on others: the international Trotskyite clique, world imperialism, hangovers from the prerevolutionary period—all these have been used to excuse the shortcomings in Soviet development. In presenting history in this fashion and restricting the circulation of alternative interpretations, the party is able to glorify its own role in the process of development and promote itself as the defender of the achievements that have derived from the country's revolutionary origins. This serves to enhance further the party's image as the leading and guiding force and hence to legitimize its rule.

In doing this, the party traces its own history back to the revolutionary tradition of the nineteenth century and associates itself with symbols from the past. Lenin, in particular, who above all others pushed the Bolshevik wing of the party toward revolution in the years and months leading up to October 1917, serves as the supreme symbol, uniting the party of today with the momentous days of revolution. Lenin's soulless bust watches over party congresses; the Order of Lenin is presented to the outstanding party leaders in recognition of their services; Lenin's words are repeatedly quoted by political orators and writers in support of their ideas; Lenin's portrait appears on the party membership card, number 00000001 of which was issued on March 1, 1973, in the name of V. I. Lenin; reference to 'the party of Lenin' appears in the 1977 words to the Soviet national anthem; and new entrants into the party must 'speak Leninist words' and do so sincerely, not simply in order to win benefits (*XXV s"ezd*, I, p. 89). On the assumption that what Lenin did in propelling the Russian Empire toward the socialist revolution is recognized as a positive achievement, the party of today is able to gain the political credit by perpetually linking itself with the man who established the system.

Lenin, indeed, serves as the mentor and superego in Soviet society, and all Soviet leaders since his death have attempted to demonstrate their adherence to Leninist principles and policies. Stalin established his own credibility by playing on his links with Lenin, even to the extent of publishing faked photographs showing the two men together. After Stalin's death, Khrushchev rose to a superior position by appealing for a return to Leninist principles after the distortions associated with the 'personality cult' of Stalin. He repeatedly invoked Lenin (see, for example, Linden, 1966, pp. 28, 52, 150), and he was referred to until the eve of his political demise in October 1964 as 'an outstanding Leninist, a tireless fighter for communism' (*XXII s"ezd*, I, p. 258).

Under Brezhnev, the cult of Lenin continued. 'Today's achievements of the Soviet people,' Brezhnev proclaimed to prolonged applause at the Twenty-Fifth Party Congress, 'are the direct continuation of the cause of October. They are the practical embodiment of the ideas of the great Lenin. To this cause, to these ideas, our party is true and will always remain true!' (*XXV s"ezd*, I, p. 28). Later at the same congress, Brezhnev himself was held up by Eduard Shevardnadze (first secretary of the party in Georgia) as a model 'from whom we must learn to work in the Leninist style, to think in the Leninist style, to live in the Leninist style.'

Moreover, he went on to declare that, although Lenin had never personally addressed the Georgian communists, since the Twenty-Fourth Congress two 'genuinely Leninist documents' had been directed by the CPSU Central Committee on the initiative of Brezhnev (*XXV s' 'ezd*, I, pp. 186–7; reference is to severely critical statements on the 'Georgian scandals' that involved protectionism, bribery, and a host of other un-Leninist ills that had been prevalent in the republic under Shevardnadze's predecessor, V. P. Mzhavanadze). More recently, as the party celebrated the 110th anniversary of his birth, Lenin was referred to as 'a Titan of scientific thought and a genuine leader of the people' (*Partiinaya zhizn'*, 1980, no. 7, p. 22).

Sincere or cynical, the Soviet leaders assiduously foster an impression of believing that their way is the Leninist way, and that it is the best way. Few Soviet citizens are old enough to have been even aware of Lenin's existence during his lifetime; the new generation of leaders have all been born since his death. Yet by their appeals to the traditions established by him, by showing an awareness of the historical origins of the regime that he founded and vowing to protect and perpetuate them, and by establishing a sense that Lenin looks, as it were, approvingly over their shoulders, the party in the present generation acquires the legitimacy that longevity and continuity confer on a system.

In its self-image, the party seized power when no other force was capable of holding it; it defended the revolutionary gains of the working class during the period of civil war and foreign intervention; it struggled to transform the face of the country, socially and economically, despite the attempts of the Trotskyites to undermine and sabotage their efforts; it successfully defended those achievements in the battleground of the Great Patriotic War (the Second World War); and it has gone on to lead the Soviet people in the creation of a powerful and sophisticated superpower, second only to the United States of America, and recognized as such around the world. In presenting Soviet history in this light—and it is portrayed thus in pageants on May Day and on the anniversary of the revolution, in towns, cities, and villages across the country—the party gains further political credit and is able to ignore the negative features that would detract from its image of sagacity and wise leadership.

### The Party and Class

The CPSU has always stressed its association with the industrial proletariat, the class that, in the Marxian analysis, occupies a special position in history as the class that will eventually carry through a revolution that would abolish classes. In the Soviet analysis of politics, all parties are said to be based on a specific class, and they attempt to gain control of the state apparatus in order to rule in the interests of that particular class. Moreover, according to Soviet writers on the theme, a party not only represents a class, but also is a part of it, and Western writers are 'unscientific' in their failure to acknowledge this fact. Parties, says M. Kh. Farukshin (1973, p. 39), channel the demands and interests of particular classes and social groups. Not all parties represent the whole of a class: different sections of a class—specifically of the bourgeoisie, in competitive systems—can be represented by different parties, which compete among themselves without, however, undermining the fundamental interests of the class (Farukshin, 1973, p. 39; Shakhnazarov, 1974, pp. 14–15). Hence, the 'catch-all' party, which appeals to all sections of society for support (Kirchheimer, 1966), is a concept bordering on the fraudulent, in the eyes of Soviet scholars.

The CPSU, by contrast, has traditionally been preoccupied with its position as the party of the industrial working class, the basic productive force in society. Lenin first came to prominence in the Russian revolutionary movement in an organization in St. Petersburg (now Leningrad) called the League of Struggle for the Emancipation of the Working Class (Keep, 1963, pp. 47–9), and the revolutionary regime set up after the October 1917 Revolution was and is referred to as the 'dictatorship of the proletariat': rule by the formerly exploited class, in friendly political union with the poor peasantry. However, 'No dictatorship by a class can be organized in such a way as to enable the whole class to exercise direct leadership of society,' and so 'The function of guiding society in the name of the class . . . is performed by its political vanguard'—that is, its party (Shakhnazarov, 1974, pp. 11–12). The CPSU saw itself as the vanguard of the working class and so exercised the dictatorship on behalf of that class.

However, there have been significant developments in Soviet society since those days, and the theory of the CPSU's class basis has also undergone a development. As society developed economically, socially, and politically, the former exploiting classes were eliminated; the kulaks (rich peasants) were destroyed as a class in the early 1930s; and, although the importance of the proletariat is still emphasized (for example, by Brezhnev, *XXV s"ezd*, I, p. 88), considerable attention has long been paid to other social classes and groups, in particular to the collective farm peasantry and the intelligentsia, who are said to be linked with the proletariat in a system of 'socialist social relations.' Soviet commentators argue that class relations in Russia underwent a transformation in the period of building socialism (from the late 1920s onward). In the current phase—referred to as 'developed socialism,' a concept that has been elaborated since the late 1960s (Evans, 1977)—a novel entity exists, namely, the Soviet people. This is characterized by 'new, harmonious relations among classes and social groups, nations and nationalities—relations of friendship and collaboration' (*XXIV s"ezd*, I, pp. 97–101). In view of this social change, the position of the party itself is radically altered. No longer does it serve as the vanguard of the proletariat in exercising its dictatorship: it has become the party of the whole Soviet people (*Programme*, p. 301; *Rules*, 1977, p. 5), which is said to be monolithically united behind it. Moreover, this change took place (according to Suslov) not because the party subjectively desired it, but 'because the aims and ideals of the working class became the aims and ideals of all classes and strata of the people that had built socialism' (quoted in Yudin, 1973, p. 245). Hence, because the interests of the proletariat are now said to be shared by all sectors of Soviet society, the party that first arose in order to defend and develop those interests can logically and easily accommodate all other classes and groups.

Thus, by a somewhat roundabout route, the CPSU appears in essence to be arguing that it *is* a kind of 'catch-all'—or at least 'serve-all'—party. Although it does not have to go out and 'catch' the votes of all sections of society, it does argue that it *can* effectively serve them all. (It should be noted, though, that some Soviet writers nowadays acknowledge the legitimacy of the communist-led multi-party systems existing in some East European countries: see, for example, Shakhnazarov, 1974, pp. 21–2.)

### The Party and Interests

The above discussion brings us to what is, for many Western political scientists, the central element in any political system: the interests that arise in society and how they are articulated, aggregated, selected, combined, and generally taken into account in the political process. Indeed, the interest-based approach to political life has come to dominate modern political science, where the concepts of demands, interest groups, and the 'authoritative allocation of values' are essential elements in how political activity is viewed. In the work of David Truman (1951), David Easton (1953, 1965), Gabriel Almond (for example, Almond and Powell, 1966), Jean Blondel (1969a), and many other Western writers, politics is 'about' this very question, and the functions of the political system are associated with selecting and accommodating perceived demands in the policy-making process. A modern, complex society in particular, it is believed, generates a wide range of distinct interests, which at least potentially are in conflict. The individual possesses interests as a worker, a housewife, or a pensioner, as a consumer, as a resident of a particular area, as a parent, as a user of leisure facilities; the citizens may join social organizations—clubs, societies—in order to satisfy their intellectual interests, so that groups of citizens organized in this way may present collective interests; as a member of a particular social category—a youth or senior citizen, a member of a nationality group, a male or a female—the citizen possesses other specific interests that he or she may wish to express in the political arena; and it is also argued that there may be overriding national interests—defense, the promotion and development of the society's culture, environmental protection, and the like. All these different interests are present in a society, vying with one another for the attention of the law-making machinery, and seeking allocations of economic resources, legislative recognition, or similar favorable 'outputs' from the political system. Such a view of the political process is now widely accepted in Western political science and indeed in society at large.

Political parties have a central role in this. Kirchheimer's concept (referred to above) of the 'catch-all' party is likewise based on a view of politics in which parties frame their policy platforms in order to incorporate the interests of as wide a spectrum as possible of special groups in society, so as to appeal to the broadest possible cross section of the electorate; parties, in this view, are involved in 'taking up grievances, ideas, and problems developed in a more searching and systematic fashion elsewhere in the body politic' and transmitting them to the political decision-making institutions of the state (Kirchheimer, 1966, p. 189).

In view of what has been said about the Soviet Communist Party's relationships with, first, the ideology and, secondly, the social classes that constitute the society, the question of interests as seen in the West would appear to be largely irrelevant. After all, the 'special understanding' of the ideology is supposed to guarantee that the party always adopts 'correct,' 'scientific' policies, geared toward the attainment of communism. Indeed, the very idea that society should move in a particular direction conflicts to some extent with the Western view of politics as essentially the free play of social forces—itself a concept that is explicitly rejected by Soviet writers (for example, Marchenko, 1973, p. 100; Topornin, 1975, p. 48). And since all social groups are said to have adopted the interests of the working class as their own interests, it follows that the conflicts of interests that characterize politics in a liberal democracy are not present in Soviet society. In other words, instead of comprising the peaceful resolution of conflict, as politics is seen in the West (Miller, 1965, p. 14; Blondel, 1969a, pp. 6–11), politics in the Soviet Union takes on a different form: that of *mobilizing* the population toward the achievement of the goals identified in the ideology and said to be in the interests of all. Such was, in essence, the totalitarian view of Soviet politics (see Friedrich and Brzezinski, 1966, for the classic statement), but it also finds expression in the work of modern Soviet authors, who likewise see the essence of the party's leadership as consisting in 'the mobilization and organization of people for fulfilling state plans and directives of the party and the government' (Lesnyi and Chernogolovkin, 1976, pp. 47–8). Otherwise expressed, the party, as the vanguard, instinctively understands what is in everyone's interests and adopts its policies accordingly. Sometimes those policies may conflict with popular desires: even though the party always claims to have the full-hearted support of the Soviet people in everything it does (*XXV s''ezd*, I, p. 114), the Soviet press and the speeches of politicians repeatedly reveal a manifest reluctance to carry out party policy with anything that could be called enthusiasm. But this is simply explained away by arguing that the party understands people's interests better than they do themselves: or, as it is sometimes expressed, there still remains under socialism a difference between the level of consciousness of the party and that of the masses (Aimbetov *et al.*, 1967, p. 82; Kadeikin *et al.*, 1974, p. 78), so that:

> not all members of the working class comprehend equally the dialectics of the life of society and the class struggle. The working class must be led by its vanguard which formulates the interests of the class and which has a clear conception of the social processes developing in each country and the world at large. (Chekharin, 1977b, p.22)

This distinction is expected to remain until the attainment of full communism (Kadeikin *et al.*, 1974, p. 78).

The argument does not end there, however. There can be little doubt that, under Stalin, that *was* the end of it, for practical purposes. The overriding 'social' or 'public' interests were given absolute priority. They consisted in building up the country's heavy industrial base as rapidly as possible, involving the transfer of millions of peasants from the land to the new industrial cities, the expansion of education, health and other welfare services, and the extraction of almost unimaginable output from the whole population, subordinating personal interests—and grossly violating individual rights—in the process; group interests were likewise suppressed by the expedient of preventing the formation of uncontrolled social organizations. Some Soviet spokesmen argue in very simplistic terms that, just because a socialist revolution has taken place, 'a political system of a new type expresses and defends the deepest needs and interests of the working class and other strata of the toilers' (Farukshin, 1973, p. 67). However, in the post-Stalin period, and especially since the mid-1950s, there has developed a much more sophisticated analysis of the question of interests in Soviet society, one that gives to the party and other institutions a role in selecting and combining them in policy making (see Hill, 1980a, ch. 5).

It is now argued that, indeed, a complex modern society leads to the creation of a great variety of specific interests; and, although all members of Soviet society share the common interest of building a communist society, these secondary interests are legitimate. Moreover, it is the task of the political system to respond to them and take them into account in policy formulation. As Georgi Shakhnazarov (1974, p. 29) has put it:

> the absence of antagonisms does not signify an identity of the needs of the different social groups. Along with the complete and permanent coincidence of the fundamental interests of all classes and social groups, there may arise, and does arise, a lack of coincidence of specific interests. That is a contradiction of a kind which, while not being antagonistic, can become aggravated unless it is resolved in good time.

Politicians too have spoken in these terms, giving the party a role not unlike that implied in the concept of 'interest aggregation.' This development is seen in the late Leonid Brezhnev's speeches on the question. He asserted in the late 1960s that the party alone is capable of taking into account the special interests of the various classes and social groups, nationalities, and generations in Soviet society and accommodating them into its policies (Brezhnev, 1970, p. 136, quoted in Yudenkov *et al.*, 1979, p. 20). At the Twenty-Fourth Congress (1971), he was a little less certain, when he told delegates that 'the party's policy brings the required results when it precisely takes into account the interests of the whole people, and also the interests of the classes and social groups that compose it, and directs them into one common stream' (*XXIV s''ezd*, I, p. 97). By the time of the Twenty-Fifth Congress, he was urging closer study of public opinion (*XXV s''ezd*, I, p. 98).

All this implies an acknowledgment that the party does not always know what is best for society, and it has implications too for the way we interpret the party's relationship with the ideology. Marxism-Leninism, instead of serving as a blueprint for building a communist society (which it has never done) or even as a means for justifying whatever policies the party hierarchy wishes to impose on Soviet society, now appears rather to offer a way of identifying which interests and demands originating in society are compatible with the overall goal. Soviet writers stress that the kinds of interests that are considered legitimate are not 'narrow, parochial interests': emphasis on those is said to be 'a distortion of the principles of planned management of the national economy,' and this can 'seriously harm the common cause' (Shakhnazarov, 1974, p. 32). The party, then, guided by the ideology, incorporates interests and demands into its policies in so far as these are not deemed to be in conflict with building communism.

Although that still leaves a great deal of discretion to the political leadership, it represents a significant change of emphasis in recent years, and it has further implications for the party's role in modern Soviet society.

## The Party in Developed Socialist Society

As noted, the 1970s witnessed the elaboration of a new concept in Soviet social analysis: 'developed' or 'mature' socialism (the two terms are used interchangeably: see Babii *et al.*, 1976, p. 9, n. 3). This is presented as recognizing that the USSR has moved to a further distinct stage in the building of communism, beyond the dictatorship of the proletariat (inaugurated by Lenin), the building of socialism (achieved under Stalin), and the 'rapid building of communism' (identified by Khrushchev, but now banished from the political rhetoric). 'Experience shows,' according to two recent Soviet writers, 'that, independently of the level from which this or that country begins its movement along the socialist road, developed socialism represents a natural and necessary stage on the road to communism' (Glezerman and Iovchuk, 1978, p. 119). The 1977 Constitution was introduced—according to Brezhnev when he presented it—to mark the new achievement (Brezhnev, 1977, pp. 34–5).

The key Article in reference to the political system is Article 6, which sums up the picture that has been and is being elaborated at far greater length by scholars and philosophers:

> The leading and guiding force of Soviet society and the nucleus of its political system, of all state organisations and public organisations, is the Communist Party of the Soviet Union. The CPSU exists for the people and serves the people. The Communist Party, armed with Marxism-Leninism, determines the general perspectives of the development of society and the course of home and foreign policy of the USSR, directs the great constructive work of the Soviet people, and imparts a planned, systematic and theoretically substantiated character to their struggle for the victory of communism.
>
> All party organisations shall function within the framework of the Constitution of the USSR.

In that Article, we find the basic elements in the Soviet political system, most of which have already been mentioned. It refers to the ideology, the party as the institutional linchpin of the system, the state organizations and public organizations; it indicates the methods of party rule (providing the nucleus in nonparty institutions); it broadly depicts the party's overall role (setting out the basic policy guidelines for the society); and it repeats the Leninist dictum that the party operates constitutionally. (This may be read as an assurance—vitally necessary, in view of the way the party has tended to operate throughout its history—to those outside the party and as a warning or reminder to party members and officials.)

Soviet writers say that the 'developed socialist society,' for which these political arrangements are said to be appropriate, is distinguished by a raising in the level of political activity. This is associated with the social and cultural development that has accompanied economic growth and diversification. In addition to the extension of widely diverse interests, which was commented on, it is argued that rising educational levels and the accumulation of political experience among the population at large have created the possibility of much greater public involvement in political life. 'Broadening and deepening socialist democracy,' asserts B. N. Topornin (1975, p. 34), 'is not simply a political slogan or the remote programmatic aim of Marxist-Leninists.' On the contrary,

> in the new historical stage, the broad strata of the population are significantly better prepared, both from the point of view of their educational level, and also from the point of view of their training in the habits of participation in the political life of society, and their interest in its affairs, so that they can with greater attention and in a qualified fashion evaluate and discuss various problems of economic and cultural development, and of managing the affairs of society and state. (Topornin, in Tikhomirov, 1975, p. 86)

As part of this political development, the representative state institutions (the soviets) and the so-called 'public organizations' have been consciously reinvigorated in the past twenty years or so (see Friedgut, 1979, pp. 156–62 and ch. 4), and the level of political culture is said to be constantly rising (Topornin, 1975, p. 31).

In a different type of society, all this might be interpreted as indicating *less* need for constant political guidance. After all, if the population is now more capable of running its own affairs, thanks to its accumulated wisdom and experience, then in principle the social and political institutions can be more reliably left to get on with the task of gathering information about demands and interests, weighing these up together with economic and other technical information, and adopting policies for implementation by the broad masses themselves. Indeed, that sounds rather like what might be understood by the term *communist self-administration*, which is one of the system's stated long-term goals, inspired by the ideology. In the Soviet Union, however, these developments have been consistently interpreted as implying not a diminished role for the party, but an enhanced one (see, for example, Kulinchenko *et al.*, 1978, p. 150).

There are several aspects to this question. The first is that the party, as a ruling party, has itself promoted these developments. It takes the credit for the economic and social advance; it has stimulated the revival of the soviets and other institutions and organizations in the post-Stalin period. And, although this might be viewed as a relinquishing of some power by the party to nonparty bodies, it in fact represents rather a change in the style of rule: the point is that these nonparty bodies are used by the party in exercising its rule (see Chapters 5 and 6). In trying to stimulate the 'initiative' of nonparty bodies, something that has long been called for by party spokesmen and in official statements, the party also feels that its own role in 'guiding' the exercise of that initiative needs to be extended, thereby ensuring the 'correct' application of its doctrines. As we saw, it is believed that communist society will not be achieved spontaneously: it has to be worked for; society has to be organized to build it. This, indeed, is where Marxism-Leninism most sharply divides from liberal democracy: the latter does not envisage a future model society toward which the present society should be guided, whereas Marxism-Leninism does; and the institution that can understand this and divine the correct course is the party. Hence, Chekharin (1977b, p. 251) can write that

> Having thoroughly analysed the experience in building socialism and communism in the Soviet Union and in the development of the socialist world system, the CPSU has concluded that with society's advance towards communism the leading role of the Communist Party must increase.

But the party, as a minority of the population, is 'a drop in the ocean' (Lenin, quoted by Shabanov, 1969a, p. 22) and cannot by inself fulfill all the tasks associated with running a modern society. In fact, even devising policies is beyond the capacity of the party alone. The point is that the party, in working out policy guidelines for the society, does not simply consult the ideology and come up with a policy: it seems reasonable to assume that the writings of Marx, Engels, and Lenin have little to say of direct relevance to, for instance, the development of a computer-run economy, or the importation of American grain, or how to deal with Afghanistan. Policy, when all is said and done, has to deal with specific situations, it has to be aimed at a particular goal, and it is arguable that the most that ideology can be expected to do is provide a means of identifying what broad directions are compatible with building communism. In other words, as Soviet representatives have come increasingly to acknowledge, the policy makers need a constant flow of information to provide a picture of the precise circumstances for which policy is being devised; and a modern society is so complex, and the scope of government so broad, that the policy makers need a vast network of institutions for implementing policy once it is adopted. For this reason, among others, the party makes use of the state, the trade unions, the Komsomol (Young Communist League), and a variety of special-interest societies and associations, both as instruments of administration and opinion formation and as a means of tapping opinion and arousing support for the system. It is in this sense that the role of the nonparty institutions is being expanded under 'developed socialism' and the role of the party becomes somewhat more restricted in scope, but more concentrated: it becomes more one of adjudicator, assessing which demands and interests are compatible with communism and encouraging certain demands and discouraging others. In other words, it exercises the role of 'leader,' 'guide,' 'co-ordinator' that Soviet scholars have been describing. Or, in Western political science terminology, it acts as 'gatekeeper' (Easton, 1965, pp. 87–99).

Such is the role of the CPSU in the Soviet system, as portrayed by its own spokesmen and apologists. And to the extent that the functioning of any system reflects the perceptions of those who are involved in it, that picture corresponds to how the CPSU wishes to perform and does in fact perform.

There are, of course, other views of the Soviet Communist Party. It has been seen as a dictator, an elite, a bureaucracy, a class. These views are examined in later chapters and summed up in our assessment of the party and its role in Chapter 7. In the intervening chapters, the party's membership, its structures, institutions and personnel are examined; its performance of political functions is analyzed; relations with the state and other institutions are explored; and a number of concepts that help to determine the party's functioning are elaborated.

# CHAPTER 2

# The Party Membership

In this chapter, we look at the ordinary membership of the CPSU. In order to appreciate the significance of this aspect of the party, a distinction needs to be drawn between the party as an institution and the party as a collection of individual members. A great deal of confusion stems from a failure to make this distinction.

As a political institution, the party has structures, rules and conventions, and authoritative bodies that issue formal statements. It has its own interests as an institution and its own internal business: the collection of subscriptions, the keeping of accounts, the promotion of members to office, the design of forms and membership cards, the maintenance of records, the running of publishing houses, and other ventures—a whole variety of items and activities that are specifically related to the party (although they may have implications for other institutions). The party, indeed, provides a highly significant (and probably fulfilling and rewarding) career structure for professional administrators and research workers, and it is a major employer of secretarial and other staff (either directly or through subsidiary enterprises, such as printing works and publishing houses), as well as being the owner or controller of much property. As such, it can and does act as 'the party.'

However, the party is not simply an institution in that sense: its members also belong to other institutions and organizations, so that they are not to be regarded as simply 'the party' in the abstract sense. It is true that the CPSU exacts unswerving loyalty and makes high demands on its members. But the image of the party as a distinct entity, separated from the rest of Soviet society, is quite misleading. As well as being members of the 'vanguard,' they are also parents, shoppers, workers; they too travel by bus and underground to and from work; they visit the theatre and cinema; they take their families to the Black Sea in August; they celebrate New Year by dancing until dawn; they have hobbies like everyone else. Even the late General Secretary Brezhnev enjoyed fast driving, hunting, and sailing, and admitted to a problem with smoking.

Mikhail Gorbachev has struck out further than all his predecessors by involving his wife Raisa in his public appearances, especially abroad, thereby creating the image of leading Soviet communists as possessing rounded personalities.

Nevertheless, it would be equally wrong to assert that the party members are not distinguished in a number of significant ways from their nonparty compatriots. They are seen as 'the more advanced, politically more conscious section' of the population, members of 'the highest form of socio-political organisation,' and characterized by 'ideological and organisational unity, monolithic cohesion . . . and a high degree of conscious discipline' (*Rules*, 1977, p. 5–6). These attributes, together with the image of the party as 'the tried and tested militant vanguard,' already imply distinctions between party members and the masses. And although there are now more than 19 million party members and probationary members, they nevertheless constitute less than one-tenth of the adult population. Membership is not open, and this results in a quite different approach to recruitment from that in conventional Western parties. In those, the initiative lies almost exclusively with the individual member, who joins and leaves with little formality. The implications of CPSU membership are more serious, and admittance procedures are involved and demanding, so it takes a long time before the advantages—and responsibilities—of full membership are acquired. (This stems from the vital necessity before the revolution for stringent scrutiny of all potential members, since the party was an illegal, proscribed organization, liable to be penetrated by police spies and *agents provocateurs*, one of whom even became an associate of Lenin: see Wolfe, 1966, ch. 31; Schapiro, 1970, pp. 137–8.)

### Joining the Party

Joining the CPSU is clearly a highly significant step: indeed, it is no exaggeration to say that it is the most significant political act an individual can perform, as momentous in its way as the decision by those of different persuasions to become 'dissidents.' Joining the party implies a fundamental commitment to the system: not necessarily an absolute and complete acceptance of every single aspect of Soviet society, but at least a willingness to operate within certain established ground rules. To expand on this comparison: dissidents may find certain aspects of the system attractive, and they certainly are not in complete agreement among themselves about the ills, as they see them, of the society and the possible remedies; nevertheless they have, on balance, opted out of that system. Those who join the party have, as it were, opted in. Not only that, they have been *invited* in. But the system of admission into the party presents a number of paradoxes that are quite revealing of how the party sees itself.

The party rules (Rule 1) state that

> Membership of the CPSU is open to any citizen of the Soviet Union who accepts the Programme and Rules of the Party, takes an active part in communist construction, works in one of the Party organisations, carries out all Party decisions, and pays membership dues.

In practice, however, membership is less easy than this formula might imply. The initiative tends to rest with the party and Komsomol authorities at local level who 'co-opt' the individual, rather than the individual acting on a desire to join. The citizen may, of course, try to draw the attention of the party's local officers to himself, thereby 'engineering' his recruitment; but beyond that, joining depends on the local party authorities. Even so, the process involves a complex procedure of application by the individual concerned, in consultation with the party officials at his place of work; it entails completing a number of documents and having these discussed and voted on by a number of different party bodies, with checking and double-checking at every stage: indeed, so thorough does the procedure appear to be, and so impressive are the hurdles, that it might seem as though the party does everything within its power to *avoid* admitting new members. The following brief account is based on an official source (*Organizatsionno-ustavnye voprosy*, 1973, pp. 74–112, 1978, pp. 97–139).

### The documents

Aspiring party members have to prepare a series of documents, beginning with three references from party members of at least five years' standing who have known them at work and socially for at least one year; in the case of Komsomol members (including all applicants up to the age of twenty-five) one of these is from the Komsomol district or city committee (*raikom* or *gorkom*: see Chapter 3). These references attest to the applicant's political qualities, his qualities as a worker, and his moral qualities. From them, it should be clear 'how the party entrant regards his work, his service or production obligations, how he participates in the collective's social life, how he is raising his own political and general educational training, and how he conducts his private and family life' (*Organizatsionno-ustavnye voprosy*, 1978, p. 128). One category of party member is not allowed to write these recommendations: CPSU Central Committee members, since a reference from one of them might unduly affect the judgment of a local organization (Rule 4; *Spravochnik sekretarya*, 1967, p. 156).

Armed with these recommendations, the applicant next prepares an application form, completed in his own hand, in ink or ballpoint, and without making corrections or using incomprehensible abbreviations. This contains such information as full name, date and place of birth, mother tongue, parents' current occupation, educational institutions attended and qualifications attained, any significant medals and other awards, languages spoken, military service record, occupational record, and whether he has lived abroad. Other details, such as social class, are added by the committee secretary. Then comes a synopsis of his career to date (an 'autobiography'). And finally a personal statement, declaring his familiarity with (and acceptance of) the party program and rules and indicating his desire to be admitted to the CPSU. It is stressed that in preparing all these documents the applicant must display precision and clarity, and normally he is expected to confer with his organization secretary in drawing them up: in any case, the secretary verifies the factual information and the signatures before forwarding them to the next stage (Khaldeev *et al.*, 1975, pp. 272–3).

### The assessment

The only forum with the authority to admit or reject applications is the party branch (PPO: see Chapter 3) general meeting. However, after initial checking by the secretary, the application documents are discussed by the PPO committee or bureau, whose informal recommendation carries great weight. In the PPO, there is supposed to be a full discussion of each applicant in turn, once more looking at candidates' political, work, and moral qualities. An interesting point in connection with this assessment stage is the preference (which is now mentioned in party Rule 4) for it normally to take place in open party meetings, attended by nonmembers. This is because 'Admittance into the party is a very responsible matter. Therefore it is important to know the opinion about the entrant not only of communists but also of nonparty people' (Khaldeev *et al.*, 1975, p. 273). It is not known how widely this is observed, nor how well attended such meetings are, nor the role played by the nonmembers (who have no vote). However, the repeated emphasis on this point clearly reflects the party authorities' intention that the wider public should signal their acceptance of the system of Communist Party rule by actively participating in its recruitment procedures; and, if it is appropriate to consider the party as an *elite* (see Chapter 7), such a procedure allows the nonelite some opportunity for influencing the nature and composition of the elite. Be that as it may, all those present have the right to question the applicant, to check facts, to determine whether he has understood the program and appreciates the obligations of a communist. Again, we know practically nothing about the nature of the discussions in these meetings; but at the end of them, a vote is held, and a two-thirds majority is required in favor of admission, otherwise the application fails.

The accepted candidate is admitted to the party, subject to confirmation by the meeting of the next higher party body: the *raikom* (district committee) or *gorkom* (city committee), or the PPO in those institutions where the party organization is so large that is has been awarded the rights of a *raikom* with regard to admissions and a number of other questions. The newly admitted member pays an entrance fee of about 2 rubles (in fact, 2 percent of monthly earnings) and begins to pay the monthly subscription, varying with earnings, from 10 kopeks (for those earning less than 70 rubles a month: that would apply to housewives and pensioners, but to practically no employed persons nowadays) to 3 percent of the salary (Rules 71 and 72). However, although the financial and other burdens of membership apply immediately, the privileges and rights do not, for he is not yet a full member. A year as a candidate or probationary member—known as the *kandidatskii stazh*—follows, at the end of which the whole application procedure has to be gone through a second time before the individual is confirmed as a CPSU member and allowed (in the party's own rhetoric) to bear 'the lofty title of communist.'

### *The* kandidatskii stazh

This period, now fixed at twelve months, with no provision for an extension, is regarded as 'a very important period in the life of a person entering the party' (*Partgruporg*, 1968, p. 38), a time when 'the party organization can thoroughly test the personal qualities of the party entrant, and also acquaint him more profoundly with the CPSU program and rules' (*Spravochnik sekretarya*, 1967, p. 157). The second admissions review, therefore, concentrates on the person's performance during the probationary year: hence, the *kandidatskii stazh* is regarded as 'a most serious test, and not an empty formality' (*Spravochnik sekretarya*, 1967, p. 157). During this period, the individual has to demonstrate that he or she possesses the personal qualities, the political maturity, and the experience deemed appropriate for members of the vanguard. There are a number of ways in which this maturity can be shown.

First, within the party group or organization, the candidate must attend meetings regularly and participate in the discussions (although he has no vote, nor may he be elected to any party office). He is immediately given party assignments (see Chapter 4), which he must carry out enthusiastically, placing himself at the party's disposal in exercising its leading and guiding role.

Secondly, the aspiring member is expected to show a 'communist attitude toward work,' constantly striving to improve the quality of his own work, to raise his output by engaging in 'socialist competition' and encouraging his fellow workers by his example. In doing so, he is obeying the instruction of Rule 2, which states that it is the party member's duty

> to be a model in work, to protect and increase socialist property, to work persistently for raising production efficiency, for the steady growth of labour productivity, the improvement of the quality of production, and the application of modern achievements in science and technology in the country's economy; to perfect his own qualifications, to be an active adherent to everything new and progressive, and to make the maximum contribution to accelerating the country's socio-economic development.

Thirdly, he must raise his level of political consciousness, by attending courses and study groups in Marxism-Leninism and similar appropriate themes. Many local party organizations put on special courses for young members and candidates, with lectures and seminars led by party secretaries, experienced older party members, and officals, to examine the party program and discuss themes related to the internal life of the party (see Shumakov and Zudin, 1973, pp. 140-1).

In short, in the course of the year, having established at the first assessment a *prima facie* case, as it were, for admission, the candidate has to prove himself sufficiently to obtain the votes of two-thirds of the members at the meeting where his case comes up for a second consideration. In some organizations, apparently, a kind of party apprenticeship is arranged whereby the candidate is attached to an experienced member (a 'party tutor') who is given responsibility for training him for full membership. However, this is frowned on, since such close supervision tends to cramp the initiative of the younger candidate: 'In a hothouse situation it is difficult for a person to show his worth, and to work up a party character' (Shumakov and Zudin, 1973, pp. 139-40). Even so, it is acknowledged that support from the party organization or group is vital and is reflected in the type of assignments meted out, the level of expectation placed on the individual, and the assistance given by members in encouraging him or helping when things go wrong: 'It is necessary that the person should see comradely interest in his growth, that he should not funk difficulties, but strive to display perseverance and initiative in his work' (Khaldeev *et al.*, 1975, p. 275). If at the end of the year the individual has himself decided not to pursue full membership and declines to reapply, he is automatically refused entry; alternatively, his party organization, subject to confirmation by the *raikom* or *gorkom*, can decline to confirm him as a full member. In either case, the individual is supposed not to be formally 'excluded' (as was the case until the early 1960s), since that would lead to 'certain consequences, [it] would place a mark on his reputation' which may be totally undeserved (*Spravochnik sekretarya*, 1967, p. 161). It is hard to estimate the scale of such failure to proceed to full membership, but between the Twenty-Fifth and Twenty-Sixth Congresses (1976–81) some 91,000 candidates were denied promotion to full member status, a rate deemed 'a more or less normal sifting' ('KPSS v tsifrakh', 1981, p. 14). Measured against a total of 3,162,372 persons admitted as candidate members during the period, we can calculate a 'failure' rate of around 3 percent, down from the 3.5 to 4 percent in evidence earlier (Rigby, 1976, p. 320); this no doubt reflects the greater stringency in assessing initial applicants. Nevertheless, significant numbers of 'unworthy' persons do slip through. This is taken as a sign of laxity on the part of local organizations and officials (see for example, 'Vysokoe zvanie,' 1976).

## The Significance of Party Membership

During the probationary year, the aspiring member has an opportunity to acquire a deeper appreciation of the significance of CPSU membership for himself and those close to him. We can fairly assume that anyone who applies for membership is already politically active and aware, and the *kandidatskii stazh* is designed to strengthen that and to prepare the individual for full-hearted commitment to the cause of communism. Party membership, he discovers, has a range of implications that will seriously affect his future life and prospects and the way he views the world: it brings both obligations and advantages.

### *The obligations of membership*

All young Soviet citizens are steadily made aware of certain features of communist life, in particular through membership in the Komsomol, the recruiting ground for the majority of party members. Seen as the party's 'direct militant reserve' (*XXV s''ezd*, I, p. 110), a massive 72.5 percent of new recruits in the early 1980s came from the Komsomol ('KPSS v tsifrakh,' 1986, p. 22), implying an average recruitment age in the early or mid-twenties, preceded by up to ten years of increasingly political training in the Komsomol (see Chapter 6).

The new party member has had a long familiarity with elements in the revolutionary tradition. At school and in children's organizations, he has learnt much of the life and work of Lenin, the radical movement, Marx and Engels, and there have been courses in Marxism-Leninism and the communist movement. The political rhetoric, with its references to and portraits of Lenin and other historic figures in the movement, has socialized practically all Soviet citizens into acceptance of the basic values and symbols of the country in which they live. Even children's literature presents Lenin as a kind of 'super-ego,' a fatherlike figure (see O'Dell, 1978, pp. 98–104), to serve as a conscience for the builder of the new society—not unlike the image of Jesus in many a home and school in Christian countries. Hence, joining the party represents an identification with this historic revolutionary tradition.

It also means identification with the worldwide workers' movement, in which the CPSU sees itself as the leading branch. All the theory of Marxism-Leninism, and the CPSU's ideological statements, serve to convince that history moves forward in the direction of success for the movement and the decline and eventual collapse of capitalism. To swim with the historic tide by joining the movement's principal component is an attraction for many.

In addition, any member coming up through the Komsomol is aware of the principles of 'communist morality' set out in the party program and formerly enshrined in the 'Moral Code of the Builder of Communism' that was prominently displayed in student hostels and Komsomol 'red corners.' 'Communist morality' is said to embody the fundamental principle of 'one for all, all for one' in place of 'egoism, self-love and self-interest'; it is imbued with profound respect for the working man, combined with interpersonal relations of 'comradely co-operation and mutual assistance, good will, honesty, simplicity and modesty in private and public life'; the morality is said to be active and vigorous in the drive for 'ever new labour achievements and creative accomplishments.' To these moral principles are appended patriotism and socialist internationalism, including a preparedness to defend the socialist homeland, atheism, and the struggle against bourgeois ideology. These principles can, of course, be obeyed by those who are not party members: however, they are implicitly binding on communists, for whom they should become second nature.

Section 1 of the party rules spells out further obligations for the member: setting an example at work, improving his qualifications, taking part in public life, and fulfilling obligations to the party itself—paying subscriptions regularly, studying the ideology, preserving party and state secrecy, engaging in criticism and self-criticism, in order to maintain the dignity of the name of 'communist.'

In other words, the Communist Party member must: (1) be an outstanding worker; (2) be well versed in the ideology; and (3) place himself at the disposal of the party authorities and be devoted to the cause.

The party is, in a sense, a very selective club, in which there is no room for idle members. It is not enough for a communist simply to agree with party decisions: he is expected to strive selflessly for their implementation (Chernenko, 1975, p. 14). As one writer put it, the party is not a club of oratorical dilettanti, and 'a party organization is not a place in which its members just come together for a meeting and then go home. . . . Belonging to the party demands from each communist a complete giving of his strength, a burning in his heart, self-sacrifice, and the fulfillment of his party duty always and in everything' (Turishchev, 1975, pp. 168, 207). The party member may not be a passive observer on the sidelines: he is expected to speak out against negligence, parochialism and 'infringements of the norms of morality' ('Mnenie kommunista,' 1980)—this, indeed, is his 'sacred duty' (Utenkov *et al.*, 1977, p. 29).

How far the members succeed in living up to these high demands is a separate question: many reports in the party press suggest that significant numbers fail to do so and join for careerist reasons, despite the threatened penalties for passivity. Once admitted, there are only two ways of leaving the party: by dying, which is somewhat drastic; and by being expelled, which is the equivalent of discharge with ignominy from the armed forces and represents a permanent stain on one's character—indeed, it is better never to have joined in the first place.

Party membership can become a burdensome obligation that involves the member in a great deal of study, political discussions, meetings, electoral work, perhaps giving talks and lectures, organizing things, and taking on a variety of public engagements. They party member may be called on to undertake any of these, and the burden will severly eat into his leisure time, and may affect family relations and disrupt social life. Even though it is an exaggeration to suggest that the party member has no private life and has to devote himself entirely to his organization, it is true that the conscientious member is charged with a range of responsibilities and a level of discipline that seriously distinguish him from other citizens.

The affairs of every party member are watched over by the party, which keeps files at central and local levels and holds branch meetings at which individuals' behavior is discussed. Even changing one's job requires the permission of the member's organization and of the committee in which his party records are kept, since the records will need to be amended and possibly transferred elsewhere (*Spravochnik sekretarya*, 1967, pp. 170–1); indeed, members are supposed to inform their organization each time they travel away, even on personal matters (*Organizatsionno-ustavnye voprosy*, 1978, p. 79). This is seen as part of the maintenance of party discipline and of the rules and norms of party life.

The formal phrase *review of a personal case* (*rassmotrenie personal'* *nogo dela*) signifies a discussion by a party committee or meeting of a member's 'unworthy behaviour' (*Organizatsionno-ustavnye voprosy*, 1978, p. 206). It is stressed that this does not mean that every single misdemeanor should be subjected to a thorough investigation: often a comradely word of warning or advice is adequate. But when there has been (or appears to have been) a severe infringement of the party rules, a formal examination of the case in instituted, which may be heard at an open party meeting, in the presence of nonmembers (pp. 217–18), and can lead to a party reprimand or severe reprimand, with possibly an endorsement of one's party record card, or even expulsion from the party. (Demotion to candidate membership was also formerly used as a form of punishment.) The slogan of the Gorbachev era is 'pure and honest,' and bchavior that contradicts the 'party ethic' leads to disciplinary action: 565 members were expelled in Omsk province between April and November 1985, 250 of them for the abuse of alcohol (Manyakin, 1985, p. 45). Periodically in the party's history—most recently in the early 1970s—reviews of membership have taken place, involving discussions between members and their local officers, prior to the replacement of old membership documents by new ones. This 'exchange of party documents,' as it is called, is supposed not to be a 'purge' in the Stalinist sense of that word, although the Russian word used (*chistka*) means precisely that. Those members who seriously infringe party discipline are deemed to have forfeited the rights and privileges conferred by CPSU membership. For, as well as imposing substantial burdens, being a communist also brings its benefits, even though Lenin's warning is still repeated, to the effect that attempts to use party membership to gain advantages or benefits are impermissible (Tikhomirov, 1975, p. 100).

### The benefits of membership

Some of the psychological benefits have already been touched on: the sense of belonging to a great tradition, a worldwide historic movement, a massive national and international institution; the knowledge that one has been identified and recognized as one of the 'top 10 percent' of the Soviet nation, the 'vanguard' of the people.

There are also certain political rights, as prescribed in Party Rule 3. First, there is the right to elect and be elected to party office, which gives the ordinary member a greater voice than the nonparty citizen has in influencing the selection of party officers and a remote chance of influencing policy. The party provides a channel of communication that is not available to outsiders. Secondly, there exists the right to discuss the workings of the party at meetings and in the party press. Although care is needed in exercising this right (so as not to draw critical attention to oneself as a troublemaker), this again is something not allowed to nonmembers. Thirdly, the member has the right to criticize in party meetings 'any communist, no matter what position he holds.' Fourthly, he may take part in party meetings and committee sessions when his own behavior is being discussed—a right, one might note, that adds nothing to the provisions of natural justice, but one that might be valuable in the light of the well-known 'infringements of socialist legality' under Stalin. And, fifthly, he may make suggestions and proposals to higher party bodies, up to the Central Committee, and demand a reply. Those are the prescribed rights of members. However, they are tempered by practice, which severely inhibits upward communication: party superiors have too much power over individual careers for one to make frequent use of some of these rights. The principle of democratic centralism gives the higher bodies the effective power to stifle critical discussion at lower levels, and anyone who made a habit of criticizing leading local or national politicians, or kept on sending statements to higher bodies, would soon be singled out as an actual or potential troublemaker and probably be disciplined for it. So in practice these rights are not quite what they seem on paper.

More valuable are the unwritten benefits of membership, stemming from the association of party membership with the occupancy of positions of responsibility throughout Soviet society. Although in law there is nothing that requires it, practice has long held that party membership is a necessary qualification, in addition to competence (sometimes instead of it), for promotion to managerial and similar positions. This point will become clear later in this chapter: suffice it at this stage to note that a nonparty person may become a schoolteacher, but promotion to a school directorship will at least be helped by party membership. Similarly, appointment to a university chair, a factory directorship, a farm chairmanship, a trade union secretaryship, and so on, normally requires CPSU membership. Moreover, in view of the rapid expansion of such 'managerial' positions, associated with the modernization and development of the economy and society, the demand for such competent and loyal individuals continues to grow, and party membership is attractive for people ambitious for career promotion. The periodic purges are intended in part to rid the party of this 'harmful and impeding ballast' (Marchenko, 1973, p. 129)—the careerists who do not pull their weight in the everyday work of the party. Obviously, then, it is 'useful' to join the party, but this is balanced by the burden of constant activity at the party's behest.

Most significantly, though, CPSU membership opens up access to a career in the country's most important institution, the party itself. Obviously, party office is open only to party members, and although the proportion of officers and officials to ordinary members is small, it is regarded as a profession (Rush, 1968, p. 255), and one that requires early membership and the acquisition of suitable experience: without it, one is automatically excluded from a political career—the notion of an 'independent' politician does not exist in the Soviet Union. Furthermore, although in the past the party treated its disgraced members with notorious harshness, today there are signs that it acts much more charitably toward its discarded long-serving officers, even to the extent, in the Brezhnev years, of protecting them from state prosecution (see Brown and Kaser, 1978, p. 273, n. 79). Rule 12, as revised in 1986, appears to remove this special protection for communists: it now reads 'A party member bears a double responsibility for the infringement of Soviet laws—to the state and to the party. Persons who have committed indictable offences are expelled from the CPSU.'

## Characteristics of Membership

So far, we have looked at party membership mainly from the viewpoint of the individual citizen or party member. We have seen how involved the process of joining the party is, and the high demands placed on members. Neither is there any certainty that a person who meets the political, moral, and working-reputation criteria will be admitted to the party, since other factors affect recruitment at particular times: notably a desire on the part of the leadership to balance the membership of the party according to sociological and other characteristics. This is reflected in recruitment policies aimed at specific groups in society. Soviet commentators openly write that not everyone who might desire to do so may become a party member (for example, Yudin *et al.*, 1973, p. 67; Tikhomirov, 1975, p. 98); and, in addition to the general stipulation that admittance is restricted to 'only the foremost, most class-conscious and active representatives of the people, the self-sacrificing builders of communism' (Yudin, 1973, p. 267), the party pursues a differentiated policy on recruitment in order to achieve an appropriate balance. This faces the party with a genuine dilemma, stemming from its many-sided self-image. It aims to fulfill several different roles in society, and these are not entirely compatible with one another: indeed, they may be contradictory.

First, the CPSU began its existence and intends to remain the party of the working class. It thus needs to stress its proletarian element by recruiting production workers and not become elitist. Secondly, as a ruling party, it needs to have within its ranks those whose expertise is indispensable in running a sophisticated modern industrial economy: the managers, the technocrats, the bureaucrats. Moreover, these groups need to be brought under the discipline of party membership, so that they do not use their power as wielders of expert skills against the interests of the system: hence, thirdly, the party today has to take into account the tradition, established over many years, that key administrative positions are reserved for party members — and the corollary that party membership is a *sine qua non* for advancement into well-paid positions of responsibility in Soviet society. Fourthly, since 1961, the CPSU has proclaimed itself to be 'the party of the whole people,' which leads to a desire to be representative of all groups in society, including non-proletarians, the various nationalities, different age-groups, women, and so on; moreover, the social structure of Soviet society itself is constantly in flux (Shapko *et al.*, 1979, p. 147). Fifthly, as the vanguard of Soviet society, it needs to regulate its total size, in order to avoid becoming 'some amorphous, unscrupulous organization' (Marchenko, 1973, p. 127). And finally, educational and cultural standards in Soviet society are constantly rising, and wider circles of citizens nowadays attain what would once have been suitable qualifications for admission (see Kadeikin *et al.*, 1974, pp. 169–70): so the party has to adjust its standards in order to avoid alienating the ambitious younger generation and also to avoid swamping the less sophisticated but loyal and experienced older generation of party members.

Clearly, it is not an easy task to elaborate an admissions and recruitment policy that will satisfy all these goals. How has the party fared in the past, and what are the current trends in recruitment and membership?

### Size

In the eighty-odd years of its existence, the party has varied enormously both in overall size and in social composition. Thus, how it would most aptly be characterized has changed markedly over the years, from a small, select 'elite' to a large, mass institution of more than 19 million communists today. Indeed, the clearest tendency is the party's propensity to expand (see Figure 2.1). However, even this trend has not been uniform, and a variety of changes have taken place over the years in the party's composition. The most thorough examination of this question is to be found in the writings of Rigby (1968, 1976, 1977); this section draws on Rigby's important work.

Before the revolution, the party was forced to operate clandestinely, at a time when all party political activity was prohibited by the tsarist authorities. The secrecy and danger that accompanied membership of the party affected the organization's nature in several ways, among them its organizational basis (party cells were set up in industrial and other enterprises: see Chapter 3) and also its highly selective and restrictive membership, a tradition that has continued, as we saw. A natural concomitant of

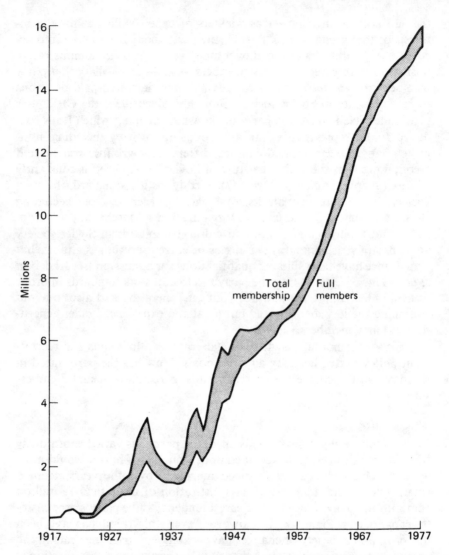

*Note:*   Party size at 1 January, except for 1917 (October), 1918–21 (March).
*Source:*   Based on figures in 'KPSS v tsifrakh,' *Partiinaya zhizn'*, 1977, no.21, pp. 20–1.

FIGURE 2.1   *The growth of the CPSU, 1917–77.*

this was the party's small size, which amounted to fewer than 24,000
members at the beginning of the fateful year 1917 (Rigby, 1968, p. 59).
Much of the crucial argument at the Second Party Congress, held in
Brussels and London in 1903, when the party split into the Bolsheviks
(Lenin's faction) and the Mensheviks (whose spokesman on the issue was

Julius Martov), was over the question of who should be allowed to join the party. The argument, which hinged on the degree of 'activism' that should be required of members, had implications for the nature of party membership, the quality of individual members, and the party's size (see Schapiro, 1970, pp. 50–4). Lenin's more restrictive policy, implying a small party of dedicated revolutionaries rather than a somewhat larger body of more general supporters, was seen by his faction as the only way of successfully organizing an illegal party. The Bolshevik party — now the CPSU — adopted this policy, which it has broadly retained.

Even so, at certain times, the party has gone out to recruit members. Numbers rose rapidly during 1917, so that by the time of the October Revolution, the Bolsheviks could claim perhaps one-third of a million adherents (estimates vary substantially: see Rigby, 1968, pp. 61–2). In 1924, following the death of Lenin, the so-called 'Lenin enrolment' brought in some 200,000 working-class members, as part of an attempt to 'proletarianize' the party's ranks. Rapid expansion during the late 1920s and particularly the early 1930s was part of the attempt to bring the new intelligentsia — the managers and specialists who held a key place in the industrialization drive — under the discipline of political control that party membership implies. From 1934 onward, however, party membership suffered dramatically in the bloody purges sparked off by the assassination of the Leningrad party leader, Sergei Kirov, on December 1, 1934. Successive waves of purges hit the party from top to bottom, removing from membership — and frequently from the face of the earth — prerevolutionary Bolsheviks, Central Committee members, leaders of the armed forces, and party, state, and economic officials and managers, as well as scores of thousands of rank-and-file members, whose fabricated connections with the 'worldwide Trotskyite clique,' with 'Zinovievites,' and with 'spies' and 'wreckers' of various hues, served as a pretext for expulsion from the party and perhaps a show trial, followed by imprisonment, forced labor, or death. Half a million members were expelled in the two years 1935–36 and nearly 100,000 more in 1937.

Whatever the reasons for this devastation — deliberate design by Stalin to rid the country of any potential for opposition to his personal power, or Stalin's losing control of a secret police that began ultimately to devour even itself — its effects on the party were disastrous, for not only were undesirable elements rooted out, but a four-year moratorium on fresh recruitment, initiated in January 1933, also meant that the members were not being replaced. Hence, by the late 1930s there was a need for the rapid replenishment of party ranks, a task that was ac-celerated during 1938 and 1939, with more than a million new admissions in the latter year. By the time of the German invasion in June 1941,

Rigby (1968, p. 220) estimates, the party stood at about 3,900,000; the officially recorded figure for January 1941 is 3,872,465 members and candidates ('KPSS v tsifrakh,' 1977, p. 21).

The first year of war saw a fall of 808,589 members between January 1941 and January 1942, many of them presumably killed in action, others possibly belonging to Soviet armies that surrendered to the Germans or were cut off from Soviet control (Armstrong, 1961, p. 140). It was as a leavening in the armed forces that the party performed its 'leading' role during the war years. Communists under arms constituted more than half of the members for much of the war, for, as Soviet President M. I. Kalinin put it, 'when the Red Army man sees that he is about to participate in a harsh battle, he puts in an application to join the party, wishing to go into battle a communist' (quoted in Rigby, 1968, p. 238). Special conditions made it easier for gallant soldiers to join the party, so that there was a surge of new recruits; but, as one might expect, losses were high, with many would-be party members not even surviving to be formally admitted after submitting their applications for membership. Turnover was dramatic, amounting to more than 50 percent in the period 1941–45, so that the overall effect of the war was, in Rigby's phrase, 'cataclysmic' (1968, p. 236).

Since the war, apart from an initial 'cleansing' and consolidation in the aftermath of the rapid and somewhat lax admissions policy of the war years, recruitment has been fairly steady, punctuated by periodic minor 'purges' and expulsion campaigns, sometimes affecting specific areas of the country, sometimes applied to the whole membership. Thus, there were 13,600 expulsions of passive members in 1962; 14,400 in 1963; 15,800 in 1964; 17,200 in 1966; and 12,000 in 1967 (Yudin *et al.*, 1973, p. 80; for a comment, see Hammer, 1971, pp. 19–21); the overall rate of expulsion may have reached 100,000 a year in the 1970s (Unger, 1977, p. 308). The last purge, initiated at the Twenty-Fourth Congress (1971) and completed in 1974, took the form of an exchange of party documents. All party members were interviewed and their suitability for continued membership tested prior to the issue of a new membership card. In 1976, Brezhnev reported that 347,000 members and candidates had been refused new cards: persons 'who had committed breaches of the norms of party life, violated discipline or lost contact with their party organisations' (*XXV s''ezd*, I, pp. 89–90). In effect, they had resigned, by not paying their subscriptions or not attending meetings. Under Brezhnev, indeed, a much more active policy of regulating party membership was adopted, so that up to half of those 347,000 might have been expelled in any case (Rigby, 1976, p. 322; Unger, 1977, p. 308); a higher level of expulsions and of refusals to confirm candidates after their probationary year may perhaps be expected in the future.

This trend reflects one element in the dilemma that we posed earlier, relating to the party's total size and recruitment policies and its desire to remain a 'vanguard': as Hammer (1971, p. 21) has expressed it, the question is how large the party can grow while remaining a Leninist party. It now accounts for 9.7 percent of the adult population (Miller, 1982, p. 6): a very large 'vanguard' indeed. It is, by any standards, a mass party, although not an open one, with complex internal structures and relationships such as did not occur at earlier stages of its existence (see Chapter 3). Soviet spokesmen envisage that the party will continue to expand. As Brezhnev expressed it in 1976:

> Over thirty years the size of the CPSU has almost tripled. It is perfectly obvious that the growth of its ranks will continue. Such is the objective tendency, flowing from the whole course of social development under socialism, and from the rise in the leading role of the party, from its authority. (*XXV s"ezd*, I, p. 89)

But equally obviously, not everyone can become a member, since the effect would be to abolish the party: if all adults were to join the party once they attained a certain level of educational training and political maturity, CPSU membership would become identified with citizenship, and its role as a vanguard would be lost — a point made by M. I. Kalinin (see Shabanov, 1969b, p. 42). Indeed, that quality may be impaired if the party expands much further beyond its present size. Hence, in devising a recruitment policy, the party leadership now finds itself with increasingly less room to maneuver, caught as it is between the party as it currently exists — the result of past policies and trends — and the party as they might perhaps wish to see it in the era of developed socialism on the road to communism. In attempting to control the party's composition, in order to make it more representative of Soviet society — seen as an essential element in developing intraparty democracy and improving the party's performance (Yudin *et al.*, 1973, p. 57) — the party is obliged to rely on a careful program that cannot be expected to yield results in a short time. We now turn to the question of the party's composition.

### Composition

The CPSU has always proclaimed itself to be a party of the working class. Indeed, as a *communist* party, which adheres to the doctrines of Marxism, its very existence is based on the need for a working-class political organization. There are, of course, several ways in which a party might be considered to be 'of the working class': it might pursue policies that favored the economic, cultural, and other interests of the proletariat, at the expense of other groups in society; it might seek to integrate the working class into society by creating opportunities for educational and social advancement (that is, it might seek to make the proletariat 'middle class'); or, most obviously, it might favor the working class within its own ranks, either excluding other groups completely, or at least somehow arranging for proletarian dominance; in addition, it might also seek to maintain working-class control over the party apparatus. If we examine the CPSU's composition over the years, we can see that it has pursued markedly ambiguous policies on this question (see Table 2.1). Periods when other groups — particularly white-collar workers — have been favored have been followed by attempts to reproletarianize the party, as the party struggled to counteract the 'upward seepage' of proletarian elements (Rigby, 1976, pp. 334–5) and to maintain the balance between conflicting goals.

Before 1917, only about 60 percent of members were workers, with a third or so drawn from among students, white-collar workers, professional people, and similar groups (Rigby, 1968, p. 63); significantly, a good number of the leaders were from this section, including Lenin, whose schools inspector father had worked his way up the tsarist civil service to a minor rank in the nobility. Throughout the party's history, these two groups have formed the bulk of party membership, with the peasantry never accounting for even 30 percent — and, indeed, working peasants never even reached the figure of 27.3 percent officially recorded for 1927.

This brings us to a peculiar difficulty in trying to analyze the composition of the CPSU, which obviously reflects an ideological problem associated with the development of the CPSU into a party of government. The question is precisely what the social categories of party

TABLE 2.1   *Party composition by social class, 1917–82*

| Year | Workers % | Peasants % | White collar, etc. % |
|------|-----------|------------|----------------------|
| 1917 | 60.2 | 7.5 | 32.2 |
| 1927 | 55.1 | 27.3 | 17.6 |
| 1947 | 33.7 | 18.0 | 48.3 |
| 1957 | 32.0 | 17.3 | 50.7 |
| 1967 | 38.1 | 16.0 | 45.9 |
| 1977 | 42.0 | 13.6 | 44.4 |
| 1982 | 43.7 | 12.6 | 43.7 |

*Sources:*   1917, 1927: Rigby, 1968, p. 85, Table 1, and p. 116, Table 2; 1942–77: 'KPSS v tsifrakh,' 1977, p. 28; 1982: 'Nekotorye dannye,' 1982, p. 36. No figures available for 1937.

members refer to: social origin, or current employment. The discrepancy is well illustrated by comparing the distribution of the membership according to the two classifications, again taking 1927 as an example (Table 2.2). Obviously, in a period of rapid social change, following a revolution aimed at advancement for the working classes, one would expect to see social mobility of those groups into supervisory and administrative posts, which is what these figures represent. The industrialization drive, initiated in 1928 with the inauguration of the First Five Year Plan, accelerated the process, the expanded managerial and administrative apparatus being staffed through the recruitment of competent and politically loyal elements from the working class, and the working class expanding rapidly at the expense of the peasantry (Sorlin, 1969, ch. 4). Hence, it can be surmised that the discrepancy between the social origins of party members and their current occupation became very marked indeed — which may be an important reason for the absence of statistics for the 1930s, in addition to the chaos caused by the purges. The 'new elite,' as Rigby (1968, ch. 6) has called the Soviet-trained intelligentsia (a term that is much broader in Russian than in common English usage), clearly came to dominate the party and continued to do so after the war and into the 1950s, as the figures in Table 2.1 again illustrate. In 1961, as we have seen, Khrushchev made a virtue out of the situation by declaring that the CPSU had become the party of the Soviet people as a whole. Under Brezhnev, there has been continued stress on the proletarian element, and the majority of new recruits in recent years have been drawn from the working class (Rigby, 1976, pp. 329–30). According to official figures, workers constituted 52.0 percent of new entrants in the years 1966–70 inclusive, 57.6 percent in the next five years, and 59.5 percent in 1981 ('KPSS v tsifrakh,' 1981, p. 15; 'Nekotorye dannye', 1982, p. 36). Party leaders take satisfaction from the trend (see *XXV s"ezd*, I, p. 88).

Even so, it has also been pointed out that, as educational levels in Soviet society continue to rise, including the training qualifications of the

TABLE 2.2 *Party composition, 1927*

|  | By class | By occupation |
|---|---|---|
|  | % | % |
| Workers | 55.1 | 39.4 |
| Peasants | 27.3 | 13.7 |
| White collar, etc. | 17.6 | 46.9 |

*Source:* Rigby, 1968, p. 116, Table 2.

working class (many of whom are now approaching technician status), the 'working-class' recruits into the party are somewhat removed from the traditional image of 'workers.' They are, moreover, perhaps the kind of workers most likely for early promotion out of the ranks of the proletariat (Rigby, 1976, pp. 331–2), and many are occupied, not in the traditional working-class industries, but in the technologically oriented fields of chemicals and petrochemicals, equipment-building, oil, instrument-making, electronics, automobiles, radio technology and the like (Kadeikin *et al.*, 1974, p. 168). By contrast, the proportion of peasants — collective farmers — in the party continues to decline steadily, and as the economy becomes still more urbanized members employed in agriculture will be further reduced.

When membership was analyzed according to sector of the economy in which members were employed, 39.2 percent were found to be in industry and construction in 1983 (a rise over the previous decade); 8.1 percent were in transport and communications (a decline); 20.0 percent in agriculture (in steady decline since the late 1950s); 4.7 percent in trade, public catering, etc. (a slight increase); 16.0 percent in science, health, and education (a slight reduction); 8.9 percent in state, party, and similar administrative employment (up slightly); and the remainder in various productive and service fields ('KPSS v tsifrakh,' 1983, p. 26).

Occupation is only one of the characteristics of membership that are of concern: another is the balance between the sexes, in a society that claims to have achieved complete emanicipation for women. In fact, as far as membership of the country's central political institution is concerned, women still have a long way to go before they attain equality with men. Women played a key role in the revolutionary movement: Vera Zasulich was one of the first Russian Marxists; Lenin's wife, Nadezhda Krupskaya, was a remarkable figure in her own right; Aleksandra Kollontai played a leading role in the revolution and in the early years of the regime. Yet as rank-and-file members of the party, they have always fallen well behind their strength in the population. Women accounted for a mere 7.4 percent in 1920 and 12.2 percent in 1927, rising to 14.8 percent in 1937, 18.2 percent a decade later (after the war had brought women fully into the workforce), 19.7 percent in 1957, 20.9 percent in 1967, and 24.7 percent in 1977 ('KPSS v tsifrakh,' 1977, p. 32); by January 1986 they accounted for 28.8 percent of party members and 34.7 percent of recruits ('KPSS v tsifrakh,' 1986, pp. 22, 24). Thus, we see a steady rise in women's strength, but they are nowhere near parity with men. The reasons reflect, on the one hand, reticence on the part of women, particularly in the Muslim areas, toward participating in public and political affairs, and on the other hand the continued pressure of the so-called 'double burden' or 'double shift': in addition to doing a full-time job, Soviet women are expected also to perform the normal household duties, so that little free time remains for either raising their political knowledge to the level required of party recruits, or carrying out the considerable burden of obligations that party membership bestows (Danilova *et al.*, 1975, pp. 68–9).

In national representation, too, we see a marked divergence from standard norms of representation. Although figures are patchy, those available suggest that the Russians are significantly overrepresented, with around 60 percent of the membership, as against something over 50 percent of the total population; Georgians, and to some extent Armenians, have also had greater strength in the party than in the population (see Rigby, 1976, p. 325), while other nationalities are consequently underrepresented, Jews being another notable exception (see Jacobs, 1976, p. 115). The figures in Table 2.3 show how far the CPSU is a Russian party. Slavs constitute about 80 percent of members, whereas perhaps 10 million members (up to 60 percent) live in the Russian republic (see Miller, 1982, p. 32, n. 45). Everywhere, it seems, party organizations are becoming increasingly international. This is seen as a manifestation of the 'drawing together' (*sblizhenie*) of the nationalities ('KPSS v tsifrakh,' 1977, p. 31). However, the principle enunciated by

TABLE 2.3  *Party composition by titular nationality, 1986*

| Nationality | Number | Percent |
|---|---|---|
| Russians | 11,241,958 | 59.1 |
| Ukrainians | 3,041,736 | 16.0 |
| Belorussians | 726,108 | 3.8 |
| Uzbeks | 465,443 | 2.4 |
| Kazakhs | 387,837 | 2.0 |
| Georgians | 321,922 | 1.7 |
| Azerbaidzhanis | 337,904 | 1.8 |
| Lithuanians | 147,068 | 0.8 |
| Moldavians | 110,715 | 0.6 |
| Latvians | 78,193 | 0.4 |
| Kirghiz | 78,064 | 0.4 |
| Tadzhiks | 87,759 | 0.5 |
| Armenians | 291,081 | 1.5 |
| Turkmenians | 76,786 | 0.4 |
| Estonians | 61,277 | 0.3 |
| Others | 1,550,527 | 8.2 |
| Total | 19,004,378 | 100.0 |

*Source:*  'KPSS v tsifrakh,' 1986, p. 24.

Petrovichev (1979, p. 71), that the composition of the party in any given area should reflect the national composition of that territory's population, adds a further complication to the task of balancing the membership of the CPSU. Recent figures (for example, in Shapko *et al.*, 1979, pp. 160–4) reveal that the CPSU is indeed a multinational organization, with broad representation of more than 100 national groups across the country; moreover, the expansion of membership among ethnic Russians appears to be at a slower pace than among some of the other groups so there is a perceptible decline in their proportionate strength. Even so, it will be a long time before the party is 'representative' of the nationalities in a sociological sense.

Two further features of membership on which information is made available are age and education. As to the former, we find what Rigby (1976, p. 323) has called a 'maturing' membership. This reflects a slowdown in the rate of recruitment, particularly of very young members, and also the greater longevity of a population enjoying better living conditions and health care and spared the devastating effects of purges and war: in 1986, 17.0 percent of the party—more than 3.2 million individuals—were aged over sixty ('KPSS v tsifrakh,' 1986, p. 24). A further result of this is that the party is maturing as an institution, with the average length of service also creeping up. In 1986, 67.9 percent of the members had been in the party for longer than ten years, whereas in 1967 the figure was 51.7 percent; of the 1986 members, 0.8 percent (i.e., approximately 152,000 individuals) had been members for longer than fifty years, although, by contrast, more than 90 percent had joined since the Second World War (1986 figures from 'KPSS v tsifrakh,' 1986, p. 25). Despite a tendency to allow membership to lapse as communists retire from employment (Miller, 1982, p. 8), the slowdown in recruitment is bound to emphasize the trend toward maturation.

This trend is not without its potential problems. On the one hand, the party needs to be able to offer membership to the best representatives of the younger generation in order to discipline them, to incorporate them politically, and to have direct access to their skills. And indeed it is asserted that the number of persons wishing to join the party is constantly growing (Shapko *et al.*, 1979, p. 153). Nevertheless, scarcely any individuals join at the minimum age of 18 years, and many recent recruits appear to have been over forty, with expulsions among younger members (Miller, 1982, p. 8). Even so, still only 15.1 percent of the party members were aged over sixty in 1983, and some two-thirds of today's communists were not even born in 1931, the year of Gorbachev's birth. Until the mid-1980s, the leaders were growing increasingly aged, continuing a clear rise in the Politburo's average age since the revolution (Taagepera and

Chapman, 1977). Just before Brezhnev died in November 1982, the average age of the whole Politburo was 68 years; only two full members (Gorbachev and Romanov, shortly joined by Aliev) were under 60, and several leading figures had passed 75. His death, followed within 28 months by those of his two immediate successors, opened the way for a significant rejuvenation, as power passed to a new generation. By the conclusion of the Twenty-Seventh Congress in March 1986, the average age had fallen to 63. This implies that the new leaders' experiences are quite different from those of the passing generation. Politically, they belong to the post-Stalin generation, which has enjoyed more than three decades of relative stability and security: this marks them sharply from their predecessors, who were scarred by the purges, the war, and postwar hardship, and it may affect the way they view the world and approach problems.

As the pace of recruitment slows down, so the qualifications for entry tend to be raised, and in practical terms that means formal educational qualifications as much as demonstrated political maturity; moreover, those already in the party are encouraged to continue their educational training. The results are clearly seen in the official figures ('KPSS v tsifrakh,' 1977, p. 29). In 1927, on the eve of the industrialization drive, 27.1 percent of communists had not even primary education, and that category had disappeared by 1967. In 1927 a mere 0.8 percent of party members had higher education, a figure that had risen to 25.1 percent half a century later. In the earlier year 9.1 percent had completed secondary education, and 63.0 percent primary, whereas by 1977 these figures were 39.2 percent and 13.6 percent respectively; the trend has continued, and by 1986, 31.8 percent of members had complete higher training, 2.1 percent incomplete higher, and 44.5 percent secondary education, with fewer than 8 percent possessing only a primary school qualification; moreover, the number of members with higher degrees (candidate and doctor of science) had increased by more than 40,000 since 1981 ('KPSS v tsifrakh,' 1986, p. 23). The party is clearly coming to consist of relatively well-educated citizens, reflecting the educational opportunities available in Soviet society, but also (as we saw) making the party much less recognizably 'proletarian' in its membership.

### Party Saturation

These figures can also be presented in another way, as implied in our discussion of the strength of women and of the nationalities in the party. The strength of various social categories among the party membership gives an indication of the nature of the party as an organization, and it may perhaps have implications for policy making within the party's structure, if the various groups are seen as in some sense 'representative' of the interests of those groups in society: there is some evidence that this is the case (see, for example, Kadeikin *et al.*, 1974, p. 164; Utenkov *et al.*, 1977, p. 43). The strength of various groups within the party may also have a bearing on the efficiency with which party policy is implemented, since it is the members who are ultimately responsible for that. It is also instructive, however, to see the extent to which the party embraces different categories within the population, as a measure of how far it has 'penetrated' society. The overall strength among the total population is about 6 to 7 percent (19 million out of about 279 million), or 9.7 percent of the adult population. These are not particularly revealing statistics; neither is it adequate to say, for example, that Jews form a small (and declining) proportion of the party membership, since it is equally significant that Jewish party membership is among the highest for any nationality. Similarly, we saw that women are weakly represented in the party compared with men; as a corollary, the party is relatively weak among women. The collective farm peasantry form a relatively small segment of the party's membership, and this reflects, in turn, the relative weakness of the party in the countryside. To analyze party–society relations in these terms, Rigby (1968) has coined the term 'party saturation,' and Hough too (1977, pp. 125–39) has examined the question in some detail. Owing to the inadequacies of Soviet statistical sources, some of the more interesting conclusions about the levels of party saturation depend on complex calculations that in turn are based on a range of assumptions about the structure of Soviet society: the interested reader is urged to read Hough, in particular. For our purposes, in order to illustrate some of the patterns, we briefly mention a few points, some of which have already been made in passing.

On the basis of his analysis of trends in party saturation among occupational groups, Rigby (1968, pp. 449–53) considered that there were three basic categories that could be identified: party-restricted occupations, high-saturation occupations, and low-saturation occupations.

Party-restricted occupations, to which Rigby added 'virtually party-restricted,' are occupations in which all or almost all members are in the CPSU. They include party officials (by definition), Komsomol officers, senior officers and officials of state bodies (ministries, soviet executive committees, administrative departments), and the directors of state-owned economic enterprises (factory and plant managers, state farm directors), army and secret police officers.

High-saturation occupations, with saturation levels in the 20 to 50 percent range, include those employed in general management, scholars and academics (with highest saturation among social scientists), school headteachers, hospital directors, and similarly responsible personnel at the middle and upper levels.

Low-saturation occupations are those that normally require no professional qualification and involve little or no managerial or administrative responsibility. They include the vast bulk of the working class and peasantry, as well as rank-and-file teachers, doctors, and others with only modest professional training and fairly low prestige. Within these broad categories, however, there are wide divergencies, with extremely low saturation among the less skilled (say, field workers on collective farms) and much higher levels among the skilled industrial workers and the equipment operators among agricultural workers and peasants. A zero level of saturation (again, by definition) is recorded among priests and other religious leaders and church officers.

Hough (1977) goes further than Rigby in examining categories other than occupation. For example, he shows that saturation levels among women in all age groups are far below those of men (p. 129); that saturation is positively correlated with advanced educational qualifications (pp. 130–1); and that this factor holds among both men and women (pp. 131–2).

An interesting article in *Pravda* ('Kto prikhodit,' 1983) gave some figures that indicate the degree of saturation of some specific professions: 'practically one specialist in three with higher and specialized secondary education'; one engineer and technician in four; one agricultural specialist in four or five; a quarter of teachers; and one doctor in six. Half of all those people with higher degrees are in the party, as are half of writers, a third of composers, one artist in five, and three-quarters of all journalists. Moreover, there are different recruitment rates for different social categories across the country: more workers in areas along the route of the Baikal-Amur Mainline railway construction; more agricultural workers in the non-Black Earth zone.

We have also noted distinctions among the different nationality groups, with the Jews, Russians, Georgians, and Armenians standing out as relatively well saturated and the peoples of Central Asia—Tadzhiks, Uzbeks, Turkmenians, and Kirghiz—as relatively undersaturated. To some extent, however, the pattern of saturation among the nationalities and in the various union republics is distorted by differentials in birth rates, and published figures make calculations of saturation among the eligible (i.e., adult) population difficult (but see McAuley, 1980, p. 470).

Enough has been said, however, to indicate the divergencies that have appeared in the strength of the party among various groups, quite apart from their strength within the party's ranks. Clearly, in view of the marked differences in the size of the various social groups—particularly those of age, occupation, nationality, and gender—the level of party saturation is likely to vary substantially in the future. Indeed, it seems most improbable that an even distribution could be obtained, since those charged with admissions appear to concentrate on the composition of the party's ranks. Nevertheless, it should not be overlooked that both ways of examining the statistics have a bearing on the total relationship between party and society and have in turn implications for recruitment policy. To conclude this chapter, we now discuss this question.

### Recruitment Policy

These trends in the composition of the party and in party saturation of various groups in Soviet society bring us back to the dilemma that faces the party authorities in formulating a suitable admissions policy. The party has expressed its wish to remain a vanguard, to remain a workers' party, to introduce more women into its ranks, more representatives of the smaller nationalities. The fundamental question is, how can all these goals be achieved? One answer might be to restrict new admissions to female workers of the non-Russian nationalities, but that is scarcely a practical policy, if only for the reason that it would leave outside the area of party discipline well-qualified male Russians in positions of influence and responsibility—individuals, moreover, who might hitherto have legitimately looked forward to the benefits that party membership confers. A simplified example illustrates the magnitude of the problem (see also Miller, 1982, pp. 4–6).

Consider the two aims of increasing worker representation and enhancing the party strength of women. With a total party membership in the mid-1970s of about 16 million, including about 4 million women, it would take the recruitment of 8 million women *and no men* to bring women up to half of the party (12 million women out of 24 million). It might be difficult to find suitably qualified women in such numbers; it would exclude millions of potential male members; and the party's character would change dramatically, with the increase in size of 50 percent. Clearly, such a crash program would not work. We calculated that, if women's recruitment proceeded at the average rate for the decade 1967–77 (3.8 percentage points annual increase), their strength would not reach 50 percent until the year 2043. Similarly, a projection of membership trends among the workers would have brought them up to 50 percent in 1997; by that year, the strength of the peasantry would have declined from 13.6 percent to 8.8 percent, while no appreciable impact would have been made on the strength of white-collar workers (a decline from 44.4 percent to 41.4 percent). As we saw, the problem is further complicated by the multiplicity of occupations within the working class, each with its own skills and graduations of status (see Matthews, 1972, ch. 5; Lane, 1978, ch. 12). The party has to decide whether recruitment should be more or less random, or according to the perceived significance of the occupation to the national economy, or perhaps even according to tradition, favoring, say, miners and railwaymen, the backbone of the 'traditional' proletarian occupations. Among the peasantry, too, should the party concentrate on recruiting the 'best'—the mechanized workers, highly skilled animal husbandrymen or agronomists—at the expense of the field workers and laborers who bear the brunt of the manual work on the farms and are therefore closer to the 'working class'?

We have said enough to illustrate the complexities involved in trying to devise a coherent, equitable, and ideologically consistent recruitment policy, and it would be presumptuous to propose remedies to what is essentially an insoluble dilemma. The evidence of recent years, however, seems to suggest that the party in its recruitment policies reflects the view that the nature of 'working-class' employment is changing, as Soviet sociologists have been arguing for some years now (see, for example, Stepanyan *et al.*, 1968, ch. 3; Blyakhman and Shkaratan, 1977, ch. 4). It recruits mainly from among the 'foremost' segments, the industries of the future, while ensuring that individuals in key managerial and administrative positions also remain under the CPSU umbrella and hence under the party's direct control and influence.

How much longer the current policies can be allowed to endure is, of course, impossible to predict. It may be that changes will have to be made in order to head off the risk that certain forms of dissatisfaction could turn into political protest. More than likely, the party will have to entrust positions of responsibility to persons outside its own ranks: indeed, this may already be happening (see Yudin *et al.*, 1973, pp. 68–69; Tikhomirov, 1975, p. 108; also Hill, 1977, pp. 173, 207, n.2). So long as the party remains the most important forum for both symbolic and practical involvement in Soviet political life, the problem is likely to persist. Since membership is not self-selecting but is subject to central policy, virtually amounting to co-option, the party leaders themselves must bear the responsibility for devising appropriate standards for recruitment and expulsion. The occasional article in the party press discusses the question of the composition of the party and its recruits. For example, a very informative article in *Pravda* indicated that readers had queried the policy of favoring the working class, since this appeared to contravene the principle of individual selection ('Kto prikhodit,' 1983). The party's leaders have so far barely acknowledged that such a problem exists; yet it is evident that these matters will remain a cause for concern in the remainder of this century.

To sum up: the composition of the CPSU is diverse and heterogeneous. Like society, it is in flux, yet party membership and society are not always reflected in each other in a precisely proportional way. On the other hand, the party's ideology demands homogeneity, unity, unanimity, and harmony. So far, the CPSU has managed to preserve a reasonable equilibrium between unity and diversity, homogeneity and heterogeneity, and we would not wish to imply that the party is in danger of fragmenting or disintegrating. But we *are* saying that party membership and composition, far from being a passive, inert phenomenon, are in fact vital aspects of the CPSU's existence, and factors that are becoming increasingly difficult to manipulate. Hence, we would agree with Soviet assertions that 'The correct resolution of this task is a matter of political importance of the first order' (Shapko *et al.*, 1979, p. 147). Moreover, we would say that the problem is likely to grow, as the Soviet economy and society become yet more complex and sophisticated. In that situation, the revolutionary ideology becomes less and less obviously appropriate in an electronic and technological age, and its requirements provide a more elusive framework in which to contain the concept of Communist Party membership.

# CHAPTER 3

# Structures, Institutions, and Personnel

After examining the party membership, our attention now turns toward the party as an institution rather than as a collection of members. Clearly, an organization of this nature requires a complex set of offices, committees, structures, and personnel through which to perform its functions and by means of which to conduct its own internal business and regulate relationships among members. How, then, is the CPSU organized to cope with the daunting tasks it has set itself? What are its structures? How is it staffed?

## Party Structure

In broad terms, the party can be thought of as a pyramid (see Figure 3.1). At the apex stand the party's central bodies, notably the Politburo, the Central Committee, and the central Secretariat. It is here that supreme political power resides, matters of doctrine are authoritatively interpreted, and all major policies are formulated. At the base lie the grassroots organizations, the primary (or basic) party organizations (PPOs), to which communists are affiliated. Within the PPO is carried out much of the work of recruiting, training, and disciplining members, allocating them to tasks connected with the implementation of policy and mobilizing the nonparty masses. Between the apex and the base are several organizational tiers: these direct and control inferior bodies but themselves receive instructions from above. This whole structure serves as the organism that leads, controls, and directs Soviet society, and we shall examine it in detail.

### The primary party organizations (PPOs)

Every member of the CPSU, without exception, must belong to a primary party organization. The special characteristic of the PPOs is that

47

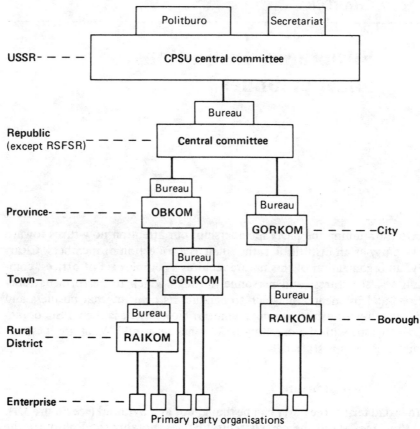

*Note:* This figure omits the levels of *krai* (territory), with its *kraikom*, and *okrug* (national area), with its *okruzhkom*; for most purposes these are best regarded as forms of *obkom*.

FIGURE 3.1    *Simplified hierarchical structure of CPSU organs.*

they are practically all located in the members' places of work. In most societies, mass parties base their primary branch organizations on a geographical area—a ward or constituency. This is because in competitive systems political power is gained through elections, and so parties organize themselves so as to maximize their chances of winning electoral contests: the major function of party branches, then, is to persuade the electors of the area to vote for their candidates. The different organizational basis of the CPSU (like the stringent admissions procedures discussed in the previous chapter) is a throwback to the conditions of secrecy and danger in which the party operated in its early years. An illegal organization of 'professional revolutionaries,' it had to disguise its existence and make sure its members could meet one another without drawing the suspicious attention of the tsarist police. In an industrial setting, informal meetings can be held and messages passed on relatively securely: there is nothing suspicious about a group of workmates chatting between shifts, whereas a group of disparate workers converging on a private home or apartment is more conspicuous. In addition, and most significantly, a party with its basic organizations in economic institutions could inflict damage at a point at which the capitalist system was most susceptible: strikes, disturbances, working-class discontent, and so forth sap the will of the system, whereas open political activities—street processions and demonstrations—are extremely vulnerable to police or army attack.

Ideas such as these in favor of such a party organizational basis were resolutely propounded over the years by Lenin, most notably in his *What Is to Be Done?* published in 1902, and the Bolsheviks were far better placed than other political parties when the opportunity came in 1917. This form of basic organization has remained until today.

The question arises: why, nearly seventy years after the successful revolution, does the Communist Party still maintain organizational practices designed for application by an illegal, underground, revolutionary party? There are a number of reasons for it.

First, tradition plays an important part, in particular, the fact that this was the structure proposed by Lenin, who remains a powerful political symbol in the Soviet Union and particularly within the party. It would thus take considerable political courage to abandon a feature of party life that was so closely identified with the party's founder. Second, as an organizational principle, a centralized hierarchy of control and authority, supported by branches situated at the very point at which policy is applied, is a very effective means of getting things done. Party cells at places of work can feed information on the current position into the center as a basis for decision making, and they can react swiftly to orders when action is required (on these points, see Chapter 4). For much of the regime's history, a crisis of one sort or another has been the overriding characteristic: civil war, the New Economic Policy (which risked a return to capitalism), industrial recovery and expansion, war, reconstruction. Each of these periods placed heavy demands on party and population, and a ruling party that had links with practically every production unit in the country—a position the CPSU built up gradually over the years— possessed a powerful means of mobilization and control. These advantages are still appreciated today, when the party's overriding goal is to create the 'material and technical basis for communism.' Indeed, one of the major tasks of PPOs, as defined in Party Rule 58, concerns the mobilization of the masses in industrial and agricultural production, raising productivity and quality, and increasing and protecting social wealth. At the same time, by locating its basic units and their officers at places of work, the party's task of educating the masses politically is greatly facilitated: the lunch break can be used for a reading and discussion of the day's editorial in *Pravda*, whereas it might be much more difficult (as party branches in pluralist systems discover to their constant frustration) to persuade workers to go out to an evening or Sunday morning political meeting.

On January 1, 1986, the CPSU had 440,363 PPOs, distributed as follows: in industry, transport, communications, and construction—112,646 (25.6 percent); in state farms—22,682 (5.2 percent); in collective farms—26,846 (6.1 percent); in educational, health, cultural, and scientific institutions—104,401 (20.1 percent); in economic and administrative institutions—76,805 (17.4 percent); and in trade and public catering establishments—15,848 (3.6 percent); the remaining 81,135 (18.4 percent) were attached to small villages, blocks of flats, and so on, on a territorial basis ('KPSS v tsifrakh,' 1986, p. 26). These organizations varied greatly in size, from 3 members (the minimum) to several thousand; more than four-fifths had fewer than 50 members, however, and only one in fourteen more than 100. In 1983, the average size in industry was 103 members; on the state farms, 68; on collective farms, 60; and in construction concerns, 39 ('KPSS v tsifrakh,' 1983, p. 28). These figures correspond to the distribution of party membership.

In view of the different types of unit in which they are located—from mines and triple-shift industrial plants, to offices, construction sites, ships at sea, embassies abroad, and even symphony orchestras—the internal structure of PPOs varies enormously, and with it, one presumes, political relationships among members and between them and officers of the party. At its simplest, the PPO is a nucleus, a cell of members personally known to one another; they meet periodically to elect a secretary, who then keeps the organization's records, collects the subscriptions, and maintains contact with the party committee above. Such a PPO might be found in, say, a retail shop or a restaurant. In 1947, almost two-thirds of all PPOs were of this type, consisting of fewer than fifteen members; thirty years later, the figure was 40.9 percent, and the clear trend is for party organizations to grow larger, so that the typical party member is likely to be found is an organization with a more elaborate structure. Its precise nature depends on two factors: (1) the number of communists (which to some extent varies with the size of the workforce); and (2) the internal organization of the enterprise itself. Let us consider two examples: a collective farm (*kolkhoz*) and a complex industrial plant.

*The collective farm.* Depending on its geographical location, a *kolkhoz* might be engaged in growing cereals and root crops; grazing and rearing livestock; perhaps (in the south) a certain acreage would be given over to vineyards; there might also be an intensive pig or poultry unit, or a dairy herd and calf-rearing set-up. The whole enterprise is administered by a chairman, an accountant, a veterinary surgeon, and a chief agronomist. The production workforce consists of livestock specialists; mechanized workers who operate, service, and maintain equipment—tractors, combine harvesters, irrigation equipment, and other farm machinery; and finally, fieldworkers, unspecialized in their skills, organized in brigades headed by brigadiers.

If such a *kolkhoz*, with a workforce of some 500 to 600, has 40 communists, their distribution among the various grades would be uneven: the level of saturation among the administrators and the mechanized workers will be markedly higher than among the general fieldworkers. Since the work patterns on a farm tend to split up the workforce, the PPO will be organized to take this into account: a party group will be set up in, say, the dairy unit, another in the equipment depot, and another in the administrative office; further groups will be established in any field brigades with three or more party members in them. Each party group is headed by an organizer (the *partgruporg*), who liaises with the PPO secretary (who frequently doubles as deputy chairman of the farm), and the work of the various groups is co-ordinated by a bureau. This structure is indicated in Figure 3.2.

Since the Second World War, the growth in the number of party groups has been dramatic, reflecting the growing sophistication of the Soviet economy and the greater penetration of the party among the workforce. At the beginning of 1946, there were slightly fewer than 29,000 groups; by 1986, the number had risen to some 721,000, and there has been a parallel increase in the workshop party organizations, similar to party groups and found mainly in industrial enterprises.

*The industrial plant.* A chemical combine, a mine, a heavy engineering works, an automobile factory—enterprises such as these in a modern economy employ thousands of workers, technicians, engineers and administrators. The manufacturing processes being carried out are usually diverse, numerous, and complicated, and normally the workforce is divided and subdivided and allocated to special workshops that broadly correspond to various production processes. Sometimes, all these workshops are concentrated on one huge site—as at a steelworks, for instance—and sometimes the various component units are scattered about a city or district. In a further complication, workshops themselves are

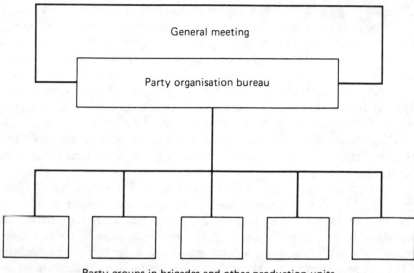

General meeting

Party organisation bureau

Party groups in brigades and other production units.

FIGURE 3.2   *Collective farm PPO structure.*

often subdivided into smaller units, each fulfilling a particular production assignment, often working on a shift basis.

In the Soviet context, a PPO is attached to the enterprise as a whole, and all the party members in the workforce — perhaps several hundred or more than a thousand administrative workers, control engineers, maintenance technicians, production workers, canteen staff, and so forth — belong to that organization. However, the chances are that many members will rarely know or even meet all the others, from whom they may be separated by the location of the workplace, the kind of task performed, and possibly the shift worked. Such a PPO is quite different from the simple cell-like structure described earlier and from the PPO on the *kolkhoz* described above. It is likely to have a complex hierarchical set of institutions, such as that depicted in Figure 3.3, which is taken from a Soviet source. Such a massive organization is given rights that bypass some of the stages in membership recruitment described in Chapter 2 by giving the PPO committee the right to confirm new members admitted at the level of the workshop party organization, which in turn is given the right to admit new members, rather like a smaller PPO. Many members may rarely set eyes on the PPO secretary, who thus becomes a remote and powerful figure for the mass membership. In many ways, this complex structure, with multiple tiers and a centralized chain of command, is a virtual microcosm of the overall structure of the party.

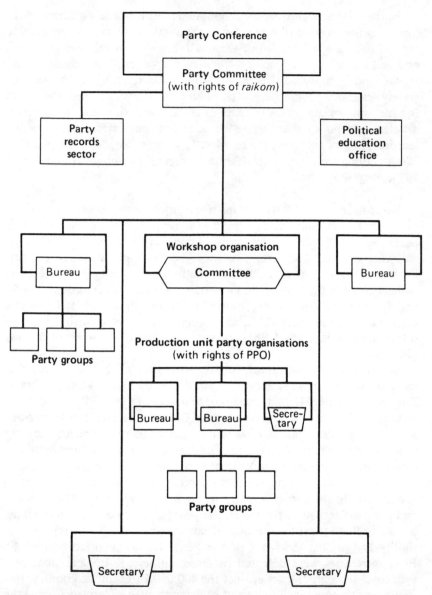

*Source:* Adapted from *KPSS — naglyadnoe posobie po partiinomu stroitel'stvu* (Moscow: Politizdat, 1973), pp. 116–17.

FIGURE 3.3 *Large industrial plant PPO structure.*

On top of this, following the economic reforms of the 1960s and 1970s involving the creation of new types of production units — the production associations (*ob"edineniya*) of various types — new relationships have had to be worked out among different lower-level units, some of them spread widely among different administrative territories, occasionally widely separated geographically (see Dunmore, 1980). Indeed, the search for the appropriate forms is continuing, and experiments, conferences, articles, and books that discuss the question have become a common feature of party experience in the past few years (see, for example, *Partiinaya organizatsiya v usloviyakh proizvodstvennogo ob"edinenya*, 1977; also Chapter 4).

*Political functions of PPOs.*   One implication of this diversity of structure is that it is meaningless to speak of a 'typical' PPO, or even a typical party member. Clearly, different party members' experience of party life will vary markedly according to the type, location, and size of their organization; and, as noted above, relationships among party members —most notably those between local officials and officers and the rank-and-file membership — are bound to differ significantly from one organization to another. This, as it were, introduces a further form of differentiation into the CPSU, apart from the social diversity already discussed.

Nevertheless, whatever the formal structure, all PPOs function in more or less the same fashion and are governed by the same rulebook. This states (Rule 54) that the highest organ of the PPO is the party meeting, held monthly or (in the case of the complex structures described above) every second month or as required. This forum alone has the right to admit new members and is responsible for disciplining any members who fail to uphold the 'lofty title of communist.' The meeting formally elects the committee or bureau and the secretary (who is a full-time party functionary in the case of organizations with more than 150 members), and these officers serve for either one year (in the case of small bureaus) or two to three years (in the case of larger committees), sharing responsibility for guiding the work of the PPO. It was reported in 1979 88 PPO secretaries were defeated in these ballots ('K itogam otchëtov i vyborov,' 1980, p. 28); set against the 400,000 PPOs in the country, this figure reveals how far this element of democracy is effectively used at the lowest levels in the party hierarchy.

This same 'accounting and election' meeting (*otchëtno-vybornoe sobranie*) also elects delegates to the party conference of the district or town in which the PPO is situated and to which its own organs are subordinated. It is here that the PPO is linked with the superior organs and apparatus of the CPSU, and the production principle in the party's

organization is linked with the territorial principle, for the permanent apparatus of the party consists of organs that are responsible for a given
territory (Petrovichev *et al.*, 1972, p. 133). (Between November 1962 and
November 1964, the whole party apparatus was divided along production lines into an industrial and an agricultural structure; however, this
was among the first measures to be abandoned by Khrushchev's successors.) We now discuss the formal apparatus and the superior organs
of the party.

## Party Institutions

Party institutions can be divided into two broad types: the largely formal
and ceremonial conferences and congresses and the more functional
committees at various levels, which together with the apparatus of administrative departments constitute 'the party' as an institution for most
practical purposes. In the description that follows, note that the uniformity of structure at the union republic level is broken by the absence of
the highest organs in the largest republic, the Russian federation
(RSFSR): hence, there is no RSFSR party congress, central committee,
political bureau, or secretariat. Under Khrushchev the affairs of the party in the RSFSR were supervised by a Central Committee Bureau for the
RSFSR, but this was abolished at the Twenty-Third Congress (1966).

### *Conferences and congresses*

For any given territorial unit — district, province, city, territory, republic
(except as noted above), and USSR — the highest party forum is
technically the party conference for that area; at the republican and All-
Union levels, it is called the congress. Conferences meet every two or
three years, and congresses every five years, and they conduct a range of
apparently important business. Indeed, the most prestigious of these
gatherings — the CPSU congresses, held in the plush setting of the
Palace of Congresses, the one modern building in the Moscow Kremlin
— are significant international events, attended by scores of fraternal
delegations from foreign communist and workers' parties, as well as up
to 5,000 delegates from various local and republican branches of the
CPSU itself. These delegations are selected, at all levels, at the conferences of party organizations at the next lower level: *oblast* (province)
conferences are attended by delegates elected at the city, town, and
district party conferences within the province; city conferences are composed of delegations from the borough conferences within the city; and
the borough conferences in turn comprise representatives of the PPOs,
elected at the same meeting that elects the secretary and the committee or
bureau members. Thus, we can see that the elective principle in the party

is indirect: the ordinary members of a PPO in, say, a factory in a city in the Urals have no direct say in who shall attend the CPSU congresses in Moscow.

At the lower levels — town and district — the conferences bear the characteristics of a political rally, 'at which well-known local political leaders affirm the appropriate line, taking their cue from the . . . first secretary, under the watchful eyes of a representative of higher authority' (Hill, 1977, p. 139). More weighty matters are debated at the conferences of major cities and provinces and at the congresses in the union republics, relating to the success of the area's economy and sometimes giving local representatives a chance to voice dissatisfaction; in addition, the conference serves as a 'school or training session' for the representatives of the lower levels in party and state (Stewart, 1968, pp. 31–3). Such conferences rarely last more than two or three days (one day at the very local level).

By contrast, CPSU congresses — 'the supreme organ of the Leninist party' (Apollonov, 1976) — nowadays endure for a week or more and attract the country's whole attention, with live broadcasting of the proceedings, supplemented by saturation coverage in the printed media. The Twenty-Seventh Congress ran from February 25 until March 6, 1986, and 5,000 delegates were elected to attend, all but 7 of whom did so. These delegates included representatives of a wide range of occupations, social groups, and nationalities as well as the most powerful and politically influential men and women in the land. The majority had joined the party since 1945 (including 948 in the last ten years), and more than three-quarters were attending their first congress; one was a pre-revolutionary party member; moreover, at 27 percent of the delegates, women achieved their highest-ever representation. These CPSU delegates were joined by 152 fraternal delegations representing communist, labor, workers' and social-democratic parties in 113 countries (*Pravda*, February 26 and 28, 1986).

After preliminaries, the bulk of the first day was given over to the political report of the party's Central Committee, delivered by Mikhail Gorbachev as General Secretary. This is always regarded as the major item on the congress agenda, a 'State of the Party' address, in which the party leader traditionally surveys the country and the world, as seen from the Kremlin, reporting on the party's successes in economic and cultural development at home, and of the movement's progress around the world, and giving details of intraparty developments. Sometimes, too, new items of legislation are promised, such as, at the Twenty-Fifth Congress, the long-awaited USSR Constitution (*XXV s''ezd*, I, p. 112). A second major report, which became a standard item during the Brezhnev era, is the prime minister's presentation of economic 'guidelines' that act as parameters in devising the five-year plans in the subsequent decade (Chapter 4). These two reports, together with a third, on the state of the party's finances, form the basis for the debates that follow, in which the leaders of delegations endorse the line adopted in the reports, perhaps with mild criticism of a ministry or the planning authority, and frequently vie with one another in their praise of the leadership, especially the General Secretary. Little is known of how the speakers are selected, although at the Twenty-Fifth Congress, 139 delegates had indicated their wish to speak on Brezhnev's report and the Auditing Commission's report, and only 44 did so before debate was called to a halt on the sixth day of the congress (*XXV s"ezd*, I, p. 462); at the 1981 congress, only 40 delegates were given an opportunity to speak in the debate (*XXVI s"ezd*, I, p. 375). At the end of the congress, statements are adopted endorsing the reports, which then become binding on all party members and form party policy until the next congress. In practice, apart from specific measures, these statements encourage the leadership in doing whatever it considers necessary and appropriate for guiding the party and the country toward communism.

In recent years, these congresses seem to have become very predictable events, with few signs on the surface that would indicate anything but complete unity and satisfaction with the Soviet leaders' performance and policies. Controversy and arguments over different policy lines never occur in the public sessions. The response of the West to these massive rallies is epitomized by Leonard Schapiro's description of the Twenty-Fourth Congress (1971) as 'bland, uneventful, colorless and smooth as a play being performed on the stage for the third year running' (Schapiro, 1971, p. 2). This was not always the case, and a handful of the older delegates at the Twenty-Seventh Congress may have remembered some of the notable congresses of the past.

There was the Twentieth (February 1956), at which the then First Secretary, Nikita Khrushchev, in a 'secret' speech, launched a reassessment of Stalin's 'personality cult' that shook the movement (text in Christman, 1969, pp. 158–228). The Seventeenth (1934), dubbed the 'Congress of the Victors,' celebrated the collectivization of agriculture and the remarkable successes of the First Five Year Plan for industrializing the country and established Joseph Stalin as the supreme leader in the Soviet Union. In his 'secret' speech in 1956, Khrushchev revealed that 1,108 of the 1,966 delegates to the 1934 congress were subsequently removed from office and in many cases put to death on the orders of the 'victor'; 70 percent of the Central Committee members elected at the same congress were arrested and shot, mostly in the great purge of 1937–38 (see Christman, 1969, p. 175). That is one reason very few party members today recall the Tenth Congress, held in 1921, which Schapiro

(1970, p. 235) has referred to as 'a watershed in the party's development.' It opened shortly after a rebellion by the naval garrison at Kronstadt (one of the Bolshevik strongholds at the time of the revolution), and it inaugurated the New Economic Policy — a deliberate retreat from the policies of the Civil War period in the direction of capitalism, particularly in the field of agriculture — and, most significantly for the future, it adopted a measure outlawing the establishment of different factions within the party. This was the resolution 'On Party Unity,' introduced by Lenin to end the bitter policy conflict that had characterized the congress, and subsequently seen in the West as 'a milestone in the history of the party' (Schapiro, 1970, p. 214). So effective was this resolution that no subsequent congress has witnessed the genuine political debate that characterized that congress and indeed congresses before it. Having achieved dominance, Stalin subsequently turned this supposed 'supreme organ' of the party into a rallying of the sycophantic faithful and failed even to call one between March 1939 (the Eighteenth) and October 1952 (the Nineteenth). This was in flagrant breach of the party rules, which required congresses every four years; this rule was amended to five years at the Twenty-Fourth Congress, in 1971, partly because of the custom of planning the economy in five-year periods: a significant point when the congress has become a platform for announcing the main directions of the economy in the forthcoming quinquennium.

A final significant function of conferences and congresses — 'an exceptionally responsible point' (Apollonov, 1976, p. 177) — is the formal election of the party's leading organs for the territory concerned. These are the Central Committee at the All-Union and republican levels, and the committee at other levels: *obkom* (short for *oblastnoi komitet*) for a province; *kraikom* (*kraevoi komitet*) for a territory; *gorkom* (*gorodskoi komitet*) for a town or city; and *raikom* (*raionnyi komitet*) for an urban borough or a rural district. Little is known about how these elections are conducted, since they are considered to be internal party affairs and are covered in a special memorandum circulated by the central party authorities. At each level, the conference decides on the number of voting and nonvoting (candidate) members to be elected; there is supposed to be open discussion of candidatures and election by secret ballot, with each candidate who receives more than 50 percent of the delegates' votes being elected. This rule was introduced at the Twenty-Second Congress (1961): previously, the number of persons elected was determined by the overall size of the committee as decided by congress, with perhaps some strongly supported nominees failing to be elected; the present arrangement allows more flexibility (see Kadeikin *et al.*, 1974, p.

150). There can be no doubt that the elections to party organs are carefully controlled; at the lower levels the conference (or the accounting and election meeting of a PPO) always takes place in the presence of a representative of the next higher level, who has the right to comment on the suitability of individual candidates and make his own (that is, the higher organ's) nominations: this is said not to contradict the norms and principles of party life (*Organizatsionno-ustavnye voprosy*, 1978, pp. 152–3) — indeed, it is fully consistent with the principles of democratic centralism and *nomenklatura*, which are discussed below. The basic rule in these as in any other elections in the USSR is that 'anarchy and free-for-all [*samotëk*] are impermissible in elections,' and the composition is worked out in advance, the purpose of the meeting being to convince those present to vote in favor of the agreed nominees. Research in Novosibirsk *oblast* has revealed that 'active discussion' of candidates takes place in only 35.5 percent of cases, with a further 17.9 percent when a candidate declines to stand; some respondents said the elections were a formality, with no real discussion, and 'a significant number' of members did not even take part in committee elections (Utenkov *et al.*, 1977, pp. 55–6).

At their first meeting, usually held before the conference or congress disperses, the newly elected committee meets to elect an inner body, a bureau (the Politburo, in the case of the CPSU Central Committee), responsible for the day-to-day running of the party's affairs between sessions of the committee. The congress or conference also elects an auditing commission (*revizionnaya komissiya*), responsible for keeping the party's accounts and financial affairs in good order, and this commission reports back to the congress.

We have now described the formation of the basic structure of the CPSU, which was presented diagramatically in Figure 3.1. The PPOs support a permanent hierarchical structure of committees and bureaus, indirectly elected by conferences and congresses, and also the auditing commissions, likewise elected by conference. Note again that the ordinary members have no direct voice in the election of the party's central bodies, and their influence over the choice of party leader is practically nil. However, one should also add that more than a quarter of party members (5.3 million: see 'KPSS v tsifrakh,' 1986, p. 28) serve on committees at one level or another; even allowing for a measure of overlap between one level and another, the proportion is quite substantial. The committees with their bureaus are the most important elements in the CPSU: these are the party's organs, attached to which are administrative offices that together form the party apparatus, whose employees in turn are known as *apparatchiki*.

### The party organs

As an organization of some 19 million members, the CPSU requires a substantial apparatus simply in order to run its own internal affairs: keeping records, collecting funds (about 57 percent of which now come from membership subscriptions: *Pravda*, February 26, 1986, p. 11), issuing documents, training officials. In addition, as an institution that takes ultimate responsibility for everything that goes on in the country, the party requires an extensive system of research departments and similar organs that can gather, sift, analyze, and evaluate information for presentation to the country's leaders in their policy-making activities. It also requires a similar set of organs for supervising the implementation of policy. The role of the party in performing these functions is discussed in Chapter 4, but it is appropriate here to examine the apparatus, taking as an example the relatively simple structure of the district committee or *raikom*, strategically situated between the powerful intermediate organs of the province and republic and the PPOs where policy is ultimately implemented. Our account is based on a useful Soviet source, called simply 'The Party District Committee' (*Raionnyi komitet partii*, 1974).

The structure of a typical *raikom* is shown in Figure 3.4. There, we see the committee itself, an elected body with perhaps up to 100 members, divided into full or voting members (say, 70 to 80) and candidate or non-voting members: these, who are all full members of the party, have a consultative voice and form a reserve from which full members are replaced when they die in office or are transferred elsewhere or dropped from membership. The typical *raikom* consists of officials from the state, the party, the Komsomol, and trade union organizations in the area; the chairmen of the major collective farms, state farms, and industrial enterprises in the district, and the PPO secretaries of some of these; representatives of scientific and educational establishments; and a leavening of 'ordinary' party members — outstanding workers from the peasantry or the industrial workforce. It meets at least four times a year in plenary session (plenum) to discuss the latest edicts from the central party authorities or to monitor the spring sowing or the harvest or the progress of industrial enterprises in fulfilling their plans. These committees issue statements, which are then taken back to the individual PPOs for implementation.

Clearly, with such infrequent meetings, the *raikom* cannot as a body keep a close check on the day-to-day affairs of the party organization, and for this purpose it elects, on a show of hands, the bureau of around a dozen leading party workers, most of them full-time employees of the party, but also including a number of important state officials and representatives of the major economic enterprises. This body meets

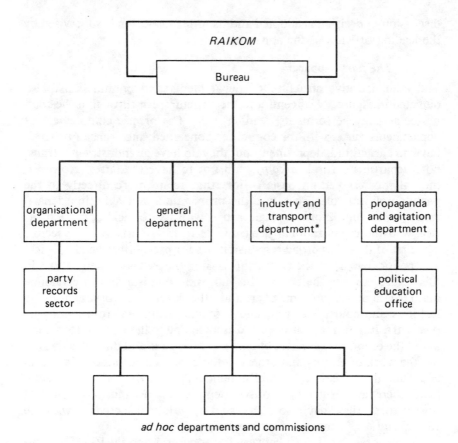

ad hoc departments and commissions

*May be replaced by an agricultural department in a rural *raikom*. Source*: Adapted from
*KPSS — naglyadnoe posobie*, 1973, p. 63.

FIGURE 3.4    *Structure of* raikom *(district or borough committee)*.

periodically — usually two or three times a month — to discuss 'the most
important questions of the economic and political activity of the district
party organization' and to receive reports on the work of party committees and bureaus at the PPO level; it also discusses 'questions connected
with checking on the fulfilment of the decisions of party committees'
(*Raionnyi komitet partii*, 1974, p. 41). Questions for discussion by the
bureau are prepared by *ad hoc* commissions, comprising party functionaries and specialists drawn from the party apparatus; interested parties may be invited to attend the discussions — PPO officers, scholars,
economists, and so on, depending on the nature of the topic; after

discussion, a decision is adopted and its implementation is supervised by
the leading officials of the apparatus.

### The party apparat

The administrative structure of departments and commissions, also
depicted in Figure 3.4, is central to the structure, for through it the committee actually performs its 'leading' role. The precise complement of
departments varies with the committee concerned: most urban *raikomy*
have no agricultural department, but they do have an industry and transport department; rural *raikomy* tend not to have the latter. However,
they all possess certain basic offices that relate more directly to the
party's political role. These are the propaganda and agitation department (commonly known as 'agitprop'), with its political education office; and the organizational department, with its party records sector.
The first of these has broad responsibilities for promoting the ideological
and political goals of the party, supervising the PPOs in their efforts in
this regard; vetting the courses in Marxism-Leninism and in economic
matters laid on for party members and other interested workers; training
lecturers and course teachers; and providing lecturers from among its
own staff. It is also responsible for disseminating to the PPOs information
about the economic successes of leading enterprises and directly supervising the work of editors and others in the communications media and in
educational and cultural establishments. Apart from a departmental
head, there are normally one or two deputies and a handful of so-called
'instructors'; they may also be assisted by volunteer activists, with the
formal status of 'nonstaff instructors.'

The most regular contact between the apparatus and the PPOs is maintained by the organizational department, in many ways the key element
in the *raikom* apparatus, responsible for arranging and supervising the
implementation of party decrees and decisions. Above all, it has control
over the staffing of secretaryships at the PPO level, selecting and placing
suitable recruits, training them, arranging for their election, and generally supervising their work. Instructors from this department regularly visit
the PPOs in the individual enterprises; it is, of course, desirable for these
officials to possess a substantial amount of industrial, agricultural, or
technical and scientific expertise (*Raionnyi komitet partii*, 1974, p. 131).
The role of this department in allocating party members to posts — its involvement, in other words, in the process of *nomenklatura*, discussed
below — is what gives it its importance, and this function is performed
on the basis of the information on the record cards of all party members,
submitted on initial application, regularly updated, and maintained by
the party records sector attached to the department.

Further contact with the PPOs is maintained by the staff of the agricultural and the industry and transport departments, whose concerns are more directly associated with stimulating production in the enterprises under their supervision. Quite often, they are called on to deal with fairly minute details of production, constantly running the risk of trespassing on the territory of industrial management, leading to interference and 'substitution' (*podmena*), which is a constant problem in the party's relations with other institutions (see Chapter 5).

The final department depicted in Figure 3.4, the general department, is responsible for organizing the business of the *raikom*: preparing the agenda and materials for conferences, plenums, meetings of the bureau; duplicating and circulating documents, draft resolutions, and the texts of decisions; keeping minutes; arranging for the filing, transfer, and destruction of party records as appropriate; handling correspondence. In short, this department is the workhorse that is expected to see to the smooth running of the party's work at this level.

A similar arrangement applies at higher levels, where the complexity and range of responsibility is reflected in a greater number of more powerful departments. An *obkom*, for example, has a separate secretariat, distinct from the bureau (at *raikom* level, the secretaries are all incorporated into the bureau), and special departments that handle business with scientific and educational institutions, with administrative and financial organs, with economic institutions; separate departments deal with the construction industry, industry in general (with sometimes a distinct transport and communications department) and agriculture, and there may be special departments to handle the party's relations with especially important industries — coal, oil, timber, chemicals, and so on; some *obkomy* possess a department for light industry, the food processing industry, and trade. These are in addition to the political and organizational departments common to all party committees (see *KPSS — naglyadnoe posobie*, 1973, p. 59). At republican level, the structure is still more complex and specific, with (notably) a department of culture. At this level, in particular, the party apparatus departments largely parallel and closely monitor the fields of responsibility and the work of the ministries.

The same applies to the central party apparatus, which is, in the words of Hough, 'structured like a miniature government, staffed by highly trained and experienced personnel, involved in such sensitive questions as personnel selection, inspection of ministerial performance, and the drafting of decisions and policy memoranda' (Hough and Fainsod, 1979, p. 438). The precise relationship between officials in the party apparatus and those in the governmental apparatus over whom in principle they have political authority is a very complex one. It is certainly not a case of the dominance of the officials in the party's central apparatus — again, as Hough has convincingly argued (Hough and Fainsod, 1979, pp. 438–48) — and there may be closer co-operation than has been generally assumed in Western notions of a rivalry between party and state. But there can be no doubt about the enormous power the party apparatus and its officials wield, at any level in the hierarchy, stemming in large part from the fact that the party has paramount influence in appointments to positions of responsibility throughout Soviet society (see Chapter 4).

### Central Party Organs

Before moving on to examine the party personnel, as such, in greater detail, it is important to look at the central equivalent of the party organs at district level — the Central Committee, the Politburo, and the central Secretariat — for it is among the members of these central institutions that the Soviet 'establishment' is to be identified.

#### The Central Committee

After the party congress, the Central Committee that it elects is the most authoritative political body in the Soviet system. In Lenin's day, it was small enough to carry out the day-to-day business of the party. Since then, it has expanded, its meetings have become less frequent (they have settled down to a twice-yearly routine, with additional meetings at crucial times), and its original role has been surrendered to the Politburo. The Central Committee elected in 1976 consisted of 287 full and 139 candidate members; 5 years later, at the Twenty-Sixth Congress, this was raised to 319 full members and 151 candidates; and the 1986 congress expanded the size of the committee slightly to 477, of whom 307 were full members and 170 candidates. This is clearly a very large body, and the word *committee* scarcely indicates its nature. Its plenums are perhaps more like conferences than committee meetings, although proceedings are confidential, apart from the communiqué that follows and press summaries of the main speeches. (In the Khrushchev years, purportedly verbatim accounts were published, in the manner of CPSU congress records; however, the practice was discontinued under Brezhnev and, although briefly revived during Andropov's period in office, it has not been resumed.)

The Central Committee's composition reflects the authority which it is reckoned to possess. Among its members are top leaders in the party itself, ministers and other top governmental and state officials, leaders of the trade unions and the Komsomol, party and state leaders from the republics and provinces, ambassadors, scientists and scholars, famous writers and artists, a cosmonaut or two, and a sprinkling of outstanding workers to represent the 'ordinary' party membership. Analysis of the 307 voting members elected in 1986 reveals that it comprises approximately 10 percent national party apparatus representatives, about 33 percent republic and provincial party apparatus, 27 percent all-Union and 5 percent regional government officials; 3.6 percent were ambassadors, 3.9 percent writers and others in culture, science, journalism, and the like; 3 percent were employed in the Komsomol, the trade unions, or economic management, and about 8 percent industrial or agricultural workers; 9 percent had a direct link with the military and security services. (Figures are approximate, in part reflecting overlapping functions and offices held.)

Little is known about the selection process, although it seems most likely that a list of candidates is drawn up before the congress and is discussed by the leaders of the main delegations (Apollonov, 1976, pp. 185-6) before being presented to the voting delegates in a secret session. The crucial question, of course, is how the names are selected for the list, and here we are largely in the dark. One would speculate, however, that the Central Committee is selected on the basis of a combination of personal merit and position occupied, and the two are obviously not entirely separate. Famous figures such as the writer Mikhail Sholokhov or the cosmonaut Valentina Nikolaeva-Tereshkova are perhaps selected for their individual merit; but the bulk of members, it appears, are chosen (as at lower levels) for their tenure of a particular post in the central or provincial administration: the 'job-slot,' as Daniels (1976) has called it. Indeed, analyses of the Central Committee in the late 1960s and 1970s indicated that there were a fair number of posts that carried, as it were, *ex officio* Central Committee membership and others that conferred candidate membership. These included a number of republican and *obkom* first secretaryships, the chairmanships of republican, provincial and major city government bodies, and other similar posts (Gehlen and McBride, 1968, pp. 1235-6; Daniels, 1976). One can conclude, therefore, that the Central Committee 'has in large part come to be an assembly of representatives of institutions and regions rather than of individuals' (Hough and Fainsod, 1979, p. 453, citing Daniels, 1976). As such, the Central Committee contains within it an impressive array of skills, expertise, and experience on which the top leadership may draw in its policy making.

Although the formal sessions are too infrequent and too brief for full-scale policy debates, allowing only a minority of members to voice their opinions, the role of committee members as 'incorporated' experts may be quite a significant one. It seems at least plausible that this is a body of prestigious individuals (mainly men; the voting members of the 1986 committee included thirteen women, or 4.2 percent) who are consulted by the officials of the central party apparatus in preparing policy proposals and draft resolutions for endorsement in the plenum itself. Moreover, their membership of the committee enhances the individuals' prestige and reputation in their localities, a factor that is perhaps material in the implementation of policy. This informal role for the Central Committee members is, however, shrouded in obscurity, and we have little concrete information beyond what is contained in the brief reports. Plenums are held immediately before major state and party events: Supreme Soviet sessions, the introduction of new economic plans, the promulgation (in 1977) of the new Constitution; also to discuss particularly grave problems, such as, occasionally, the international situation or agriculture. On each occasion, the committee issues a formal decree, which represents party policy and is binding on all party members.

It seems probable that these sessions serve two functions: first, as a body that gives authoritative endorsement to policies agreed on by the top leadership; and second, as a forum at which the broad consensus of the party throughout the country can be gauged as a basis for future policy-making (Hough and Fainsod, 1979, p. 465–6). It also seems clear that on certain critical occasions, the Central Committee is able to exercise its party-constitutional authority to resolve conflict within the Politburo, as appears to have happened in 1957, when Khrushchev appealed to the committee against the 'anti-party group,' and again in 1964, when Khrushchev was ousted after failing in a similar appeal from the Politburo to the larger forum (Armstrong, 1973, p. 89). For much of the time, however, its public face is largely ceremonial, and responsibility for the everyday running of the party's and the country's affairs is entrusted to a smaller body, the Politburo.

### The Politburo

The Politburo (political bureau) is elected by the Central Committee at the end of each party congress, and the names are read out before delegates disperse. Subsequent changes in membership are made at Central Committee plenums — including the dramatic change of leadership, when Brezhnev replaced Khrushchev in October 1964. In the crucially important sense of decision making and policy determination, the Politburo is the government of the USSR, deciding priorities, allocating resources, and defining broad policies — and perhaps occasionally dealing with specific items of business that require quick, authoritative resolution. However, as a small body, obviously the Politburo cannot govern the country directly, and in an increasingly developed society the complexity of the issues confronting it implies a quite different working style from what may have been adequate at earlier stages of Soviet development. Today, in the decision-making process various governmental, ministerial, and state bureaucracies, as well as lower party bodies and representatives of the party's own central secretariat and apparatus, make substantial inputs of advice and information. But the final decision rests with the Politburo, the institutional apex of the Soviet political structure.

It consists of some two dozen men (only one woman has ever been a member), divided into full and candidate members, and headed by the General Secretary. All those in the Politburo are full members of the Central Committee, and they form the most powerful, select body of politicians in the country, the 'super-elite' (Löwenhardt, 1982, p. 74). Their portraits are hung in the streets and carried on placards in May Day and November 7 parades, and they are nominated as election candidates and to various honorary positions throughout the country; until the mid-1950s, they had factories, farms, and even towns and cities named after them during their lifetime.

The changes in the kind of individuals who reach such high office, since the days when it contained those who actually led the revolution, can be analyzed in various ways (see Hough and Fainsod, 1979, pp. 466–71; Löwenhardt, 1982, ch. 2), and relations among the members vary over time. Following a change of leader, the body's composition tends to reflect fairly accurately the balance of forces at the summit of the party structure. The General Secretary is little more than *primus inter pares*, and the allocation of functional roles within the 'collective' leadership has usually been arranged to make this clear. But gradually, changes take place; under Brezhnev by the mid-1970s, something like a Western cabinet seemed to be developing in the Politburo's make-up, with major sectoral and geographical areas 'represented' among the party and governmental officials who sat on this top policy-making organ. Rigby (1970) wrote of the possible emergence of a 'self-stabilizing oligarchy,' in which interests and individuals were carefully balanced to avoid the need for sudden changes in the team. Subsequently, however, the dominance of the General Secretary became apparent, and it can now be seen that this was achieved by a skillfully manipulated process of gradual, seemingly piecemeal dismissal of personal rivals and political opponents, and their replacement by supporters and clients, sometimes of long standing, who also happened to occupy key positions in government. The result is that the Politburo entered the 1980s under the secure leadership of the ailing and elderly Leonid Brezhnev.

Brezhnev gave to Soviet politics order and stability (see Bialer, 1981), virtues in accord with the mood of society following years of flux and turbulence, and ones that were welcomed by employees in the party apparatus, on whom the leadership relies for implementing its policies. But order and stability, if prolonged too long, can become inertia and stagnation, and this appears to have happened from the late 1970s (Brown, 1982), avoiding new initiatives to resolve increasingly pressing issues (see, for example, Gustafson, 1981). Following two ailing, interim leaders, Gorbachev firmly abandoned Brezhnev's personal style to inject dynamism into the system, speedily removing elderly colleagues from influential posts and replacing them with younger, more competent, and energetic colleagues.

To a considerable degree, how the Politburo operates depends on the proclivities of the General Secretary and the extent to which he chooses (and is able) to dominate his colleagues. From the late 1930s, Stalin virtually disregarded the statutory provisions concerning the Politburo and surrounded himself with men who were in or out of favor according to whim: they were divided into smaller bodies, which met separately, and — according to Khrushchev (1971, p. 307) — they enjoyed no security in their lofty office. Khrushchev, too, after the defeat of the 'anti-party group' in 1957, promoted his own personality cult, which cast his colleagues into the shadows. Brezhnev, although dominant, apparently treated his colleagues with consideration and resolved genuine differences by appointing special working parties (*XXVI s''ezd*, I, p. 88) rather than imposing his own opinions. The Politburo now meets regularly, usually once a week, on Thursdays (see Löwenhardt, 1982, pp. 95–6; Brown, 1982, p. 226), and its members may be in touch more often during crises. The working relationship within Gorbachev's Politburo is not yet clear, but regularity and a businesslike style seem likely to continue, with the General Secretary's authority over policy growing, boosted by his forceful personality.

### The Party Control Committee

Another central institution, the Party Control Committee, is responsible for investigating and ruling on infringements of party discipline and expulsions from the party; in a sense, it is the party's 'supreme court' (Hough and Fainsod, 1979, pp. 249, 418). Reports of its activities are regularly published in the press. For example, *Pravda* (10 March 1980) contained two accounts of investigations by the committee into poor work discipline by party members in responsible industrial managerial posts. In one case, two officials in the soap manufacturing business were 'strictly punished' for irresponsibility and lack of concern. In the second case, an administrator in the oil industry ministry was expelled from the party for financial and other mismanagement, including the award of bonuses for simply fulfilling normal quotas; the party organization secretary was reprimanded for not exercising sufficiently tight supervision over the activities of his members; and a third official was reprimanded for taking no action. These examples show how far this committee can become involved in the detail of economic management, seen as a legitimate area of concern for all party organs. In other cases, the Party Control Committee may have a role in redressing the genuine grievances of party members who have suffered from the high-handed action of their local secretary and committee.

### The Central Secretariat

Finally, among the top party institutions, mention must be made of the central Secretariat, headed by Gorbachev as General Secretary, and containing usually ten to a dozen secretaries in all, some of whom (like Ligachev) are in the Politburo and all of them powerful and influential individuals in their own right. The Secretariat meets weekly on Wednesdays. Its members supervise the departments of the Central Committee apparatus, alongside department heads who are usually members of the Central Committee or other important party bodies. Each secretary supervises a particular range of activity. Gorbachev, as General Secretary, is ultimately responsible for all aspects of party life; Ye. K. Ligachev, the second most influential secretary in the hierarchy, assumes closer supervision over the appointment of party cadres, ideology, discipline, and certain aspects of foreign policy. The other full member of the Politburo who is also a secretary is L. N. Zaikov, in charge of the defense industries, and perhaps also the military and security apparatus. Politburo candidate member V. I. Dolgikh has for many years supervised heavy industry, and more recently the USSR's energy program has been added to his responsibilities. The 'portfolios' of the remaining seven non-Politburo secretaries range from agriculture (V. P. Nikonov) to propaganda (A. N. Yakovlev); and from consumer affairs and social services (the remit of the central leadership's sole woman, A. P. Biryukova) to ideology and culture (M. V. Zimyanin), science and education (V. A. Medvedev) and party-organizational work (G. P. Razumovskii). It was expected that A. F. Dobrynin, for many years the USSR's ambassador in Washington), might take over the International Department following the retirement of the long-serving B. N. Ponomarev. However, there was talk at the Twenty-Seventh Congress of a major restructuring of the central Secretariat, which could result in significant changes in several areas of responsibility.

Work in the central Secretariat and its offices frequently serves as an important training experience in the careers of rising political leaders, and in the past appointment to the Politburo itself has frequently been made from among the secretaries, who clearly should be considered, along with the Politburo members themselves, as part of the top leadership.

It is convenient to note here the office of the General Secretary, with his team of personal assistants. These are believed to brief the top leader, write reports and speeches for him, and generally prepare him for meetings and negotiations, particularly with foreign visitors (see Hough and Fainsod, 1979, pp. 418–19).

All these officers and officials are properly thought of as part of the party personnel, those who staff the *apparat*, known in Russian as *kadry* (cadres) or *apparatchiki*.

## Party Personnel

We have already seen something of the role of the workers in the party apparatus: ministering to the internal needs of the party as a mass organization; stimulating and supervising the political education of the party members and the population at large; overseeing the performance of the various economic and cultural enterprises; and, at the higher levels, becoming directly involved in policy making. Clearly, these party workers are an important link in the political system.

The number of such officials is uncertain. In a recent estimate, taking into account various Western computations that range from 100,000 to twice that figure, Hough suggested a figure of around 90,000 for the staff of the 'lower party apparatus,' bringing the total apparatus staff to not more than 100,000 (Hough and Fainsod, 1979, pp. 495–6). These are the people who are making a career of party work, as it were, placing their considerable expertise at the disposal of the party in the most direct way possible. In some cases, this employment in the party apparatus is a temporary secondment; but in others, it becomes permanent, as successful experts who show administrative or political flair may be recruited into the pool of local political leaders, given special training by the party, and launched on a career as a party administrator, perhaps being placed in the position of *raikom* first secretary, whence he or she may work upward through promotion.

At the local level, there is evidence of a recruitment policy that regards party, state, and economic managerial cadres as part of a common pool, with individuals being moved around to give them experience in a range of spheres (see Hill, 1977, pp. 165–7). Subsequently, they may specialize within the party or the state or economic management (Frolic, 1972, p. 51). But by whatever route they reach the position, the key post at any level in the hierarchy is that of party committee first secretary, and it is generally recognized that the occupant of that position is the most powerful official in the locality (Stewart, 1968, p. 133; Scott, 1969, p. 140; Hough and Fainsod, 1979, pp. 497, 501). At *obkom* level, Hough (1969) has compared them to the prefect in the French administrative system: plenipotentiary representatives of the central political authority, responsible for maintaining economic success and political peace in their territory. For success, the reward will be further promotion; for failure, an abrupt end to a career, although the impact will be more gentle than it was for a previous generation of disgraced party officers.

As regards the routes to the top, John Reshetar (1972, pp. 164-8) identifies four broad career patterns. First, the career of the central party apparatus official, exemplified by Georgi Malenkov and by Aleksandr Shelepin; these individuals rise through obtaining a position in the central apparatus, which leads on to membership of the central Secretariat. The second pattern is that of the 'ideocrat,' of which Suslov was an example, whose career is strongly oriented toward ideology, theory, and propaganda. A third type if the specialist—Anastas Mikoyan, Aleksei Kosygin, Nikolai Ryzhkov—whose technical expertise brings Central Committee and Politburo membership. And finally, some individuals pursue a successful career in party or government posts in the provinces and then are called to Moscow for responsible posts in the central apparatus: Khrushchev, Brezhnev, Chernenko, and Gorbachev are examples of that pattern. Other types of career pattern might also be identified (see, for example, Fleron, 1970; Moses, 1981; Rigby, 1985, pp. 153-7).

In each of these cases, reaching the top means sitting on all the influential and ceremonial committees and other bodies, including soviets and party committees, attending countless meetings, delivering regular speeches (perhaps to inattentive audiences), negotiating with higher authority on behalf of one's area, and all the other functions of leadership in a complex society. Furthermore, for aspiring political leaders, educational qualifications and professional training and experience seem to be increasingly necessary. Statistics for the past decade or more have indicated that those chosen for election as secretaries at any level are generally better educated on average than the mass party membership, and substantially so in comparison with the population as a whole: they are, indeed, 'the cream of the CPSU membership' in their general and technical education (Harasymiw, 1971, p. 319). Among PPO secretaries, a record 99.3 percent of those in office in January 1986 had third-level or secondary education ('KPSS v tsifrakh,' 1986, p. 31). *Obkom* secretaries in the late 1960s were likely to be Russian or Ukrainian, to be about fifty years old, to have joined the party at around twenty-five years of age about the time of the Second World War, and—significantly—to have higher education, acquired through, or supplemented by, the party's own educational system (Frank, 1971, pp. 182–4, 190). In order to improve the standards of training for future leaders, in March 1978 the party restructured its top training institution, the Central Committee Academy of the Social Sciences (Shapko *et al.*, 1979, p. 195).

The fact is that the modern leader requires a much more sophisticated view of his role than was ever thought necessary under Stalin, or even under Khrushchev—and certainly by Lenin, who believed in the gradual simplification of all the processes of government, so that ordinary citizens could run the affairs of society themselves, and the elite group of professional politicians and administrators could be dispensed with, alongside the 'withering away' of the state. Trends in the organization of the economy and society in the twentieth century have made the attainment of that goal most unlikely in the foreseeable future, if ever, and the CPSU seems to have recognized this fact in its leadership recruitment policies. We return to this question in Chapter 4.

### Democratic Centralism

Finally in this chapter, we consider the principle that cements together the structural pyramid and its various components and determines the formal relationship between those who function within it. That principle is *democratic centralism*, and it would be hard to overestimate its importance. It figures prominently in Lenin's writings on party organization; he contrasted it with bureaucratic centralism and with anarchism, stressing the need for both centralism in order to ensure discipline and democracy in order to involve all party members in the institution's work (see the various quotations from Lenin's work in Smirnov *et al.*, 1973, pp. 55–8). Modern Soviet writers, referring to this 'firm Leninist principle,' assert that the CPSU was the first workers' party to implement the policy in full measure and to test its force and effectiveness in the most varied historical conditions (Kadeikin *et al.*, 1974, p. 108). Writers on the development of the party point out that the emphasis in the balance between democracy and centralization in the concept has varied in different conditions over the years, but they say that the principle has remained intact: even Stalin's personality cult, which 'had a certain negative influence, as a result of which infringements of the norms of party life took place,' did not, it is claimed, destroy the party's democratic character (Petrovichev *et al.*, 1972, pp. 102–3; also Utenkov *et al.*, 1977, pp. 9–22).

Democratic centralism as a doctrine exists independently of its specific use in the USSR, as virtually an element of the ideology (see Waller,

1981); however, in its modern Soviet form, it is defined in Party Rule 19 as consisting of four elements:

- all leading party bodies are elected;
- party bodies report periodically to their organizations and to higher bodies;
- there is strict party discipline and subordination of the minority to the majority;
- the decisions of higher bodies are obligatory for lower bodies.

In practice, one finds that these various elements are not all observed with the same degree of scrupulousness: indeed, a recurring theme in Soviet literature in the past few years has been the need to develop 'intra-party democracy' (see Hill, 1980a, ch. 7). At the Twenty-Sixth Congress, Brezhnev emphasized that the democratic centralist link between center and localities is two-way (*XXVI s"ezd*, I, p. 92).

We saw above that 'leading party bodies'—including delegations to congresses and conferences, members of committees, and bureaus—are formally elected, in accordance with the first element in democratic centralism. However, we also saw that elections to all 'leading bodies' above the PPO level are indirect, so that democratic control becomes less effective the closer one goes to the center of power. Party secretaries also are formally elected; but at all but the very highest level, the candidates are subject to the approval—in effect, the selection—of the apparatus at the higher level, exercising its prerogative of *nomenklatura* (see Chapter 4). Moreover, party conferences and the first plenary session of a newly elected committee are always attended by a representative of higher authority, 'in order to exercise proper control over the conduct of reports and elections' (*Organizatsionno-ustavnye voprosy*, 1978, p. 152). It is inconceivable that the delegates to, say, a town party conference could decline to elect a secretary who had been nominated by the *obkom*; neither could they elect to the *gorkom* a party member whom the higher body thought unsuitable, for whatever reason.

Party committees report on their work to the conference that has the power to re-elect them; bureaus deliver accounts of their work to the committees. Yet it is doubtful whether these occasions can serve as a genuine forum for examining the work of the elective organs. As we saw, congresses and conferences tend to be rather like rallies, gathered to acclaim successes. There may be criticism voiced, particularly at the lower levels (see, for example, Hill, 1977, pp. 137–8); yet rarely, if ever, is a party organ genuinely censured for its performance, except by higher bodies. Then, criticism may be devastating. An investigation by the Central Committee into the Yaroslavl city organization revealed an extremely lax state of affairs, with meetings being held irregularly, highly formalistic proceedings, low turnout, insignificant and too specific topics discussed, poor preparation, use of the occasion for criticizing ordinary party members, and a range of further indicators of poor performance (text in Smirnov *et al.*, 1973, pp. 104–9). But this criticism from *above* indicates the emphasis on the centralist, rather than the democratic, form of control.

The other two elements—discipline, and the binding nature of decisions on lower bodies—are, by contrast, firmly applied, subject only to inefficiencies in application and control. These various principles are supposed to allow for completely free discussion and criticism up to the point when a decision is taken, after which it becomes obligatory. In practice, over the years, criticism from below has been at best frowned on and disregarded, and critics often persecuted, and discussion has been effectively stifled, a point raised more than once by Soviet scholars in recent years. Thus, Petrovichev pointed out that criticism tends to go 'from above, directed toward the lower organs,' rather than in the opposite direction (in Kadeikin *et al.*, 1974, p. 14). In the same book (pp. 97–8), Kadeikin notes that officials at the intermediate and higher levels disapproved of unpalatable information coming up from below and instead encouraged their inferiors to 'prettify' the true position. Shakhnazarov (1972, p. 57) pointed out that Lenin said there would always be argument and struggle within the party, so that no disciplinary measures should be taken against party members who criticize—provided their comments do not contradict the principles of the party program. The problem arises, however, over who is to determine what contradicts the program; and, in presenting his argument in this way, Shakhnazarov is revealing that some members have indeed suffered for being outspoken: 'rocking the boat' is something not permitted in the CPSU.

Democratic centralism, as applied in practice, therefore, has a number of negative and positive sides. On the one hand, it narrows the boundaries of legitimate debate within the party (and in other institutions to which it is applied). This can harm the party's functioning, by preventing genuine criticism and fresh, challenging ideas from reaching the ears of the party's policy makers. It also has the effect of inducing complacency on the part of those officials, particularly in the middle ranks, who take advantage of it for self-protection, asserting their authority by invoking the principle as a means of stifling the opinions of those below them, and deflecting censure from themselves. This negative effect could be overcome only by the party's taking positive measures to encourage discussion and debate and to stimulate flows of information and opinion, upward, downward and horizontally. More positively, perhaps, democratic centralism ensures discipline in the application of policy and lends a coherence and unity that such a diffuse organization might otherwise lack. For these reasons, among others, it has been identified as one of the 'pillars' of the Soviet system, along with the party's leading role and censorship, that is most unlikely to be abandoned in the search for political reform (Brown, 1979, p. 152).

# CHAPTER 4

# The Party's Functions and Performance

We turn in this chapter to review the various political functions performed by the CPSU and the arrangements by which it organizes its operation. We begin with an examination of the relationship between the party and the Soviet political culture.

## The Party and the Political Culture

The attention of Western students of communist and Soviet politics has turned significantly toward the concept of political culture in recent years (see, for example, Brown, 1974, ch. 4; Brown and Gray, 1977; White, 1979; Brown, 1984); Soviet scholars too have begun to make use of the concept (for example, Kerimov, 1979, pp. 123–8; Keizerov, 1983; see also Brown, 1984, ch. 5). This concept, which refers to the psychological dimension of the political system's functioning, may indeed be thought of as a 'natural' one for understanding certain central aspects of Soviet politics. This, as well argued by Tucker (1973), is because of the explicit and clear general goals of the regime, which are derived from the ideology and aim to create a completely different *type* of political system, characterized by different fundamental relations among the members of society: those members will be examples of the 'new Soviet man.'

### Bringing up Soviet man

The general characteristics of this 'new man' can be inferred from the qualities of the communist society in which he will exist. Phrases such as 'from each according to his abilities, to each according to his needs' and various altruistic elements contained in the 'communist morality,' as expounded in the party program, give some idea of what is expected of Soviet citizens—indeed, the whole human race—when eventually they live under communism. A more explicit description of the moral qualities of the 'new man' was given by the veteran ideologist and Politburo member Mikhail Suslov, referring to the qualities that the work collective is expected to instill in its members: concern about the public interest; a conscientious and creative attitude toward work; political activeness; socialist patriotism; a high civic consciousness; a spirit of collectivism; a readiness to offer comradely mutual assistance; impatience with relics of the past; and lofty moral qualities (Suslov, 1977, pp. 510–11, quoted in Yudenkov *et al.*, 1979, pp. 22–3).

Given that aim, in 1917 the Bolsheviks were faced with the most un-promising social material: a largely illiterate, poor, ignorant peasant population almost totally excluded from public affairs and ruled by an autocrat of notorious aloofness and a corrupt, half-competent bureaucracy, disrupted by war and hostile to the revolution (see Lewin, 1985). Starting off with such material, the party has been faced with a massive task of education in civic matters, as well as in the knowledge and skills required in an industrializing society. Giving people an understanding of the ideas contained in the ideology has thus been a basic requirement, and associated with it has been the attempt to eradicate 'relics of the past' in the consciousness of the citizenry and to arm them mentally against subversion by the competing ideology and in-deed by competing interpretations of Marxism. It is in such activities that the party sees an important part of its ideological function (Lesnyi and Chernogolovkin, 1976, p. 48).

In addition to such lofty moral qualities, supposedly characteristic of developed socialism and communism, other qualities will also be demanded, if 'the government of people' is to be replaced by 'the ad-ministration of things' under the communist system of self-administration. The writings of the founding fathers first asserted and in recent times the 1961 CPSU program reaffirmed that the functions hitherto performed by the apparatus of the state would gradually be taken over by the population and the state itself would, in the classic phrase, 'wither away.' The 1986 version of the program, less exuberant than its predecessor about the transformation of the state into organs of public self-administration, observes:

> The CPSU believes that at the present stage the strategic avenue of development of society's political system lies through advancing Soviet democracy and increasingly promoting the people's socialist self-government on the basis of the day-to-day active and effective participa-tion of the working people, their collectives and organisations, in decision-making on the affairs of state and social life.

In the longer run, citizens' involvement in the running of society clearly requires a very special set of attitudes, knowledge, skills, and experience on the part of the population if the process is to be pursued smoothly. Here, the literature on political development can help us understand what is involved. There may be a strong element of culture-bias in some of the assumptions underlying the concept of political development — specifically, much of the literature of the 1960s seemed to assume that 'modernity' and the politically developed nation are synonymous with what exists in the United States and, to a lesser extent, Western Europe (see, for example, Sherrill, 1969). Such views are, of course, rejected — with contempt — by Soviet commentators. Nevertheless, the notion of political development is one that ties in well with what the CPSU sees as the underlying aim or goal of the Soviet system: the developed, democratic political system is one in which citizens are involved, in which they participate, and popular participation in the running of society has been one of the elements emphasized in 'developed socialism' (Babiy and Zabigailo, 1979).

Western students of political development are not alone in stressing that effective participation in government requires a range of appropriate skills, attitudes, and experience — in short, a *participant political culture* — on the part of all members of society, citizens and officials alike (Almond and Verba, 1963, p. 19; Pye, 1966, ch. 5). Soviet scholars, too, have observed that people need a basic knowledge of the political system in which they are to participate: a familiarity with the institutional structure, the constitution, and other basic laws, and at least a rudimentary knowledge of modern methods of government (Shakhnazarov, 1972, p. 132). Indeed, this elementary fact was noted by Lenin, who commented:

> We are not utopians. We know that an unskilled labourer or a cook cannot immediately get on with the job of state administration. . . . Politics is a science and an art that does not fall from the skies or come gratis. . . . A vast amount of educational, organizational and cultural work is required; this cannot be done rapidly by legislation but demands a vast amount of work over a long period. (Quoted in Kerimov, 1979, pp. 123, 125, 127)

Hence there is need for people to be *taught* how to govern, as a necessary condition for 'serious' participation by the masses (Shakhnazarov, 1972, p. 132), and the Communist Party, as 'the organizer and educator of the masses,' takes on this role of political culture-development (Kerimov, 1979, p. 125).

In any case, even without the stated aim of trying to involve citizens positively in the country's political life, any regime, including that of the

Soviet Union, needs to inculcate in citizens attitudes of acceptance of and support for the system: even dictators need to win some sort of acceptance, or at least acquiescence, on the part of those whom they rule (and they frequently do so by flamboyant methods, including cults of their own personalities).

For these various reasons, the Soviet Communist Party has long engaged in the task of 'socializing,' of educating, the Soviet public into the values and norms of the ideology and the system of government.

## Political Socialization

Political socialization has been characterized as 'primarily a teaching or training function by which the party or organization persuades the general public of the legitimacy and correctness of the system and of the goals articulated by the system's leadership' (Gehlen, 1969, p. 71). To that end, the party uses a whole variety of methods and techniques in order to win the minds and hearts of citizens.

In addition to exercising enormous influence over the content of the mass media (see Chapter 6), the local party organs, directed by the central apparatus, run an impressive program of lectures, evening courses, discussion groups, and group and individual agitation, under the aegis of agitprop departments; on top of that, full use is made of election campaigns and other suitable occasions as a vehicle for trying to stimulate citizens' political knowledge, awareness, and commitment to the party's values.

From the earliest years, the party has mounted a co-ordinated effort at political enlightenment, which today embraces a system of political schools and academies that take students through the biography of Lenin and the history of the CPSU and more advanced courses in Marxist philosophy and practical political training. This program lasts for several years and has an enrollment counted in millions. The formal courses of instruction are supplemented by series of classes by well over a million 'propagandists' (a word that has positive connotations in Soviet usage) and supported by the work of 'agitators' — 4.8 million of them in 1984 — who work in groups to hold discussions among their workmates on issues of current concern. One-off lectures are given by 'political informers' — 1.8 million in 1976 — and members of universities or the Academy of Sciences are also drawn in to give advanced lectures in their special field of expertise. These efforts are co-ordinated at local level and follow programs outlined by the central party authorities: for example, in January 1980, the journal *Party Life* contained a list of lecture titles considered suitable for a course in the year of the 110th anniversary of

Lenin's birth ('Delo Lenina . . .,' 1980). A range of other organizations and informal channels, likewise under direct or indirect party or Komsomol supervision, completes the picture. Millions of lectures are attended in a year by millions of party members and the interested public (for these points, see White, 1979, ch. 4, 1985).

The impact of this effort is hard to measure, but the indications are that the results are far from what might be desired by the leaders. A great deal of scattered information suggests that many lecturers are ineffective in putting across their message, and audiences are composed of unwilling draftees, except perhaps for lectures and discussions on current themes, particularly the international situation. When agitators spend a workgroup's lunch break reading aloud the morning's *Pravda* editorial, one can appreciate the marginal impact that the experience is likely to have on the level of political socialization. Similar lack of enthusiasm characterizes the more formal party education system, so that there, too, the impact is at best dubious (see White, 1979, ch. 6). At his first important Central Committee plenum, in April 1985, Gorbachev (1985a, p. 15) noted the irrelevance of much propaganda work, so that 'a person hears one thing, but in his life sees something else.'

In view of this, the party authorities are redoubling their efforts in this field. A new decree of April 1979 attempted to put the whole propaganda effort on a fresh footing (see *XXVI s''ezd*, p. 94), and a Central Committee plenum in June 1983, followed by an important conference in December 1984, further emphasized the importance of this aspect of the party's work — a point stressed also in the massive literature on the topic (White, 1985, p. 10). Yet even those party members chosen to sit on party committees — the cream of the politically conscious, one would have thought — in many cases, according to *Pravda*, lack the appropriate skills that would enable them to perform as competent and effective committee members ('Vybornyi aktiv,' 1980), so that service on a PPO committee, or even a *gorkom* or *raikom*, is coming to serve as an adjunct to the mechanisms for political socialization used by the party.

### The effects of political socialization

Thus it would seem as though the CPSU has a long way to go before it can claim success in instilling the appropriate culture in Soviet citizens. For, while some writers already report with enthusiasm the development in political participation by the masses in recent years, the same individuals also comment on negative elements that also remain — and may even be increasing — in Soviet society: passivity, consumerism, political indifference, selfishness, and philistinism (G. N. Manov, in Tikhomirov, 1975, pp. 277–8, and in Tikhomirov, 1978, p. 58). This has led Stephen White (1977) to suggest that the whole effort must be considered a failure.

Moreover, the CPSU has so far failed to instill the appropriate high-minded principles even in its own officers and officials. This is well illustrated by the catalogue of evils noted in the Georgian Communist Party, which came to light in the early 1970s, and were recited at the Georgian party's Twenty-Fifth Congress: misappropriation of public property, bribery, protectionism, sponging, red tape, careerism, private property tendencies, harmful traditions and customs (quoted in Kharchev *et al.*, 1976, p. 60). Two years previously, the Georgian central committee had adopted a statement aimed at combating protectionism, which contained the following revealing passage:

> In life there still take place phenomena alien to the nature of socialism, in relation to which criminal responsibility is not envisaged and which — in conditions of a weakening of party and state discipline, a blunting of the vigilance of communists, a lack of organisation, and the irresponsibility of some leaders — are able to cause serious harm both to the national economy and to [the cause of] forming the consciousness of people on the basis of the Moral Code of the Builder of Communism. (Quoted in Kharchev *et al.*, 1976, p. 59)

It is not out of place to note that these infringements of party and state discipline took place at a time when the then Georgian party first secretary, V. P. Mzhavanadze, was a candidate member of the CPSU Politburo and a close colleague of Leonid Brezhnev. A series of investigations, by the new party leadership in Georgia and by journalists from *Pravda* and other powerful organs, revealed widespread corruption in the republic, excused on the ostensibly altruistic ground of 'helping one's neighbor' (Kharchev *et al.*, 1976, pp. 59–60). It was in order to root out those guilty of such uncommunist behavior that the 'exchange of party documents' was undertaken by the party in the early 1970s. This episode illustrates the protection from prosecution that party members can obtain, for Mzhavanadze was allowed to retire with a certain dignity. In other cases, too, even where a party member is found guilty of an offense and punished by the courts, both the party meeting and the PPO bureau sometimes turn a blind eye, to the chagrin of more conscientious members (see Makarov, 1980). If the party and its responsible officials are so poorly socialized into the norms of socialist society, one should not be surprised if the mass of the public also display low levels of civic responsibility and a weakly developed political culture.

## Information and Political Communication

We have already referred to one important form of political communication engaged in by the CPSU: communication of political ideas and concepts to the mass membership and the population at large. This same process can also be seen as directly connected with the earlier function of developing and interpreting the ideology (see Chapter 1), for much of the content of the political socialization and education is concerned with transmitting ideas related to Marxism-Leninism. Apart from the propagation of the works of Marx, Engels, and Lenin, the party also issues various forms of programmatic statements that encapsulate new interpretations and new concepts and incorporate new emphases in the party line. These are widely broadcast and published and form the basis for general discussion within party organizations and study groups. The party program, the rulebook, congress and conference resolutions and decisions, statements adopted by the Central Committee: these and other forms of communication serve as a regular mechanism for bringing new ideological insights to the attention of the party and the world (Lesnyi and Chernogolovkin, 1976, pp. 48–9); indeed, such authoritative statements have been referred to as 'part of the treasure-house of Marxist science' (Chekharin, 1977b, p. 34).

However, 'political communication' is a much broader concept than simply the use of various media for transmitting propaganda to the masses: it is, indeed, a process that links all parts of the political system, and without it 'politics' as a human activity could scarcely exist (Deutsch, 1966, p. 77). In common with other organizations, the CPSU is held together by communication, and in recent years there has been a growing awareness of the need for effective information flows within the party as the basic requirement for 'competent leadership, well-founded and timely decisions' (Kulinchenko et al., 1978, p. 126; see also Hoffmann, 1978). As a recent book on the PPOs put it:

> It is hard to imagine the successful work of any party committee if it does not know what is happening in the organisations subordinated to it, if it does not know what cares and problems are causing concern to the mass of communists, and how the works collectives are getting on. In their turn, it is difficult, even impossible, for primary party organisations to conduct their affairs properly if they have not got appropriate information from the superior leading organ. (Khaldeev and Krivoshein, 1979, p. 260)

It is revealing of the fresh attention being paid to this question that the first edition of this handbook (Khaldeev et al., 1975) contained no section on intraparty information, although some writers now recall that Lenin stressed the party's need for 'complete and truthful information' (Yudin et al., 1973, pp. 205–6). It has also been argued that the flows of information from below will develop as the level of activity of party members increases, and that the development of adequate upward communication is necessary in the process of formulating policy (Reutskii and Yevdokimov, 1974, pp. 14–15). Western scholars would endorse these perceptions.

### Vertical communication

As a centralized, hierarchical institution, the CPSU possesses a ready-made structure for vertical communication: from primary organization up to the Central Committee and back again. The major form of *downward* communication is the resolution of the party committee, at whatever level. Such resolutions are published in the party press, or passed on down the party hierarchy until they reach the lowest levels. Some highly important documents are, in fact, never published, although they are circulated along intraparty channels. For example, Khrushchev's 'secret' speech to the Twentieth Party Congress was one such document. Again, at the Twenty-Fifth Congress, Brezhnev revealed that the CPSU Politburo had circulated a 'special letter' concerning the implementation of party decisions (*XXV s"ezd*, I, p. 94). Other internal matters are regulated by Instructions, also circulated through intraparty channels: these include procedures for electing party committees, covered by an Instruction that was apparently amended in August 1973 (*Raionnyi komitet partii*, 1974, p. 309); another Instruction, telling PPOs how to prepare and keep records of their business, was approved by the central Secretariat on December 3, 1974, and came into operation in the following March (Khaldeev and Krivoshein, 1979, p. 376). A less formal but frequently used and vitally important communication channel is the telephone: it is in constant use at local level, between officials and officers of the district or city committee and primary organization secretaries, economic managers, and so forth; and a special telephone network links provincial (*obkom*) and republican party leaders with the Kremlin (Pravdin, 1974, pp. 97–8).

Hence, we see that the party makes use of both formal, public, and also informal, private channels of communication downward, the particular mode on any occasion depending on the nature of the message, reflecting and emphasizing its significance. The most authoritative statements, to which the party leadership attaches the greatest importance, are given full publicity: congress resolutions appear in all newspapers and many journals as well as in collections of documents and official records. Central Committee meetings are reported in summary in the press, but presumably these accounts for mass consumption are amplified in private communication to party workers and, as appropriate, the mass membership, through the PPOs, where they may be discussed. Information internal to the party — on party finances, for example, or on how to conduct the party's affairs — is kept essentially private. Specific directions from one party organ to another are passed on by 'instructors' (so called because they instruct, they pass on instructions: Pravdin, 1974, p. 98) by letter or telephone.

The channels for *upward* communication are not so well developed. In principle, all party members have the right to address themselves directly to superior party organs 'up to the Central Committee,' to criticize any communist 'no matter what position he holds,' and to make use of the party press for expressing their views (rights given by Party Rule 3); in practice, the exercise of these rights is severely circumscribed by political custom. PPO secretaries bear responsibility for providing superior party organs with 'timely, complete and objective' information (Khaldeev and Krivoshein, 1979, p. 267). However, as has been observed, information coming from below 'frequently bears a superficial, formal character, does not contain a deep analysis of the facts and phenomena of life; in it, the situation is not always objectively illuminated, and serious deficiencies and omissions are passed over in silence' (Kadeikin *et al.*, 1974, pp. 97–8). This is because lower officials' careers depend on their being able to report 'success' to their party superiors; 'failure' in the past meant disaster. Hence, there is a tendency to report what they think the center would like to hear and pass over the problems (Kadeikin *et al.*, 1974, p. 98). At the PPO level, many party members are either too shy to voice their opinions or deliberately avoid discussing contentious issues, since their ideas are at best ignored (Petrovichev, 1979, p. 78). The difficulty is that any criticism from the ranks has long been regarded as subversive or as evidence of sabotage: criticism has tended to become the prerogative of higher bodies, a weapon to be used against their inferiors (Kadeikin *et al.*, 1974, pp. 14–15). A sad case was reported in the journal *Party Life* in June 1978, when a PPO bureau member who complained because responsible party officers failed to turn up to an important party meeting was rudely told 'not to poke his nose into other people's business' (Poladich, 1978).

An undesirable effect of all this is that the center has no rational basis on which to make decisions since it fails to acquire an accurate picture of the situation for which it is supposedly producing policy; hence, the recent calls for opening up the party to freer discussion and debate, rather than interpreting all criticism as evidence of fractionalism within the party's ranks: after all, Lenin had said that party decisions must be based on the widest possible exchange of opinions (Shakhnazarov, 1972, pp. 56–7).

Even downward communication has not always been effectively carried out. A survey in Moscow *oblast* in 1969 revealed serious failures on the part of the smaller committees, in particular, in bringing their own decisions to the attention of party members. In one small town, some PPOs in the course of a whole year never received notification of a single *gorkom* bureau decision, so that rank-and-file members were not given a chance to take part in implementing them (Reutskii and Yevdokimov, 1974, pp. 17–18; also *Raionnyi komitet partii*, 1974, p. 39): small wonder that the party authorities complained of ordinary members' low levels of activity.

In recent years, local party offices have been exhorted to be more conscientious about informing their inferior bodies about party business and also to be more willing to listen to just criticism. Even more publicity has been given to the need to acquire information from the localities — from ordinary members and the public at large. Sociological methods, including surveys, questionnaires, statistical analysis, and other techniques, have been used since the mid-1960s as a means of learning about the state of the party at the lower levels (Yudin *et al.*, 1973, pp. 221–6; also Hill, 1980a, pp. 142–5). As far as the party's relations with the public go, since at least the early 1970s, the central party authorities have on several occasions issued statements criticizing the inadequacies in the party organs' response to letters from the public, and the party-directed press has frequently drawn attention to the question. An editorial in the Moscow newspaper *Moskovskaya pravda* noted that some officials failed to appreciate the political significance of such letters, adding that 'many of them are evoked by the absence among the population of sufficient information on how current tasks of economic, social and cultural development are being resolved' ('Partiinye komitety i pis'ma trudyashchikhsya,' 1975). At the Twenty-Fifth Congress, Leonid Brezhnev stressed the value of such communications from the public in devising legislation and policy statements, and he called for the closer study of public opinion (*XXV s"ezd*, I, p. 92). Thereupon, party committees in a number of areas set up special commissions for that purpose (Utenkov *et al.*, 1977, p. 109), supplementing computerized information-handling systems reportedly in operation for some years (see Yudin *et al.*, 1973, p. 225). In 1981, Brezhnev again stressed the importance of letters from the public, 'many of which, unfortunately, indicate serious deficiencies in the localities'; he reported that some 1,500 letters a day reach the central party organs, which had established their own letters department to process them, but Brezhnev added a word of contempt for anonymous communications (*XXVI s"ezd*, I, p. 93). Still more recently, the Central Committee in June 1983 authorized the establishment of an All-Union Center for public opinion research (*Pravda*, June 16, 1983).

One should not be too sanguine about these various developments: calls to study the needs and opinions of the masses are not new, and the tendency of local officials to jump on trendy bandwagons in order to please their political superiors is no recent phenomenon. There is perhaps some promise in the trend, and certainly Gorbachev has continued the rhetoric: his administration has been much more receptive to expressions of public opinion, but so far this has been barely reflected in specific policies.

### Lateral communication

A further form of communication is *horizontal* or *lateral* communication among party organs and organizations at the same level in the hierarchy. As we have noted, existing channels within the CPSU are essentially vertical, and the principle of subordination means that party organs can communicate with their superior (or inferior) organizations, but links with their lateral equivalents tend to be routed through the higher office. Thus, links among separate PPOs in a city are carried on essentially through the *raikom* or *gorkom*; *obkomy* communicate via the Central Committee and its apparatus. One effect of this — of political benefit to the center — is that it impedes the development of local coalitions that might threaten stability. However, the problem became acute at local level in the 1970s following the creation of industrial and other production associations — variously structured conglomerates involving several separate production or processing units under a unified management. Where such associations have their various member-enterprises spread over several districts, or even in different parts of the country, the problem of devising appropriate party structures and linkages becomes complicated, and the mid-1970s saw much experimentation in this area (Dunmore, 1980). When a dozen or more formerly independent enterprises, each with its own internal party institutions (PPO, party groups, workshop organizations, committees and bureaus), were combined, there was no obvious party hierarchy into which they could fit, particularly if, as was often the case, their PPOs were subordinated to different *raikomy*. How could they be kept in touch? What channels for lateral communication could be devised?

Various solutions to the problem have been experimented with in different parts of the country. However, one body that has emerged is the council of secretaries, consisting of the secretaries of the PPOs in the various enterprises in the association, chaired by the secretary of the head enterprise's PPO (when there is a head enterprise). This is a specific adaptation of a practice that existed in the 1960s, whereby similar councils were set up under *raikom* sponsorship, linking PPOs in small towns and large villages to co-ordinate their individual efforts; the council of secretaries, chaired by one of their number, met as necessary for consultation and issued recommendations, although no formal records were kept (*Spravochnik sekretarya*, 1967, pp. 223–5). At a seminar for the secretaries of such organizations, held in April 1977 in the city of Gorky (where the Gorky automobile works, one of the biggest such associations, is situated), several speakers emphasized the growing value of the council of secretaries for conducting party business within the association. The councils meet quarterly, their sessions usually coinciding with similar meetings of the managements of the various enterprises. They have no formal power or authority, and their recommendations need to be adopted and implemented by their members' respective PPOs. Nevertheless, their work seems to be appreciated by their members, was endorsed by the central party organs in a statement of August 16, 1976, and has established local channels for intraparty communication that effectively bypass the territorial organs: some *raikomy*, it is complained, now seem to pay no attention to the PPOs in the branch enterprises of economic associations (for these points see *Partiinaya organizatsiya v usloviyakh proizvodstvennogo ob"edineniya*, 1977, pp. 5-11, 49-54, 55-9, 126-31, 132-6). Clearly, the structural problems are to continue for a while yet.

A trend appears to be developing toward considerably greater exchange of information on an informal basis, through personal contacts, over the telephone, by sending teams to study the experience of nearby committees, and studying the local press; some *obkomy* have bilateral arrangements to send one another various materials and documentation, which may furnish valuable materials for future scholars of the party, as well as influencing the party's performance, perhaps in the direction of greater uniformity. Much of the communication at the local level is concerned with the party's role in implementing policy, which is discussed below. First, we examine the function of leadership recruitment.

### The Party and Leadership Recruitment

A central function performed by the CPSU in Soviet society is political recruitment: bringing citizens into active political life (as opposed to socialization, which equips citizens with the capacity to play a positive but essentially receptive role). Political recruitment takes place on two basic levels: the recruitment of activists, including (most obviously) members of the party itself (dealt with in Chapter 2); and the recruitment of leaders, at all levels in society.

Soviet writers, notably Farukshin (1973, pp. 58-61), reject the concept of 'recruitment,' preferring the phrase 'selection, training and placement of cadres' (*podbor, podgotovka i rasstanovka kadrov*), essentially because the latter is a more purposeful notion, applicable to a particular class — the very basis, he asserts, on which *all* parties recruit particular individuals. Indeed, the Soviet concept may be more appropriate in depicting the relationship between the CPSU and those whom it 'recruits': those entrusted with the responsibilities of leadership are indeed selected from among suitable party members (and occasionally others) and placed throughout the system as the party judges necessary. Party Rule 42 defines as a basic duty of party organs above the PPO level 'the execution of personnel policy, the education of cadres in the spirit of communist ideology, moral purity and a high sense of responsibility before the party and the people for the work entrusted to them.' But whatever term is used for the concept, it relates to the party's involvement in placing citizens in leading posts.

A key feature of the party's recruitment function is that it extends throughout Soviet society, through a principle known as *nomenklatura*. This is not often discussed openly in the Soviet Union, yet it certainly exists and has been examined in the West, notably by Harasymiw (1969, 1984; see also Moses, 1981; Voslensky, 1984; for an informative Soviet account, see Razumov, 1983, pp. 56–82).

The essence of the system is simple. Every party committee, from the *raikom* to the CPSU Central Committee, possesses two lists, which it compiles itself in the light of local needs (Shapko *et al.*, 1979, p. 185.) The first of these (the basic: *osnovnaya*) specifies posts in the political and administrative network which that committee has ultimate responsibility for filling; the second (registered: *uchëtnaya*) is a list of names of persons regarded as suitable to fill those posts. The system is supervised by the party secretariat at whatever level, on the basis of files on members and of contacts between the likely recruits and the officials responsible (second secretaries frequently have special responsibility for cadres appointments).

The precise function of the party organ in a particular case will depend on the position to be filled: in sensitive posts, it may have the right to nominate for appointment or election; in less sensitive positions, it may exercise a veto (that might apply to some managerial posts in the economy); in still other cases, the party committee might simply be required to confirm that an individual is suitable (in, say, the case of a parent–teachers' association secretary, or an economic post that is filled by a ministry). But the principle of party involvement is present, and it applies to both appointive and elective positions; moreover, at PPO level, the party is constantly on the lookout for suitable leadership talent.

Whatever the precise details in given cases, the scope of party control over recruitment through *nomenklatura* is massive, covering several million executive positions in Soviet society, including posts in the party apparatus itself, in the soviets and state administration, public organizations such as the Komsomol, the trade unions and other associations, and posts in educational, scientific, and creative institutions (see the discussion in Harasymiw, 1984, pp. 160–73; also Shapko *et al.*, 1979, p. 185). Razumov (1983, p. 60) gives details of the size and range of the *nomenklatura* of the Kursk *obkom* and the Gur'evo *raikom* in Kaliningrad *oblast*: the first of these contained 1,840 posts, 26 percent of which were occupied by party workers and 22 percent by workers in the Soviet apparatus; 4 percent related to Komsomol and trade union posts, 12 percent to cadres in industry, transport, construction, and communications, and a massive 36 percent to agricultural personnel. Out of 341 *nomenklatura* positions at the *raikom* level, there were 84 party and 23 Soviet apparatus posts, and 134 managerial and administrative posts in agriculture. Moreover, even where a post is not formally covered by *nomenklatura,* the party is expected to give 'guidance.' According to one Soviet author, a benefit of the system is that it supposedly prevents local bodies from capriciously and mistakenly transferring personnel (Voronovskii, 1967, p. 30), although more recently the decentralization of *nomenklatura* in other socialist countries has been welcomed, on the grounds that it is better to decide about a person where he is best known, that is, in the localities (Shapko *et al.*, 1979, pp. 347–8).

The effect of all this is to ensure that leaders are appointed through co-option, rather than through competition that would ensure priority's being given to competence and excellence. As Harasymiw (1969, p. 512) observes, 'it is an intramural recruitment system. It is not open to talent alone. Advancement depends more on political than on professional qualities.' Moreover, it can easily be used in order to protect the incompetent. For example, in the Georgian case, more than 120 out of 313 *nomenklatura* officials did not possess the appropriate educational qualifications, and 280 with supposed higher training were ordinary workers (Kharchev *et al.*, 1976, pp. 59–60). It has also been pointed out that people are often appointed purely on the basis of their application form, without taking their personal qualities into account (Kadeikin *et al.*, 1974, p. 202).

Nevertheless, since the mid-1970s the CPSU has been paying increasing attention to the question of leadership recruitment and engaging in a change of generations. Many of the older leaders, recruited during the Stalin period, were selected for their political reliability rather than for their skill as administrators; they were given an inadequate training of a few months and then sent with authority to do whatever was needed to keep their patch in order (Yudin *et al.*, 1975, p. 160). At that time, the country's political leadership was concerned almost exclusively with mobilizing the population to superhuman effort in building up the economy and winning the war, and the standard party secretary was at best an unsentimental and tough taskmaster, at worst an unsophisticated, sycophantic bully who used cruel methods in order to be able to report 'success.'

More recently, as Soviet society has continued to grow in complexity and sophistication, greater demands have been made on leaders, and training courses for cadres have had to be revised, extended, and updated. More than once in recent years, the party has taken to task its personnel in particular parts of the country. For example, a statement issued on January 30, 1967, criticized the party authorities in Estonia for the low demands made on party officials, for making hasty appointments of poorly trained persons, weak organizers, people of no initiative, and few women (*KPSS v rez.*, Vol. 9, pp. 215–21). In February 1972, the central committee in Uzbekistan noted precisely similar weaknesses in that republic (Yudin *et al.*, 1975, p. 168). Brezhnev more than once turned his attention to this question. At the Twenty-Fifth Congress, for example, he stressed that the leader of today must combine the qualities of party commitment (*partiinost'*), professional competence, discipline, initiative, a creative approach, and sensitivity to people's needs and requirements, and he must set an example in his work and everyday life (*XXV s"ezd*, I, pp. 95–6). At a Central Committee plenum in November 1979, he again pressed home the need to weed out undisciplined and incompetent personnel. Speaking toward the end of an appallingly bad year for the Soviet economy, he even named ministers whose sector of the economy had performed especially poorly. To the prolonged applause of the Central Committee members, he referred to personnel with whom 'no matter how much you speak, no matter how much you appeal to their conscience, their sense of duty and responsibility, nothing helps. Here,' he said, 'we must act more decisively, apply other measures, replace those who are not equal to the task assigned to them, and more boldly promote energetic, creatively thinking comrades with initiative' (Brezhnev, 1979, p. 2). The notion of 'political flair'—taken from Lenin's writings—has also been mentioned lately as a desirable characteristic, alongside the observation that mere paper qualifications are not enough (Shapko *et al.*, 1979, pp. 134, 177).

There is a further point. In the war and early postwar years, the apparatus in the peripheral areas was staffed by persons assigned by the center: 291 cadres were sent to party work in Belorussia in 1944 and the first half of 1945; 430 party workers were sent to Lithuania when it was incorporated into the USSR; 16,000 'evacuated' communists were sent to the Uzbek party organization in the first year of the war in the Soviet Union (Yudin *et al.*, 1975, p. 158). Now, there is a policy of recruiting local nationals to staff the apparatus—administrators who 'know the life, mores, customs and language of the local population' (Kadeikin *et al.*, 1974, p. 193). In 1971, Brezhnev said that the allocation of nonlocal personnel was now a device used 'only as an exception' (*XXV s"ezd*, I, p. 124), although it has become established practice for *second* secretaries in the republics to be recruited from outside, normally Russians (Bilinsky, 1967, pp. 20–1; Miller, 1977, pp. 19–20, 1982, pp. 22–3).

The move toward sophistication and competence on the part of cadres must be applauded as positive developments, again signifying that the authorities recognize the need for the CPSU to change with the times and reflect important developments in society at large. How successfully these policies are being implemented is an open question at this stage. The party asserts that it is engaged in weeding out its older cadres, treating them with the respect due to those who have loyally served the cause for the best part of their lives, and replacing them with a new generation of 'promising young workers' (*XXIV s"ezd*, I, pp. 124–5). Yet the tough talking by Brezhnev and others is also tempered by a reminder that, when individuals are removed from their posts, they should not be painted only in dark colors, since they are 'living people' after all; and, equally, 'stability' among personnel has been praised as conducive to efficiency (Shapko *et al.*, 1979, pp. 179, 186). At the same time, into the 1980s, senior leaders grew older in their posts, blocking opportunities for promotion and frustrating the career aspirations of thousands beneath them, and widening the age gap between the top leadership and those being promoted to posts lower down (see Frank, 1978; Miller, 1982, p. 24). Rapid turnover and promotion under Andropov, interrupted by Chernenko but quickly resumed by Gorbachev, has at last started to unblock the system.

There is one more important point that affects competence. Although it is undoubtedly true that the party cadres are on average much better trained than ever before, it appears that those disciplines from which they are recruited—the technical fields and the humanities—do not attract the country's best brains, who are drawn toward the prestigious fields of natural science (Kaiser, 1977, p. 413). The Lithuanian minister for higher and specialized secondary education implicitly endorsed this interpretation, when he wrote in *Pravda* that bright students who failed to enter the best faculties of the best universities tended not to go to university at all, whereas 'average' students set their sights lower, at 'production-oriented' disciplines (Zabulis, 1980). On top of that, anecdotal evidence suggests widespread cynicism among those who are drawn toward a career in administration (Kaiser, 1977, pp. 413–15), and it is certainly true that the substantial material and other privileges that accrue to those who successfully operate within the system (see Matthews, 1978) might be sufficient to attract careerists out to make good—a feature not unique to the USSR.

These trends, if widespread (and if accurately reported), have serious implications, both for the quality of government and administration in the USSR in future years and for the likelihood that the party will be able to guide Soviet society in the direction of 'communism'—assuming (which not all observers would concede) that that aspiration is not itself an empty rhetorical device manipulated by a leadership that is itself overcome by the same cynicism.

## The Party and Policy Making

Among the various functions performed by the Soviet Communist Party, that of directing policy is the most important. Politics, after all, is concerned with choices over policies, with ordering priorities, with taking decisions that affect the use of resources and the distribution of rewards in society. When we say that the CPSU is a ruling party, we are saying that it possesses the power to take such decisions for Soviet society. This is, moreover, a role that the party readily acknowledges, indeed asserts: 'The party determines and elaborates the political line on all the basic questions of the internal and foreign policy of the Soviet state' (Lesnyi and Chernogolovkin, 1976, p. 43). In other words, one element in the party's 'leading and guiding' role is the determination of the broad policy goals for Soviet society. To some extent, in fulfilling this function, the party is also exercising its role as the interpreter of the ideology.

### Ideology and policy making

The CPSU presents itself as being in control of all developments in Soviet society. Such gains as have been achieved are said to be the result of the party's unerringly correct policies, which take into account both the current situation and the requirements of the ideology, blending the two into policies for changing present circumstances in the direction indicated by Marxism-Leninism. As society continues to develop, so new policies need to be adopted in order to promote further developments in tune with the overall goal of building communism. The party, in other words, sees itself as establishing the 'course,' the 'line' to be pursued by Soviet society. This is defined and set out in the 'programs,' the current one (the third in the party's history) having been adopted at the Twenty-Second Congress in 1961 (see Schapiro, 1963). A revised edition (explicitly not seen as a fourth program) was adopted by the Twenty-Seventh Congress in March 1986, following four months of discussion of a draft prepared after the previous Congress.

What is unclear, though, is how far the ideology serves to guide policy and how far it is used simply to justify policy decisions arrived at for pragmatic reasons. All policies are expressed in terms of their alleged contribution to the task of building communism, with suitable quotations from the writings of the masters and firm assertions of their

'Leninist' content. Yet, it is also clear that policies are intended to deal with problems that arise in Soviet society: it is wrong to picture a Soviet leadership in the Kremlin taking policy decisions on the basis of the writings of Marx, Engels, and Lenin and imposing them by 'mobilizing' the Soviet population. It is equally wrong to suggest that the Soviet party leaders simply follow on behind socioeconomic developments, reacting by encouraging, as it were, more of the same thing, and justifying it by newly discovered concepts such as 'developed socialism.' Neither do they simply respond to the pressures of articulated interests. Determining the general 'mix' between ideological and practical influences in the policy-making process is impossible: one can at best make generalized interpretations.

It has been suggested that ideology serves more to prevent the adoption of certain policies (say, the denationalization of industry, or the decollectivization of agriculture) rather than to induce the party into following specific lines (Brown, 1974, pp. 44–6). The ideology, it seems, 'rules out whole ranges of possibilities on political grounds even though they may be feasible from a purely technical-rational point of view' (Kassof, 1968, p. 6). Be that as it may, the ideology does not rule out—indeed, is even used to justify—some rather unexpected policies. It did not prevent the invasion of a fellow socialist state in 1956 or again in 1968, nor a third at the end of 1979; it did not prevent a pact with Hitler's Germany; it does not prevent the pursuit of policies that lead to gross inequalities in living standards and privileges, and in the wielding of political power, in Soviet society—all of these being on the face of it remote from commonsense notions of 'socialism.' The ideology does not prevent the Soviet Union from engaging in profitable deals with capitalism when this is convenient, or from attempting to dissuade other communist parties from seeking power, as in China after the Second World War. Such contradictions between what the ideology ostensibly stands for and the policies of the CPSU make some critics (including the Chinese leadership under Mao Zedong) highly sceptical of Soviet proclamations of loyalty to Marxism-Leninism.

Indeed, many of the bitter arguments between the Soviet ideologists and their critics of left and right can be understood only by recognizing that the CPSU distinguishes between the ideology and the party line on specific issues. The party line represents the current official attitude toward a particular problem, reflecting not only the demands of the ideology but also the political requirements of the moment, as perceived by the party and its policy makers. The party line is therefore to be seen as a tactical and strategic guide for attaining the unchanging goal of a communist society.

Soviet commentary rules out the possibility that, in pursuing a line that appears to be incompatible with the goal, that goal itself becomes impossible to achieve. As an example, one might wish to argue that the violent methods used by Stalin ruled out all possibility of achieving 'genuine' socialism because they alienated the mass of the Soviet people and allowed unsocialist norms of behavior and political expectations to become entrenched in the political system. However, such an argument cannot even be broached in the Soviet Union, where all is justified as being a necessary tactic at the time and subordinated to the higher goal. This is one reason the post-Stalin leadership has never been able to face the problem of Stalinism head on. The result, in any event, is that Soviet writers vehemently deny any tendency for an ideologically inspired approach to be replaced by 'pragmatism': indeed, they deny the substance of any such distinction (Farukshin, 1973, p. 186).

Party policy in whatever field is said to be 'scientific,' both because it is derived from a 'scientific' ideology and because it is based on the latest discoveries of science. It is also said to enjoy the complete support of all sectors of Soviet society, whose interests it embodies. Its formulation is undoubtedly influenced to some extent by the ideology, as this is currently interpreted. But equally clearly it is based on a flow of information gathered by the state institutions, various party bodies, the Komsomol, trade unions, and other 'public' organizations. On that basis, the Politburo sometimes examines policy in very great detail, as Gorbachev (1985a, p. 11) noted with reference to the development of market gardening. It is also clear that the CPSU's policies can be strongly, in fact overwhelmingly, influenced by the will of a single leader.

### The role of the leader

Stalin's power to determine party policy, and his capacity to appoint supporters to power positions, gave him absolute domination over the top decision-making bodies (Bialer, 1980, p. 32). Khrushchev, too, was able to induce totally irrational policies, such as the notorious maize campaign, which encouraged farmers to sow maize even where it would not grow, in order to solve the country's fodder shortage (Nove, 1977, p. 128). The October 1964 Central Committee plenum (at which Khrushchev was removed from office) is said to have put an end to 'subjectivism' and 'voluntarism' (see, for example, Rodionov, 1967, pp. 218–19). Brezhnev's exercise of leadership in the Politburo was much more subtle, characterized for many years by remarkable stability among the leading figures (Blackwell, 1979). Only after he had consolidated his position, in the early 1970s, did Brezhnev begin, gradually yet systematically, to change the Politburo's composition as the opportunity presented itself (Brown, 1980, p. 150, 1982, pp. 223–5). In what appeared to be Western-style cabinet-building, Brezhnev complemented the party functionaries and the top government and state officers by introducing several ministers with specific portfolios: foreign affairs, security, defense, and agriculture. Analysis suggests that the apparent shift to quasi-cabinet government demonstrated that Brezhnev's power was being substantially enhanced and support for his policies assured. Although surrounded by grossly exaggerated adulation (see Gill, 1980, pp. 172–4), there appears to have been something genuine in Brezhnev's style that commended him to the colleagues who kept him in office despite failing health. He appears to have been a relatively congenial and effective chairman who allowed his lieutenants to take responsibility without interfering—witness the warm praise from Eduard Shevardnadze, then Georgian party secretary, in 1976 (see *XXV s"ezd*, I, p. 186). The price of this, however, was diminished efficiency.

Style may also have commended Mikhail Gorbachev in March 1985. In a manifestly spontaneous nomination speech, Andrei Gromyko (1985) referred to his forthrightness, his strong convictions:

> And whoever meets him and discusses any appropriate questions can confirm this. I personally can confirm it. He always holds at the center of his attention the essence of the question, its content, its principles, and directly states his own position, whether that pleases the person he's talking to, or perhaps doesn't quite please him. He expresses himself with directness, with a Leninist directness, and for the person he's talking to it's a case of going away with a good or bad feeling.

But style is not everything, and it is inconceivable that the General Secretary does not enjoy substantial personal influence over policy making in many areas (see Brown, 1980). Indeed, an important point concerning the top leadership is that 'no formal institutional parameters have been placed on the individual role positions at the summit of the party' (Gill, 1980, p. 177; also Bialer, 1980, p. 78). In the Soviet political system today, power alone may not be enough to guarantee political survival, and a newly incumbent General Secretary has to build his authority (see Frank, 1984; Breslauer, 1982; Gustafson, 1981, p. 24; Rigby, 1980, p. 9). This will require him to promote like-minded lieutenants and ease out rivals and opponents (and Gorbachev here moved extremely swiftly in his first year in office); but it also requires him to identify with issues and policies and gain the approval of his Politburo and Central Committee colleagues. Khrushchev, Brezhnev, and Gorbachev were all concerned with agriculture; Gorbachev, like his mentor Yuri Andropov, has promoted discipline throughout the economy and like several predecessors has taken a keen interest in foreign relations, encapsulated in the Geneva summit meeting with President Reagan in November 1985.

But no matter how influential an individual leader, policies are ultimately authorized by the party as an institution. This applies even, and in particular, to the detailed field of economic planning, a question with which it is intimately concerned.

### The party and planning

The Soviet state has a whole range of economic ministries and the massive planning authority, Gosplan, with local administrative offices at republican level and descending to every local council from the district upward. Yet the guidelines for economic development are approved in the first instance by the Communist Party and debated at Central Committee plenums and at the quinquennial party congresses. The example of the Tenth Five Year Plan, covering the years 1976–80 inclusive, illustrates the timetable, which in turn reveals the importance of the party's role.

The Twenty-Fifth Congress heard the first details of the plan from Brezhnev, speaking as head of the party; a full report was later given to the congress by the prime minister, Aleksei Kosygin, detailing draft Directives which were in turn later formally adopted by congress, together with instructions to the Council of Ministers and individual ministries to work out the specific implications for each sector of the economy and each administrative level; in this process, they were to take account of comments received from party meetings around the country, and then submit a detailed plan for ratification by the Supreme Soviet. This draft plan was approved by the party Central Committee in October, nine months after Brezhnev first revealed the party's ideas, and adopted by the Supreme Soviet a few days later. Party and state institutions later debated individual plans for republics, cities, and districts (see Hill, 1980c, p. 362). As that plan reached its final year, the Central Committee plenum of November 1979 discussed the budget for 1980 (*Pravda*, November 28, 1979), and this too was given legal force by the Supreme Soviet (*Pravda*, December 1, 1979). The party's involvement in details is illustrated by an article prosaically named 'The party's concern about saving metal' published a few months later (Bulycheva, 1980). In October 1985, the draft of the twelfth plan (1986–90) was debated in a plenum and published for discussion, four months ahead of the Twenty-Seventh Congress, which formally adopted these 'Guidelines,' following presentation by the prime minister, Nikolai Ryzhkov.

This is not to say that the central party organs devise the 'guidelines' completely on their own. Hough (1969, pp. 188–96) has shown how closely party organs and officials at all levels are engaged in trying to influence investment decisions at the highest levels and intervening in local planning decisions. Nevertheless, the party relies for information on

Gosplan and the economic ministries, as well as on its own research departments, and the state more broadly provides statistics, data, technical advice, drafting expertise, and so on. What remains true is that the central party authorities do determine the political priorities that affect the allocation of resources into one sector rather than another.

Upon being given legal force by the Supreme Soviet, the plan—as with other laws—is implemented by the state institutions. But again, the party is involved in the process, and this is discussed in the next section.

### The Implementation of Policy

Soviet writers frequently assert that the party is not engaged in the task of administration, that it 'does not possess a special apparatus for managing society' (Kerimov, 1979, p. 57). 'The party exercises political leadership,' says Farukshin (1973, p. 184), 'and is not occupied directly in the economic and technical management of production.' However, this is true in only a technical sense. The party *as an institution* is not a governing party (see Chapter 5); it does not engage in managerial decision-making. However, *as a collection of members* the party is minutely involved in the everyday running of Soviet society. We saw in Chapter 2 that practically all holders of positions of responsibility in industry, agriculture, the security forces, education, the health service, the professions, and so on, are party members. Soviet sources acknowledge this, adding the claim that this has the unfailing support of the masses (Petrenko and Shapko, 1977, p. 111). Frequently, they sit on the party committees and work closely with local officers of the CPSU. Some of them are recruited from industrial management to become committee secretaries themselves (see examples of V. S. Solov'eva and A. V. Nechaenko, in Hill, 1977, pp. 161–2). Hence, it may be strictly true that the party does not engage in management; yet most of the managers in the Soviet economy are party members, although employed by the various industrial and other ministries of the state. Moreover, the party is actively engaged in supervising the state's implementation of party policy.

#### *Party supervision*

We have already seen the party's power to control appointments and to discipline managers and state officials engaged in implementing policy, disposing of its members where and how it considers appropriate. That is a part of the CPSU's general guiding role. In addition, the party organs as such are closely involved in policy implementation, as the example of the plans again shows. The broad outlines of the national plan need to be broken down into smaller plans for each province, city, or district. This is done, technically, by the various state economic institutions at different levels in the hierarchy; but in fact this function is carried out under the direct supervision of the appropriate party committee and its apparatus, which organizes conferences and meetings, takes planning directives as a theme for its own formal plenary sessions, and arranges for press publicity. In this way, plans of all types—social, economic, local, regional, national—are worked out 'through the most active participation of Soviet, economic and public organisations *under the leadership of party committees*' (Yudin, *et al*., 1973, p. 230; our emphasis).

A number of Western writers, notably Stewart and Hough, have shown how far the party is engaged in supervising the running of the Soviet economy. At *obkom* level, plenary sessions often deal with economic matters, frequently in very specific detail, as does the *obkom* bureau (Stewart, 1968, pp. 58–64, 100–19). Hough (1969, p. 178) points out that the local party organs and their officers have expressly laid on them a wide responsibility for providing policy guidance to managers, promoting technical innovation, enforcing adherence to the law and to the plan, and ensuring that 'reserves' are identified and fully incorporated into the production schedule. Moreover, the local party office is frequently used in order to release bottlenecks in supplies, or to give a firm ruling on priorities—say, to give precedence to getting in the harvest, even if this might involve diverting manpower and transport from industrial needs (see Hough, 1969, ch. 10; also Chapter 5). McAuley (1969, pp. 87, 124–34) has shown how significant a role the party committee in a factory can play in settling labor disputes, sometimes by reference to a superior party organ for adjudication or advice.

In fact, much of the activity of provincial and local party organs is concerned with the economy in one form or another: indeed, as a 'super-mayor,' the *gorkom* provides essential co-ordination for the various segments of the bureaucracy (Taubman, 1973, ch. 6). It has, in Hough's words, 'been given the job of serving as the local "common superior" when the regulations and instructions to officials of different ministries come into conflict or when disputes about priorities in deliveries cannot be resolved by negotiation and compromise' (Hough and Fainsod, 1979, p. 509). These organs have general responsibility for the economic performance (as well as the political reliability) of their respective territories, and in 1956 Khrushchev declared that the main criterion in judging the success of a party official should be 'those results attained in the development of the economy for which he is responsible'; he added the suggestion that their earnings should be related to the success of their area in fulfilling the plans (quoted in Stewart, 1968, p. 110). It is thus easy to appreciate the emphasis that the party gives to the implementation of policy, particularly economic policy.

**Pravo kontrolya**

One of the most important principles involved in the party's role in policy implementation is the so-called *pravo kontrolya*: the 'right of verification,' or the right to check on managerial decisions, seen as one of the party's principal prerogatives (Shakhnazarov, 1974, p. 60). Particularly in economic enterprises, this right can involve the party organization deeply in the day-to-day decision-making and management of the concern. It accords to PPOs a role in checking 'how the administrators of enterprises and institutions fulfill the obligations of their position, and how correctly and successfully they organize the activity of works collectives in carrying out the party's directives' (Derbinov *et al.*, 1975, p. 97). This includes verification of a decision both after it has been made *and* before, to ensure that it corresponds with party policy. In effect, notes Hough (1969, p. 89), this makes the factory PPO bureau 'the real board of directors of the plant.'

In performing this supervisory role—which may even bring the PPO secretary into conflict with management—the party sees itself as keeping the state and economic officials up to scratch, enforcing the high standards of professional competence and public morality that the party considers necessary in a society that is building communism. The picture is of the party consisting—as it unremittingly says it does—of the vanguard, those who understand what is required, ensuring that those who run the nonparty institutions match the task that faces them. Moreover, the Twenty-Fourth Congress extended this right to PPOs in ministries and state bodies, local soviets, scientific and other institutions, thereby bringing them also more firmly under party guidance (*XXIV s''ezd*, II, p. 239; Schapiro, 1971, p. 5).

A further complication is that, as we have noted, most managers are themselves party members; a good many of them serve on party committees at district or city level, or even higher. Indeed, they are regarded as 'persons trusted by the party and the state' (Derbinov *et al.*, 1975, p. 97). Despite this, the party, as an institution, evidently does not trust these, its own members, to carry out their managerial functions loyally and conscientiously without this constant supervision by the PPO, and specifically by its secretary. The principle of the right of verification also creates a very complex relationship between manager and PPO secretary, each of whom obviously enjoys the confidence of the higher committee (both appointments are subject to *nomenklatura*), and each of whom has distinct political resources on which to draw in cases of conflict. The complexities of these relationships have been well explored by Hough (1969, pp. 86–97; Hough and Fainsod, 1979, pp. 504–10).

Apart from the economy, the party also has policies in other areas, of course, and the local party committees have specific organs for implementing them, as we saw in Chapter 3: the agitprop department, which arranges for evening classes in Marxism-Leninism and similar forms of party and public political instruction, is one such body, which engages in a great deal of activity, but with very mixed results, as we saw.

It is in the implementation of policy that PPOs come into their own. Situated as they are in the very heart of the production units—in each factory, office, farm, institute—they are directly involved in putting the party's instructions into effect, bringing them also into contact with non-party citizens (Petrovichev, 1979, p. 75). The PPO secretary is involved alongside management in supervising the running of any enterprise, and communist workers must fulfill their rulebook obligation 'to set an example of a conscientious, creative attitude toward labor, . . . to work persistently for raising production efficiency and for the steady growth of labor productivity.' They are also available to fulfill any tasks if called on by party committees and bureaus. A party policy remains little more than an aspiration until it is put into effect by party members, be they the planners of Gosplan, the deputies in the soviets, or ordinary workers and peasants; and it is from their PPO that these members get their immediate instructions related to the application of central party policy: that is the party assignment, or *poruchenie*.

### Party assignments

The party assignment is a specific task with which a communist is charged as part of his personal obligation in carrying out party policy. Party assignments can be allocated by the PPO committee or bureau, by the party meeting, or by the secretary alone; they may also be given by superior party organs (Khaldeev and Krivoshein, 1979, p. 254). They are of two types: regular and short term. Examples of the former might be selection for service as a deputy of the local soviet, or for election as trade union branch chairman or editor of a wall newspaper (Lyaporov, 1979, p. 150). A short-term, one-off assignment might be an instruction to write an article or give a lecture, on the theme of, say, the Central Committee's latest policy statement, or to assist in preparing a meeting (Lyaporov, 1979, p. 149). Ideally, all party members are engaged in these arrangements, taking into account their own capabilities, experience, age, circumstances, and inclinations—with special consideration for those undergoing courses of study, or, say, mothers with children to care for (Khaldeev and Krivoshein, 1979, p. 257). The aim is to distribute the various tasks as rationally as possible so that the best persons for particular jobs are assigned.

Furthermore, communists are encouraged to volunteer for party-approved tasks, even without specific directions, and are expected to gain enjoyment from them. This is illustrated by the following comment of a party member at the Bryansk machine-building works, in response to a survey on assignments, reported favorably in a handbook on PPOs:

> I lead a discussion circle among young people on the theme, 'Fundamentals of economic knowledge,' and on top of that I work with 'problem' youths, going on trips with them and getting in touch with their parents. This is not an easy matter, of course, but how nice it is when a youth with your help gets on to the right path. At the party meeting of our department they listened to my report on fulfilling my party assignments, and declared their gratitude. In front of my comrades it was very pleasant for me to hear such a kind evaluation of my social work. (Khaldeev and Krivoshein, 1979, p. 256)

As this statement implies, carrying out assignments successfully is also supposed to be a matter of pride for all members of the organization (Lyaporov, 1979, p. 150).

Such examples, alas, are not the norm, and in practice problems frequently arise. Reflecting what is perhaps a natural part of the human condition, the officers of local party organizations tend to rely most heavily on those party members who have proved themselves most competent and reliable, giving two or three or more assignments to this minority, and leaving aside the younger, inexperienced, or simply shy communists (Gogichaishvili, 1969, pp. 3–4). One member complained that eleven assignments had been given to him, despite his protests (Golyshev, 1975). Again, sometimes assignments are allocated to party members who, through age or indifferent health, are unable to carry them out (Khaldeev and Krivoshein, 1979, p. 257). Sometimes a 'formalistic' approach leads local party officers to allocate so-called assignments that are little more than exhortations to individuals to do their jobs conscientiously—such as telling a garage manager to ensure that his fleet is always roadworthy and not to permit drivers to work while drunk (Khaldeev and Krivoshein, 1979, p. 259). It is not unknown for party members to decline to carry out their allotted assignments, sometimes using ingenious pretexts: a party handbook of 1975 gave the example of a communist who refused to become a *druzhinnik* (unpaid, vigilante street patrol) on the grounds that this was a voluntary movement. However, the report goes on, 'if the interests of the cause demand it, then the party organization is obliged to strengthen this or that street patrol' (*Knizhka*, 1974, p. 167) and invoke party discipline against the recalcitrant member (p. 171).

There are two points here. First, the assignment is the basic instrument for carrying out party policy: 'without party assignments, without the correct distribution of public activity, work for the fulfilment of the party's directives is unthinkable, and the fighting capacity of party organizations is impossible' (*Knizhka*, 1974, p. 167). Second, these assignments are also one of the most important training devices for party members, and hence they have their place in the political culture-building function of the party. They are a means of broadening communists' horizons, disciplining them, forming in them the habits of a public figure, and generally promoting party activism (Kulinchenko *et al.*, 1978, pp. 103–4). As a handbook for party activists put it, assignments are given to a party member in order to turn him into 'a steadfast political warrior, capable of fighting against routine and stagnation, against indifference and bureaucratism, which here and there make themselves known' (*Knizhka*, 1974, p. 168).

We can see, then, that the ordinary party member's program of assignments is what brings him into contact with policy that is determined at the top; it also helps to imbue him with those 'party' qualities of activism and participation in public affairs, coupled with discipline and responsibility, that are supposedly the hallmark of the new Soviet man. A further element of party life that reinforces this process is the party meeting.

### Party meetings

The monthly meetings of the PPO, or the irregular but frequent meetings of the party group, form an important element of the political life of the party member and of the party as an institution. It is here that new policy directives are discussed by those responsible for implementing them, that the work of the various economic and other institutions over which the party exercises guidance is examined by those charged with that task, and that the performance of individual party members is assessed by their peers and their immediate superiors, in part through the practice of 'criticism and self criticism'; here, too, new members are admitted to the party's ranks, and in this forum party members may take their first steps on the road toward a political career.

Party meetings may discuss in principle practically any question of relevance for the PPO or group concerned. For example, they may be called at very short notice to discuss such 'burning questions' as the behavior of a young party member picked up by the police and taken to one of their 'sobering-up stations' (Lyaporov, 1979, pp. 65–6). More commonly, and particularly at the PPO level, meetings are formally prepared, including reports, speeches, and the adoption of a resolution drafted in advance, frequently on matters relating to the party and its role, or to an economic question: 'The tasks facing communists in implementing the decisions of the Twenty-Fifth CPSU Congress'; 'Your party membership card'; 'The tasks of ideological work'; 'Quality is the mirror of work'; 'How the collective is matching up to its socialist obligations' (Khaldeev and Krivoshein, 1979, p. 175).

In addition to regular PPO meetings, as part of the process of 'increasing its links with the masses,' the party may also organize so-called 'open' party meetings, which, as their name implies, may be attended by nonmembers. As one would expect, these deal with matters of general concern, not involving 'party and state secrets' or the party's internal business (the exception, noted in Chapter 2, being that it is considered appropriate for the admission of new recruits to be discussed in these open meetings). Again, economic questions may be raised—on the introduction of new technology, saving on materials, reducing waste, improving discipline ('Ob otkrytom partiinom sobranii,' 1980)—but other topics are reported, such as the theme 'Our children are our future,' raised at an industrial works in Moscow (*Organizatsionno-partiinaya rabota*, 1974, p. 74).

Nevertheless, although this kind of meeting has evidently enjoyed official favor in recent years, the rights of nonmembers are pretty restricted, and their significance may be small. Noncommunists may take part in the meeting itself, but no more. These are, after all, still *party* meetings, as the journal *Party Life* reminded one reader, who had inquired whether nonmembers could take part in preparing the draft resolution for an open meeting. That would be quite wrong, said the journal, since often votes had to be taken, and this excluded even party candidate members ('Mozhno li . . .,' 1978). This clearly shows how unwilling the party authorities are to share power even with those members of the public sufficiently interested to attend these meetings.

Joint party and Komsomol meetings may be held to discuss matters of mutual concern—again, often economic questions or matters related to the ideological drive. A final form of meeting at PPO level brings together party members from several organizations to co-ordinate their activities in carrying out policy (*Spravochnik sekretarya*, 1967, pp. 223–4).

According to the literature on this topic, party meetings are regarded as much a 'school of training' for party members as they are a means of organizing the implementation of policy. Indeed, through involvement in preparing, chairing, or speaking at these meetings, the party member gains valuable experience in the conduct of public business. The preparation of a meeting can take up to three weeks, and dozens of party members may be detailed to take part in its preparation, by writing a report, collecting materials, or helping to draft the resolution on the topic (Bazin *et al.*, 1968, pp. 113–23). It is in such work that secretaries, in particular, acquire organizational and public speaking experience, which they may build on as they advance politically.

Those, at any rate, are the stated aims of party meetings: training communists, and organizing and supervising the implementation of policy. In practice, as much literature on this subject makes plain, these meetings frequently fall far short of the ideal. In fact, the Central Committee issued a statement on the subject in 1969, which was still quoted a decade later. Referring specifically to the conduct of meetings in the Yaroslavl party organization, but with the intention that its contents should be read as applying throughout the country, it amounted to a devastating indictment of party organizations everywhere (text in Smirnov, 1973, pp. 104–9). The same points were already being discussed in the literature at that time. M. Gogichaishvili, in a short booklet on the topic (1969), gave examples of meetings that were arranged in such detail that 'all that communinsts had left was to vote' (p. 3); where open and closed meetings were held simultaneously, leading to an embarrassing—and politically inept—request for nonmembers to leave (p. 16); where no one said anything after the report had been read, because no one had done any preparation (p. 17); where the bureau members ran the whole show themselves (p. 27); meetings full of boring, hackneyed speeches, or at which 'staff' rapporteurs, prepared to mount the platform and make speeches on any topic, addressed those present (p. 30). These and all the other weaknesses pointed out by the Central Committee in Yaroslavl were clearly widespread in the party (Gogichaishvili's examples come from Georgia) and cast grave doubts on the effect of PPO life on the 'communist training' of party members. Party meetings, indeed, in all too many cases became a formality: something engaged in so that the *raikom* could receive reports of activity, of something going on at the grass-roots level. A more recent study of members who fail to speak at meetings suggests that many had nothing to say on the questions discussed because they were badly informed of the issues; others professed lack of skills in public speaking, and still others complained that their remarks and suggestions were greeted with indifference and were ignored (Utenkov *et al.*, 1977, pp. 49–50).

The unfortunate thing, from the party leaders' viewpoint, is that such undesirable practices have come to be regarded as the normal and accepted 'party' way of doing things; thousands, perhaps millions, of party members rarely if ever experience anything else. When they are promoted to positions of responsibility themselves, they will most likely perpetuate this style of leadership in conducting the party's business. This is one reason the party changes only slowly. It is also why the central authorities, year after year, decade after decade, have to make the same criticisms of the new generation of local leadership as they made of their predecessors—and perhaps as some of their own predecessors made of them at the start of their careers.

### System Integration

A final important function performed by the CPSU, and an obvious one, is that of system integration: bringing unity and coherence to a political system that otherwise might lack those qualities. The party's program of socialization is an important part of its integrative function, as is its exercise of political recruitment prerogatives (Gehlen, 1969, p. 71), but the issue is much wider.

The Soviet Union is a vast country, stretching over ten time-zones and thousands of miles, east to west and north to south. The problem of communication between the center and the localities is made still more difficult by the lack of roads and railways and the harsh climate that cuts off large tracts of territory (and indeed much of the countryside even in European Russia) for significant stretches of the year. Holding the system together presents formidable problems for the government, as it did for its imperial predecessor. A disciplined army of lieutenants stationed around the country can help create loyalty and ensure compliance with central directives. Even so, as we have seen, this cannot be taken for granted as it might perhaps have been under Stalin: it is not necessarily the case that 'what the Kremlin says goes' (see Hill, 1980b, p. 159).

Furthermore, the population of the USSR is differentiated in ways that might threaten the integrity of the society. Ethnically, linguistically, culturally, in traditions, in religion, in historical experiences, in levels of economic development and wealth—in these and other ways, the many peoples of the Soviet Union are distinguished from one another; few serious observers see as much more than a pious aspiration the declared emergence of 'a historic new community of people, the Soviet People,' characterized by 'new, harmonious relations' (*XXIV s"ezd*, I, p. 101). The Communist Party, at the center of the political system, serves both symbolically and practically as an instrument that can encompass these many and varied groups—and, indeed, as we saw, it has aimed to make its membership more representative of the society of which it claims to be the vanguard. It is, in fact, a symbol of the Soviet Union's uniqueness (Kaiser, 1977, p. 139). Finally, the unified structure of the CPSU serves as a powerful counterweight to balance the federal structure of the Soviet state. For, although there is a distinct party organization in all the republics except the Russian federation, with a central committee, a politburo, and secretariat, Soviet writers point out that the party is not a federal institution. It has a single rulebook, a single program, a single membership card, and 'the party organizations of the union and autonomous republics are territorial organizations of the CPSU' (Tikhomirov, 1975, p. 100). This fact—which means that republican communist parties are subordinated to the central organs, as well as represented on them—enables the political center to use *nomenklatura* to dispatch personnel anywhere in the country. In government, certain areas—notably in the cultural and educational fields—are delegated to the republican authorities, and differences in legislation reflect local traditions and needs. But the unified party apparatus, linked from top to bottom by democratic centralism, ensures that no republic or national unit steps away from the line, defined by the central authorities in Moscow. The party remains 'the sole centripetal force in a society consisting of increasingly centrifugal forces' (Hoffmann, 1980, p. 83), and it is probably inevitable that it should perform such a role.

In this chapter, we have surveyed the various functions performed by the CPSU in playing its 'leading and guiding' role in Soviet society and the Soviet political system, and we have seen the mixed level of success with which it achieves this. Indeed, there remains much scope for 'perfecting the style, forms and methods of party work' (Petrenko and Shapko, 1977, ch. 3). But whatever the limitations on the party's performance, we have seen that this self-appointed role brings it into a close relationship with other institutions. In the next chapter, the party's relations with the Soviet state are explored in greater detail; in Chapter 6 we examine the party's functioning with respect to other institutions and with the outside world.

# CHAPTER 5

# Party–State Relations

The relationship between the Communist Party and the institutions of the Soviet state may be considered a central problem in the Soviet political system. The question is complex and difficult to unravel, and its regulation is problematical (Schapiro, 1961, p. 111; Shakhnazarov, 1972, p. 76). It is also a dynamic relationship, varying over time and from one level of administration to another (Shakhnazarov, 1972, p. 76; Church-ward, 1975, p. 224). The problem is a difficult one in several senses. First, it is hard for us to work out what the relationship is at any time. Second, it is difficult for Soviet political philosophers to determine what the relationship ought to be. And third, it is hard for Soviet politicians to implement and regulate the desired relationship. Obviously, what was appropriate during the Civil War period is unlikely to be appropriate in today's industrial society (Shakhnazarov, 1972, p. 76). In consequence, the relationship has always been regulated by discretion rather than by law (Rigby, 1980, p. 12).

For Western students, struggling to disentangle party–state relations, the task was made particularly difficult because, until recent times, the Soviet writings on the state virtually ignored the party dimension: it was more or less a taboo subject and led to gross distortions in Soviet analyses. When the party was mentioned in relation to the state's activities, it was frequently with confusing, apparently contradictory statements, even within the same book. This can still be encountered. For example, in 1974 the then prime minister of Moldavia stressed that party leadership of the state organs is political, based on persuasion, not administrative; yet a few lines further on, he noted that 'this does not mean . . . that party decisions bear a purely recommendatory character. All decisions of the Communist Party on the most important questions of public life are obligatory for all organs, including the soviets' (Paskar,' 1974, p. 79). Lenin is frequently quoted: 'Not a single important political or organizational question is decided by a single state institution in our republic without the guiding directions of the party Central Committee' (cited in Naida et al., 1967, p. 10).

The ambiguity and ambivalence among Soviet writers seems to indicate a degree of confusion on their part as well. In view of the conflicting statements, it is impossible to accept the view of one scholar, writing for a Western readership:

> The political organization of socialist society in the USSR is . . . distinguished by the clarity and unambiguousness of relations between the Communist Party, on the one hand, and the state together with the mass organizations of working people, on the other. (Veselov, 1973, pp. 5–6)

Since the 1970s, however, both Western and Soviet scholars have devoted considerable attention to this question. Indeed, since the concept of 'developed socialism' was promulgated, and the 1977 Constitution introduced the broader concept of 'political system' to replace 'state structure' in the previous constitution, Soviet scholars have been able to examine the relationship more openly. A substantial body of literature now augments what has been discovered by Western specialists and adds detailed descriptions and quantitative analysis of the relationship between party and state organs. The party has, as it were, 'come out,' and a significant aspect of this development is that the question can now be discussed by the Soviet public. Much of the information now appearing, of benefit to Western students of Soviet politics, is also being presented to Soviet citizens for the first time. It can be seen as part of the trend toward reasserting the party's role in the 1970s, following the débâcle in Czechoslovakia in 1968, when the Communist Party (as viewed from Moscow) appeared to be relinquishing its political monopoly (Hill, 1980a, pp. 112–13).

The question has a number of aspects, beginning with the ideological factor.

### The Ideology and Party–State Relations

One reason this question is so fraught with difficulties is that the ideology is ambiguous about the roles of party and state. On the one hand, Marxism-Leninism sees the state as an instrument of class rule, a mechanism used by the dominant class to run affairs in its own interests; it is also an apparatus that will disappear ('wither away') as communism is reached, since in that future classless society there will be no class antagonisms that require such an instrument of class rule. It is also true, as we saw in Chapter 1, that there are already said to be no antagonistic class interests, and the Soviet state has become a 'state of the whole people.' This formulation is itself ambiguous and unclear about the 'withering away' (see Harding, 1984, pp. 104–28).

The party is seen as the vanguard of the working class, its most advanced, politically conscious section. But it now presents itself, too, as the vanguard of the whole Soviet people. It is also seen in the writings of the founding fathers of Marxism-Leninism as an instrument for seizing power in revolution: it is not clear what the party's role would be after the revolution had been achieved, particularly in the long run—would it wither away like the state?

In addition, one must consider the ideological (in this case, Leninist) view of the soviets: they were institutions created by the workers themselves during the revolutionary upheavals of 1905 and 1917, beginning their existence essentially as strike committees, to coordinate revolutionary activity (Petrovichev *et al.*, 1972, p. 398). They are therefore seen as progressive institutions, which makes it hard to argue that they should be abolished: accordingly, they became the basis of the Soviet state in 1917. Subsequently their nature has changed beyond recognition: but the continuity of their name (which identifies the country itself), and the fact that they involve the masses (over 2 million citizens serve as deputies at any one time, plus approaching 30 million activist volunteers), makes it difficult to hasten their demise, even if there were no positive political functions for them to perform. Khrushchev, it is true, attempted to hasten on the 'withering away' of the state bureaucracy by transferring functions to the trade unions and other nonstate bodies; but this has been halted and caution advocated (Stepanyan and Frish, 1979, p. 174).

Thus, the Brezhnev era brought a stabilization and revitalization to the Soviet state, and this can justify the CPSU's continuing 'leading role.' Luk'yanov (1980, p. 39) even asserts baldly that 'the Soviets can actively express the will and interests of the popular masses, and make provision for their realization, only by persistently implementing the communist party's line and acting under its leadership.' On the basis of such an analysis of the relationship, as we saw in Chapter 4, a rough division of functions operates, revolving around the policy process (see Frank, 1982).

## Party and State in Policy Making

As we saw in Chapter 4, the basis of policy in the USSR is the party program, its 'theoretical banner' (Volkov, 1985), which is said to have become 'the ideological constitution of the country': hence, the party is seen as providing not simply political but 'ideological-political' guidance (Shakhnazarov, 1974, pp. 56–7). We have also seen that the state apparatus—the 'organs of state power' and the 'organs of state administration'—do not enjoy the right to reject party policy. However, Soviet writers are emphatic that the decisions of party bodies, including the authoritative statements of the Central Committee or the Politburo, are not legally binding on anyone, except the party's own members. Thus it is stressed that only the state institutions, specifically the soviets of people's deputies, have the power to adopt decisions having the force of law and to implement those decisions by coercion, so party resolutions coming to these law-making bodies have the status of 'authoritative recommendations' (Shakhnazarov, 1974, p. 58). In constitutional theory, the soviets, including the quasi-parliamentary USSR Supreme Soviet, have the right to decline to give this legal force to party resolutions. On the basis of this legalistic argument, there is a tendency to stress that it is the duty of party member deputies in the soviets to persuade, to convince their nonparty colleagues of the merits of the proposals, and win their support: 'For the CPSU, the basic method of party leadership of the masses is, in its character and essence, a democratic method: the method of persuasion,' writes Shabanov (1969, p. 24; also Barabashev and Sheremet, 1967, p. 34).

As shown below, there are a number of ways in which the party can ensure that its policies are dutifully enacted and implemented by the state institutions. Nevertheless, there is so much emphasis on this distinction that one must conclude that the Soviet authorities—or at least Soviet scholars who write about the relationship—are anxious to give it some substance. It is aptly summed up in the image of the CPSU as a party that rules but does not govern (Ukrainets, 1976, p. 63). The implication —which is frequently made explicit—is that the party should not get bogged down in the details of administration: it should not indulge in *podmena*, or supplanting the state (see below). Extending this, it has also been suggested that the party should leave essentially current decision making to the state organs: formulating and applying specific decisions for implementing the broad policies indicated by the party (Shakhnazarov, 1972, pp. 86–7).

The general picture, then, is of a political system in which party and state institutions function complementarily: the party depicts broad policy outlines, which are given legal force by the soviets and implemented by the state administrative organs, using coercion if necessary (see Cocks, 1978, pp. 49–56).

So far, so good, perhaps; but it is not quite so simple. The distinction between policy formulation, rule making, and policy implementation cannot be sustained in theory or respected in practice. In many situations, no fine distinctions can be drawn, and sometimes the same individuals are involved in all processes (Ukrainets, 1976, p. 71). Thus, a farm chairman who is on the local *raikom* feeds in information about his farm's needs and capabilities; he is involved in adopting resolutions about agriculture in the area; and he also supervises the application of the policy on his farm after it has been approved by the soviet, of which he is, as likely as not, also a member. Moreover, even if a local soviet did the unthinkable and refused to endorse party policy, it would never-theless be binding on party members, who would have to set about im-plementing it, since for them 'party decisions have the force of law' (Ukrainets, 1976, p. 65).

Neither is this blurring of the edges between party and state, and the intricate web of political relations that it creates, restricted to the local level. As Hough has convincingly argued, 'even if the party Secretariat were to have the final say on every important question (and this is most improbable), the executive institutions would still be reservoirs of exper-tise and centers of specialized interests, and they would still be significant participants in the battle for influence over policy' (Hough and Fainsod, 1979, p. 363). At the intermediate and lower levels, state officials and economic personnel have a channel of appeal against interference by the local party representative, namely, through the apparatus of the ministry, which has more authority than provincial party organs, since it functions on instructions from the Central Committee or Secretariat (Hough and Fainsod, 1979, pp. 505–6). Complexities such as these make the relationship between party and state almost impossible to sort out.

On top of that, certain policy areas are reserved for direct party deci-sion, notably the field of foreign policy, especially when it involves inter-national crises that threaten the fate of the whole people. The party's relations with the outside world are discussed further in Chapter 6; suf-fice it here to note that the party as a party has dealings with communist parties in other countries, and this directly involves the CPSU in foreign affairs. Second, the uncertainty in Soviet and Western eyes as to where power and authority lie makes it hard to distinguish the party leader as party leader from the party leader as national leader, a problem that goes right back to Lenin (Carr, 1966, p. 193). In international crises, the par-ty's supremacy stems from its assuming responsibility for the general welfare of the Soviet people, and also from the fact that for most of the time, the supreme organ of state power—the USSR Supreme Soviet—is not in session. (For this reason, the 1977 Constitution reserves a range of decisions to the much smaller Supreme Soviet presidium, including powers to declare war, introduce martial law, and inaugurate other ex-treme measures, without even ratification by the Supreme Soviet itself.) During international crises, an *ad hoc* committee or 'team' takes charge, although no doubt nowadays the scattered members of the Politburo are kept in touch by telephone—unlike what appears to have happened dur-ing the Cuban missile crisis of 1962 (Allison, 1971, pp. 135, 215, 238).

Such events are obviously exceptional, and the party's direct involve-ment in day-to-day decision making is in principle an infrequent occur-rence. Even so, the party claims the 'authoritative right of intervention in the process of current policy-making any time this is necessary and when there is sufficient basis for it' (Shakhnazarov, 1972, p. 88). As we shall see, such a formulation leaves a great deal of latitude for interference, although it is frowned on.

How does the party ensure that the state does implement regular policy? There are a number of mechanisms, and taken together they are a formidable armory of control. They ensure a compliant state—indeed, as an institution of power, a pretty ineffectual state—which for that very reason has been described as a facade, despite its fulfilling certain significant political functions (Armstrong, 1973, p. 157).

## The Mechanics of Party Control

As we examine the links between party and state, it becomes clear that, on every plane, the party enjoys political superiority. In terms of policy toward the state institutions, their composition and functioning, it is clear that the party holds ultimate responsibility, and the state organs can do little without party sanction.

### Policy toward the state

Since the mid-1950s, and increasingly since the late 1960s, when a spate of new legislation began to be introduced, a great deal of attention has been paid to the representative and administrative organs of the Soviet state, aimed at improving their performance of their allotted role, increasing their effectiveness, and generally raising them from the moribund state into which they had declined under Stalin (see Hill, 1980a, ch. 4; Friedgut, 1979, pp. 156–62; Jacobs, 1983, ch. 1). The point about this development, however, is that it was sponsored by the Communist Party and not brought about by the spontaneous efforts of the state institutions themselves. It was the party Central Committee that adopted the trailblazing resolution, dated January 22, 1957, 'On improving the work of the Soviets of Toilers' Deputies and strengthening their links with the masses' (see *KPSS v rez.*, Vol. 7, 1971, pp. 237–48, for text); it was the party congress that proposed the adoption of a Statute on the Soviet Deputies' Status to improve the effectiveness with which deputies perform their role (*XXIV s''ezd*, I, pp. 102–3, II, p. 233); it was the CPSU that introduced the 1977 Constitution, which was discussed in draft several times by the central Secretariat and Politburo (Luk'yanov, 1980, p. 33). The party congress regularly comments on the work of the soviets (for example, *XXV s''ezd*, I, p. 107; *XXVI s''ezd*, I, p. 83).

This has two important implications. First, it implies that the party takes the state seriously. The amount of effort and financial resources expended on running the state institutions, organizing elections, and so on, is vast. A good deal of paperwork is involved in running a huge state bureaucracy and servicing the sessions of the 50,000-plus soviets across the country, and the cost in lost production that results from taking more than 2 million deputies away from their jobs on full pay to attend to state business is a further significant burden. It seems inconceivable that the party would give further encouragement to this without some faith that the state institutions can play a positive role in the system. Second, it also means, quite obviously, that the party remains firmly in charge. The pace and the direction of development in these institutions are always measured and controlled by the party, which can place limits on the extension in the soviets' role. The state enjoys no independent existence: it is, as it were, sponsored by the party, and exists in such a form as the party considers appropriate. That does not mean, however, that it cannot be thought of as a distinct political unit, at least for analytical purposes.

The point is that the party has a policy toward the state (Barabashev and Sheremet, 1967, pp. 31–3). Moreover, there have been perceptible shifts in policy over the years. Stalin's policy was to check the development of the representative institutions, while allowing the administrative side of the state—particularly the ministries—to burgeon and even virtually eclipse the party (Schapiro, 1970, pp. 621–2). In the mid-1950s, as mentioned, a process of revitalization was initiated. By the early 1960s, Khrushchev was trying to hasten the 'withering away' of the state by transferring functions from the state administration to 'nonstate' bodies such as the trade unions, and there was much speculation about transferring functions from the administrative departments to the standing commissions of deputies. The Brezhnev era witnessed a reaction to that forced withering and a tendency to stress competent management as a feature of the state under developed socialism. All these emphases in policy are justified in ideological terms, as they have to be, but they appear to reflect the mood of the time, rather than the imperatives of Marxism-Leninism.

### Control over elections

The representative institutions—the soviets of people's deputies (as they were renamed in the 1977 Constitution)—are formed through an electoral process in which the party plays a controlling role (see Hill, 1976). From the initial decision to hold elections on a particular day through the selection, nomination, and registration of candidates, right through the count and post-election scrutiny of the ballots, the party is involved, instructing the state bodies, making 'authoritative suggestions' as to who should be nominated, and leading the propaganda campaign, designed to get the voters to the poll and to refrain from voting against the one approved candidate in each constituency by crossing out the name. At the local level, the whole effort is coordinated by the *raikom*, which draws up a campaign plan of action, including even making arrangements for fire protection for the polling stations and for the supply of telephone lines, and for groups of entertainers—a troupe of musicians, for example—to visit factories and farms to enhance the campaign by bringing a little light diversion to the electors. Most of this work is not carried out directly by the *raikom* administration: the various state bodies—the fire protection service, the communications department, the department of culture—do the organizing, but on the prompting of the party committee's organizational department.

Of all the stages in the campaign, the selection of suitable candidates is the most delicate, 'the most responsible' (Shabanov, 1969b, p. 41). Soviet citizens do not possess the right to run as a matter of course: they require the formal nomination of a recognized institution, as defined in the constitution (Article 100) and the electoral laws. And an unwritten convention—a political law, perhaps—is that they must be acceptable to the party, because, as Soviet writers put it, the party takes responsibility for them and their performance (Aimbetov *et al.*, 1967, pp. 83–4; Shabanov, 1969b, pp. 42–3). All candidates since 1937 (the date of the first elections under the present system of equal representation for all classes) have campaigned as members of the 'bloc of communists and nonparty people' with the support of the party. This means that at the time of their election, at any rate, all deputies, whether or not they are party members, are at least supporters of it and its policy: the are nonparty, not antiparty (Scott, 1969, p. 97).

There is abundant evidence that the party is quite meticulous in directing the selection of candidates (see Clarke, 1967; Jacobs, 1970, 1972; Hill, 1973) in order to achieve what is regarded as 'the proper mix' of sociological characteristics among deputies (Jacobs, 1970, p. 66): a certain proportion of women, of party members, of new deputies, and so forth. Nothing is left to chance or spontaneity (Shabanov, 1969b, p. 43), electoral defeats are exceedingly rare, and they are normally confined to the village level (Gilison, 1968, p. 820; Friedgut, 1979, p. 130). Hence, the party ensures that the state representative institutions consist of persons who will carry out party policy willingly.

### Control over the deputies

One important mechanism for achieving this is the presence among the deputies of a significant proportion of party members. Although party deputies form a minority at the local level—an average of 42.8 percent in 1985—they are always in a majority at any level of importance, rising to 71.4 percent in the case of the 1984 USSR Supreme Soviet ('Soobshchenie,' 1985, p. 32; White, 1985b, p. 224, Table 2). A study of the Moldavian town of Tiraspol in the 1950s and 1960s found the party always in a stout majority: an average of 58.1 percent of deputies were full members, augmented by up to 4.4 percent who were candidate members (Hill, 1977, pp. 37–8). A further bloc of firmly 'committed' deputies are the Komsomol members, who now account for almost a quarter (see 'Soobshchenie,' 1985, p. 32): they too are effectively subject to party discipline. Clearly, if it is the duty of the party member deputies to 'persuade' the nonparty representatives to support the party's policy, the task is made somewhat easier if those are in a minority. In fact, there can never be a chance that a party-approved policy would be rejected by a soviet. It could happen only by a 'fluke' vote, taken in the absence of a significant proportion of the party deputies, after the nonparty deputies had agreed among themselves to vote against a proposal. In the USSR, such an occurrence is unthinkable.

### The party group

The activity of the party member deputies is coordinated by the party group, embracing all party members in a given soviet. In common with party groups in other political systems—say, the British—Soviet party groups meet in advance of the sessions of the soviet, discuss the agenda items, run over the arguments, and agree on their approach. They are subordinated to the local party committee, working under its direction in checking on the efficiency with which party deputies fulfill their obligations. They are an important instrument in implementing party policy through the soviets and strongly influence the allocation of deputies to standing committees (see Vinogradov, 1980, p. 265); they probably also control the nomination of officers for the sessions, who will speak on the various topics, and possibly even what they will say. Such detailed organization of sessions in advance has been criticized by Soviet writers (e.g., Bezuglov, 1971, p. 59), but it seems likely that the party group is frequently responsible for it. Its effect, of course, is to deprive the nonparty deputies (who do not have the same right to meet as a group and prepare an alternative viewpoint) of a truly effective voice in the deliberative forum. It is little wonder that the sessions have been severely criticized in recent years (see Hill, 1980a, chs. 3 and 4).

Therefore, among the other topics these groups discuss are included deputies' failure to attend sessions, their reports to their electors, and elements of bureaucracy in the work of the apparatus and the executive committee officers. They also discuss appointments, a matter on which the district committee has normally already reached a decision but over which there may occasionally be disagreement (see Shababov, 1969b, p. 73, for an example). Often, points of detailed application may be considered, such as 'the tasks of deputies in the spring sowing, the procurement of feedstuffs, the harvest, and other agricultural campaigns'

(Vinogradov, 1980, p. 256). In performing this broad supervisory function, the party group is acting as 'a kind of stimulator of positive work
by the soviet, a permanently operating organ of the party in the soviet,
an organ for generating the collective thought of communists, an organ
for checking on the behavior of communist deputies' (Shabanov, 1969b,
pp. 74–5).

The significance of all this is that it means communist deputies have a
dual burden of obligation: to their constituents, and to the party, whose
authority they also represent in the soviet. In any conflict among these
interests, party discipline would ensure that the communist deputy's
obligation toward the party would prevail.

### The executive committee

The party not only has a strong representation among the deputies: it is
also normally overwhelmingly present among the members of the executive committee (see Frolic, 1972, pp. 43, 45). In the study of Tiraspol
mentioned above, in practically all cases the executive committee
members were communists. There can be no doubt that they are hand-
picked by the organizational department of the local party committee, in
some cases working in consultation with higher party bodies, through the
*nomenklatura* system (see Chapter 4), and discussed and agreed on by the
committee: Shabanov (1969b, p. 60) cites a specific example of this. The
party's key role in selecting the officers is indicated by the fact that it is
the party committee first secretary (himself invariably a deputy) who rises
to propose the nominations for election to the most important positions.
Indeed, at the Supreme Soviet level, the chairman of the presidium is
nominated by the party Central Committee: in nominating Andrei
Gromyko to that office in 1985, party General Secretary Mikhail Gorbachev (1985b) stated that the question had been discussed at the Central
Committee plenum on the previous day; there can be no doubt that it had
previously been considered by the Politburo, of which the chairman is invariably a member. The heads of the more important administrative
departments—the ministries, at republican or All-Union level—are
likewise selected and approved by the party. The post of prime minister is
filled on the recommendation of the Central Committee (Kravchuk,
1967, p. 469), in practice of the Politburo, and in the past was filled by
the party First or General Secretary (Stalin, then Khrushchev). Although
the deputies always solemnly go through the motions of formal election
on these occasions, there is no doubt at all about which authority makes
the selection.

### Party organizations in the state apparatus

Apart from the party group that links all the party member deputies in
each soviet, there are also primary party organizations attached to state

bodies. All the state employees in the given institution who are party members belong to the appropriate PPO. This includes those state employees (essentially civil servants) who are also deputies; thus, there is some overlap between the soviet's party group and the PPOs attached to the administrative apparatus. (Other party deputies belong to the PPOs at their place of work: a factory, shop, farm, or office PPO.) Thus, each ministry, each local soviet executive committee, and each department of the large city and provincial administrations has its own primary party organization, linking representatives, officers, administrative and secretarial staff. These PPOs were given extended rights to check on the work of the administration following the Twenty-Fourth Congress (1971), and their task is to 'exercise control over how the apparatus fulfills the directives of the party and government and observes soviet laws,' reporting delinquent state officials to the party authorities (Party Rule 59). They function on the basis of regular meetings, at which the work of the state apparatus is discussed and individual officials report on their own performance of their duties; the work of their nonparty colleagues is likewise discussed by the PPO meetings (see Kulinchenko *et al.*, 1978, p. 158). This is seen as a means of keeping party-member state employees up to scratch and of ensuring that they always set the appropriate high standards for nonmembers to emulate.

### Informal contacts

In addition to this direct involvement in the state institutions, the party keeps an eye on the workings of the administrative apparatus. Local party committees regularly hold meetings of the local party *aktiv*, consisting of leading party members from the party apparatus, the state organs, the trade unions, and the Komsomol. These somewhat amorphous meetings bear some resemblance to the extended party committee plenums that were common, in particular, under Khrushchev, although they are not formal decision-making occasions in the way plenums are (Hill, 1969, pp. 205–6). They meet periodically in order to discuss broad questions of economic and social development in the town or area and to coordinate the activities of the various institutions and organizations. Furthermore, informal meetings are now regularly held between leading party figures at each level and their colleagues of similar status in the state apparatus (Kulinchenko *et al.*, 1978, pp. 159–60): the fact that party and state administrative officers are frequently housed in the same building facilitates these contacts. Sometimes semiformal reports are made by soviets to party committees directly (Shabanov, 1969, pp. 20–1). The aims of these contacts and the other measures outlined above are said to be 'to inform communists about current questions of the CPSU's internal and foreign policy, and also on questions concerning the further improvement of the work of the soviets . . .' and 'to strengthen the party committees' links with state and public organisations' (Kulinchenko *et al.*, 1978, pp. 160–1). The party organs further arrange seminars, courses, and other training facilities for employees in the state apparatus and other institutions (Shabanov, 1969b, pp. 18–19; Kulinchenko *et al.*, 1978, p. 161); and the work of communists in such positions is discussed in the bureaus of party committees (Paputin, 1970, p. 208).

### Interlocking membership

We saw that the Supreme Soviet presidium chairman is always a member of the party Politburo. That example illustrates a further element in the relationship between party and state: there is a substantial measure of overlap between the personnel sitting on party committees and state bodies. Members of party committees—say, a *gorkom*—also serve as deputies in the appropriate soviet, in that case, the town soviet. In Tiraspol town, the overlap ranged from 15.3 percent of the soviet in 1963 to a third or more in 1955; in Tiraspol rural district, the proportion of deputies on the party committee (*raikom*) ranged from 53.3 percent in 1957 to 23.8 percent in 1965. As proportions of the respective party committees, the overlap varied from 32.7 percent to 80.9 percent (town), and from 29.6 percent to 43.8 percent (rural district) (Hill, 1980c, pp. 359–60). At the All-Union level, 79.3 percent of Central Committee members, 63.9 percent of candidate members, all Politburo members, all members of the central Secretariat and 34.6 percent of the central Auditing Commission were deputies of the USSR Supreme Soviet: with the exception of the last, these figures were all higher than in other socialist countries cited for comparison by Strashun (1976, p. 96).

Interlocking membership of the executive bodies can be added to the overlapping among ordinary members. Brezhnev again illustrates the point; a member of the Politburo and the central party Secretariat, he was chairman of the Supreme Soviet presidium, and until his elevation to that position, he was an ordinary member of it. Aleksei Kosygin also, from 1964 until 1980 the chairman of the Council of Ministers and its presidium, was likewise a Politburo member (and also, of course, a member of the Central Committee, and a deputy of the Supreme Soviet). Figure 5.1 illustrates the various forms of interlocking membership among All-Union party and state institutions; similar principles apply at all levels in the hierarchy (see Hill, 1977, p. 109, fig. 6.1). This leads McAuley (1977, p. 186) to treat party and state as a single unit for analytical purposes: a neat way of side-stepping the complexities raised by the relationship.

This phenomenon further strengthens the party's hand by ensuring that those who are involved in adopting the policy are also present in force when it comes to explaining that policy and giving it legal status.

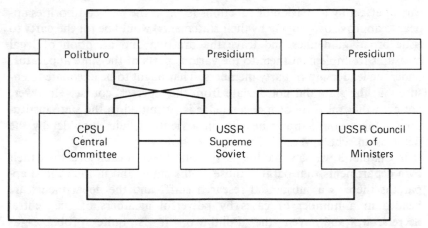

*Note:* Overlapping between the Council of Ministers and its presidium and the Supreme Soviet presidium is prohibited: see Kravchuk, 1967, pp. 469-70.

FIGURE 5.1 *Scheme of interlocking membership between top party and state bodies*

Their authority is enhanced by their participation in the work of the party body, which, in turn, also gives them a strong sense of personal responsibility for the success of the policy they helped to adopt. However, as has been argued elsewhere, the overlap can also assist the party in its policy making by ensuring that the experience of committee members gained as deputies in the soviets will be fed into the policy debates. Thus, party committee members as such have no direct awareness of the needs and feelings of ordinary citizens; nor have they any direct experience of the logistical or other aspects of implementing policy. As representatives, however, or as officers of the executive committee, they can acquire precisely that kind of information and administrative experience, which is essential if policy is to relate to the situations and problems it is intended to deal with. Already, Soviet writers have begun to mention the significance of the deputy as a supplier of information that permits governmental organs to plan and predict more effectively (Gorshenev and Kozlov, 1976, p. 91). In this way, therefore, interlocking membership between party and state bodies can serve as a two-way channel of linkage and communication, and the state institutions have some chance of influencing the course of party policy, presumably in the direction of greater rationality and acceptability (see Hill, 1977, p. 108, 1980c).

### Involvement in legislation

We saw that the party claims as its own prerogative the formulation of policy, which is based on the program and, in turn, on the ideology. One way of effecting a division of functions (such as the party authorities appear to approve of, judging by their statements) would be for the party to issue broad guidelines and leave the drafting and adoption of legal measures to implement them to the various parts of the state apparatus, under the leadership of party members. That ought to be adequate to ensure that the state did not deviate from the 'correct' course. However, not even that measure of independence is permitted to the state institutions. Our account draws heavily on a richly detailed booklet by the Belorussian scholar Yu. V. Shabanov (1969b).

In Chapter 3, we saw that the party committees at each level have their own departments that parallel those of the state, and in the central apparatus there is a substantial research staff, and the departments are headed in a number of cases by powerful members of the central Secretariat, and even the Politburo. It is quite probable—as suggested—that these party institutions obtain a fair amount of factual information from the ministerial and planning apparatus of the state, using precisely the same individuals (party members, naturally) who acquire and handle that information as civil servants. It is also probable, in view of their experience and expertise, that these same individuals are invited to give their professional opinions about the feasibility of various courses of action. They may therefore have some influence over the content of policy, although obviously not the final word.

When it comes to implementing the policy, the party again takes the initiative and at several stages in the process examines the functioning of the state institutions. Basic legislation may be drafted by the party organs themselves and introduced into the soviets for legal confirmation; otherwise, party organs at least examine the drafts prepared in the state apparatus (Shabanov, p. 14). Party organs initiate the calling of sessions of the soviets and contents of the agenda. Indeed,

> Practically all soviets, from the Supreme Soviet to the district, raise and discuss questions that have been to some extent agreed or debated in advance in party committees. And this is completely understandable, because every question introduced to a session directly or indirectly has a political tendency, affects the life and activities of the toiling masses; and the organs of political leadership, in their way the 'bandmasters' in this field, are the party committees. (Shabanov, p. 56)

At the city level, according to a secretary of the Moscow *obkom*, the Soviet executive committee's monthly and forward work plans are agreed in consultation with the *gorkom*, which also 'helps the soviets in defining the main directions of their activity' (Paputin, 1970, p. 207).

The key department in coordinating this control over the soviets' work is the organizational department, which maintains regular contact and exercises 'everyday party influence' on the soviets and their executive committees, while the 'most important' questions are discussed by the party committees themselves (Shabanov, p. 63). At the local level, where the soviets and state organs function largely within guidelines established by superior soviets (and hence they have less room to maneuver, to stray from the desired course), there is no need for such close involvement as at the central and republican levels (pp. 63–4). That, indeed, would amount to petty supervision or *podmena*: unwarranted interference by the party in the work of the state (see below). Nevertheless, certain types of issue are always, as a matter of course, submitted by the state bodies to the party for approval: draft economic plans, or the appointment of responsible officials (p. 61). In any case, before adopting any decisions affecting enterprises in their area, local soviet executive committees normally consult in advance the party secretaries of the enterprises concerned; and where there is a territorial PPO covering a whole village or settlement, 'agreement with it is practically obligatory' (p. 65). Thus, even at those levels at which there is no party committee to supervise the soviets' work directly, the party in one way or another influences what they do. The party takes the lead in the work of the standing commissions of deputies (pp. 68–70) and initiates the recall by electors of those deputies who are judged not to be adequately performing their functions (pp. 79–80).

It is clear, then, that the party committees 'are always in touch with all the affairs of the soviets' (p. 67), and the same applies to the party's relationship with all other organizations and institutions. It has long been recognized, however, that the line between 'leading and guiding' and interfering is an extremely fine one that is often overstepped in practice. This brings us to the problem of *podmena*, which has been mentioned briefly but now requires fuller elaboration.

### Podmena

In essence, *podmena* refers to a tendency on the part of the CPSU organs and officials to usurp the functions and authority of the state, to interfere in the work of professional administrators, or otherwise deal with matters that are properly the province of the state or economic management. Politburo candidate member the late P. M. Masherov (cited in Ukrainets, 1976, p. 72) referred to such matters as the allocation of fertilizers, fuel, or machinery, which are on occasion discussed at meetings of party committees, even though this business is purely administrative, and hence formally the prerogative of the state. A party member from Novosibirsk complained to the journal *Party Life* that his local *raikom* bureau had sacked the chairman of a *kolkhoz*, even though (as he pointed out) only the general meeting of the collective farmers has that right. The *raikom* can certainly give its views, but it should be careful how it expresses them: the definitive decision is taken by the economic or other organs according to the law (Chernyshev, 1978, p. 78). The practice of issuing statements jointly between party and state organs, although it can be of 'co-ordinating significance,' is also frowned on when it is applied to matters wholly within the competence of the soviets (Arutyunyan, 1970, p. 30). Associated with *podmena* are two further phrases, 'petty supervision' and 'parallelism,' both regarded as serious problems against which everyone should strive.

*Podmena* can be explained by a number of factors. Fainsod (1959, p. 93) believes the system of political institutions was deliberately designed to provide for 'overlapping, duplication and parallel functions.' Some Soviet scholars (for example, Ukrainets, 1976, p. 73) refer to 'subjective reasons' (party and state officials simply not understanding the correct delineation of functions) and 'structural problems' ('structural imperfections in the state and the economy which oblige the party to take on matters not proper to it'). But there are other explanations, some of them perhaps excusable, others that suggest an unwillingness or inability on the part of the CPSU's apologists to appreciate the implications of placing the party in such an overbearingly powerful position at the center of the system.

### Lack of managerial skills

In the past—and to some extent it still applies—there simply was not a large enough stock of managerial skills available to run a rapidly developing country effectively. When faced with managerial or administrative incompetence, it is very tempting for local secretaries to step in themselves, either directly or by prompting their committee to intervene. Many party officers themselves possess technical qualifications (Harasymiw, 1971, p. 319) and have often had direct experience of economic management or state administration (Hill, 1977, ch. 8); they also possess party authority.

### Party authority

As we have seen, the party asserts its capacity to make 'correct' decisions, to adopt 'correct' policies. The representative of party authority at local level—even a PPO secretary—can thus speak with all the authority conferred by this tradition. A further result of the tradition is that at any level, the party secretary enjoys much more authority than anyone else. Although (as we argued above) management or state administrators have alternative channels of appeal, nevertheless the party secretary in the factory, on the farm, in a town or district, has political precedence. This can, in fact, be used to the benefit of the enterprise, since it means that

the party possesses the political influence that can unblock supply channels, or even (as one of the present authors discovered to his benefit and
embarrassment) cause beds to materialize in full hotels (Hill, 1977, p.
129). However, the same coin has another side.

### Party responsibility

The point here is that the party, and not just the state, is judged in terms
of economic success. Much of the effort of party organs, particularly at
district level, is spent on stimulating economic activity (*Raionnyi komitet
partii*, 1974, pp. 72–3; see Chapter 4), and the first secretary's own career
depends largely on the economic success of his territory. The most effective way of getting things done (as we saw) is often to do them yourself.
This can be presented as not shirking responsibility, and the party
secretary can claim credit for success and advance his own career, while
placing the blame for failure on managers or state officials. This, in turn,
breeds irresponsibility on the part of those officials: knowing that the
party will always step in, and knowing that the penalties for taking a
wrong decision are grave, it is easy to shift the responsibility on to the
party.

A vicious circle develops: the party secretary or official uses his
authority and his expertise to get involved in administrative or
managerial matters; the administration becomes reluctant to take decisions, for fear of upsetting the party authorities, and in the knowledge
that, in the last analysis, the party will step in; so the party is obliged to
do so; and management does not then need to take awkward decisions.

Such are the origins of *podmena*; its effects are that the party organs
burden themselves with business they are ill-equipped to handle and have
to make adjustments to their own work patterns and even structures,
deploying their skills inappropriately; and the state or economic organs
become dependent on party organs, passing on 'difficult' questions and
thereby avoiding responsibility. The party organs come to work ineffi-
ciently; the state organs are not used to anywhere near their full potential; people become skeptical toward the soviets and their apparatus,
failing to respond until the party steps in, and this simply confirms the
party's dominant position. As Shakhnazarov (1972, pp. 80–2) puts it,
'such a state of affairs gives rise to a certain disregard for socialist legality on the part of both officials and citizens'; he argues that even when the
party's administrative decisions are correct, they are nevertheless un-
constitutional.

A book on party structures asks the question directly: what is the
danger of such phenomena? It gives the following answer:

> In the fact they give rise to undefined responsibility and irresponsibility,
> they inhibit the development of the activity of the mass organizations of

the workers and weaken them. In the fact that they lower the fighting
capacity of the party organizations themselves, rupture their links with
the masses, and create a situation where they 'do all and nothing'. In
sum, the correct organization of work is made difficult, the cause suf-
fers, and damage is caused to the interests of building communism.
(Petrovichev *et al.*, 1972, p. 435)

This is a problem long acknowledged inside the USSR, and its
undesirable consequences have been analyzed and described (see Hill,
1980a, ch. 6). Time after time, the authorities have criticized it and
warned against *podmena*, parallelism, and petty tutelage and supervision
(Petrovichev *et al.*, 1972, p. 434). The fact that they have to keep
repeating it shows how difficult it is to eradicate (and it is a problem that
cannot be appreciated if the party and the state are regarded as a single
unit). However, it may be something that flows inevitably from the basic
elements and assertions in the Soviet system: the party is always right; the
party is the vanguard; the party decides policy; and it really does matter
whether policy is carried out, because (in the Soviet view) failure to implement policy might lead to diversion from the road toward communism. Given these circumstances, the party feels a need to take steps
to ensure that the state does what is required; and too frequently that
means giving orders, it means *podmena*. Ultimately, the problem boils
down to confidence. Unless the party shows that it has faith in nonparty
bodies (which are, after all, led by its own members) and trusts them not
to engage in actions contrary to the spirit of socialism, the problem seems
likely to persist. Both party and state officials will continue to operate as
though the state were subordinate to the party, which is the same in its effects as if it were legally in such a position. This is one obvious case in
which the political reality is more instructive than legal prescriptions.

# CHAPTER 6

# The Party and Nonstate Institutions

In this chapter, we examine the party in its relations with nonstate institutions and organizations and also look briefly at the CPSU in the international arena, both in its relations with other communist parties (an essential dimension of Soviet foreign relations) and in its role in guiding the foreign policies of the state.

According to an authoritative textbook, the general aim of all the non-party institutions is to draw the masses into the process of government, uniting them around the party and involving them in building socialism and communism (Petrovichev *et al.*, 1972, p. 397). Official policy states that further improving the work of these organizations is a central task in building communism, in deepening and broadening the party's links with the masses, and in raising the population's level of political and economic activity (Shapko *et al.*, 1977, p. 241). So we immediately see a party-oriented purpose. Indeed, as Chekharin (1977b, p. 80) puts it: 'One of the basic features which marks the formation and operation of mass organisations in socialist society is that they are guided by the Communist Party and the Soviet state.' However, each has its own peculiarities, and the party supposedly takes these into account in its work with them (Petrovichev *et al.*, 1972, p. 398).

In this section, we discuss the party's relations with the Komsomol, the trade unions, and the special-interest organizations.

### The Party and the Komsomol

Apart from the state, the most significant political institution with which the CPSU has a close relationship is the Komsomol: the All-Union Leninist Communist League of Youth, or VLKSM, already mentioned in connection with recruitment into the party. Seen as a genuinely political organization (Kuftyrev, 1981, p. 210), the Komsomol is, in effect, the junior section of the CPSU, catering for young people between the ages of fourteen and twenty-eight, and its activities are closely tied with those of the party itself. As one writer on the topic wrote: 'The strength of the Komsomol consists in the fact that, being formally a nonparty organization, it is at the same time a communist organization, and is associated with the party and works under its leadership' (Korolev, 1967, p. 40). For another observer: 'Party guidance gives the Komsomol strength and is an earnest of its success' (Chekharin, 1977b, p. 88). Whether the Komsomol succeeds in its allotted tasks is a separate question; but it is true that no organization in the USSR can possibly enjoy success without party approval. This special relationship is made manifest in a number of ways, and the particular value of the Komsomol for the party can be clearly seen.

The general outlines of the relationship are defined in Party Rules 63–6, where it is stated explicitly (Rule 65) that 'The work of the local Komsomol organizations is directed and controlled by the appropriate republican, territorial, regional, area, city and district party organizations.' Rule 63 defines the Komsomol as 'an independently acting social and political organization of young people, the party's active helper and reserve,' whose duty is to 'help the party educate the youth in the communist spirit, draw it into the practical work of building the new society, and into managing state and social affairs, and to train a generation of roundly developed people, prepared for work and for the defence of the Soviet Motherland.'

The rules of the Komsomol itself spell out the principles of the relationship more fully and include in the prologue the details of the Moral Code of the Builder of Communism, which the Komsomol inculcates into its members and, indeed, the whole of Soviet youth. In other words, the Komsomol performs for the younger generation the functions of political education and socialization that the party engages in among the adult population. In doing so, it uses methods similar to those of the CPSU: meetings, talks and lectures, and the publication of daily and periodical newspapers and other printed matter, including the prestigious *Komsomol'skaya pravda*, with its network of home and foreign correspondents and a daily circulation of 10 million; indeed, the Komsomol owns three publishing houses, with an annual output of more than 50 million copies of books and brochures, and more than 230 newspapers and magazines for children and young adults, with a total print run of more than 75 million copies (Petrovichev, 1979, p. 147).

The Komsomol rulebook (*Ustav VLKSM*, 1985) is virtually identical to that of the party, making similar demands on members, although expressed in places in language that is perhaps slightly more accessible to young people. The 'rights and obligations' of Komsomol members mirror those of the party, and the structures of the organization likewise follow those of the CPSU. Primary Komsomol organizations are found in places of work or education in which there are at least three members; these hold regular meetings, elect delegates to regional conferences at which committees (*gorkomy, raikomy, obkomy,* and so on—just as in the CPSU) are elected; Komsomol congresses are held at republican and All-Union level, and the whole structure is guided by democratic centralism. Members pay a monthly subscription, a percentage of earnings, comparable with party subscriptions. In addition to its own membership, the Komsomol has formal responsibility for running the Pioneers' Organization, for younger children, in which practically all Soviet schoolchildren are enrolled.

This similarity in structures between the Komsomol and the party is obviously of great benefit in the political socialization of young people. It acquaints the rising generation of Soviet citizens with the institutional structure and terminology of the political system so that as adults they are familiar with the basic framework of the CPSU and with the organizing principle of democratic centralism and its implementation. It also prepares them for transition into the ranks of the CPSU itself, providing they as adults match up to the heightened demands made on prospective communists. The prologue of the Komsomol rulebook states that to join the party is the highest honor for a Komsomol member, and, as we saw in Chapter 2, the Komsomol has a specific role in party recruitment, since it has to provide a reference for all aspiring members up to twenty-five years of age, who may join the party only from the Komsomol. Out of more than 130 million former members in the organization's history, by 1981 some 14 million persons had progressed through the Komsomol to the CPSU (Kuftyrev, 1981, p. 210); nearly three-quarters of party recruits now come by that route.

That is one way in which the Komsomol performs the function of the party's 'reserve.' Another is through serving as a valuable training ground for party members and future party leaders: again, the similarity of the two sets of structures facilitates this. The party is said to 'preside over' the selection, training and appointment of officials in the Komsomol (Chekharin, 1977, p. 92), and in fact a high proportion of officers and committee members of the Komsomol are already party members, for whom this is a formal party assignment—one and a half million by 1982; approximately half of the country's Komsomol organizations were headed by party members and candidates (*Pravda*, 19 May 1982, p. 3). Given that delegates to congresses are in the main officers of the institution, it is clear that Komsomol congresses are in a very real sense party gatherings, and they are addressed by members of the party Politburo, including the General Secretary.

There is an even closer link between Komsomol and party: the first secretary of a Komsomol committee is invariably a member of the appropriate party committee (a Komsomol *gorkom* first secretary will normally be a member of the party *gorkom* and its bureau: see Hill, 1977, p. 131) and often at republican level a candidate member of the politburo. A number of the Soviet Union's leading politicians in recent years served in Komsomol posts early in their careers: Aleksandr Shelepin, for example, was Komsomol first secretary in 1952–58, when he was already approaching forty years old; he subsequently headed the security police (the KGB), served as CPSU Central Committee secretary, and held other significant political appointments, combining them with membership of the CPSU Politburo, before his disgrace and demotion in 1975; a similar, although less spectacular, less prolonged and ultimately less successful career was enjoyed by Shelepin's successor, Vladimir Semichastnyi. Mikhail Gorbachev, a CPSU member since 1952, began his political career in 1955 as Komsomol *gorkom* first secretary in Stavropol, later moving to the regional-level organization of the Komsomol, before transferring into the party apparatus (career details in *Kommunist*, 1985, no. 6, p. 12). The Komsomol can thus be seen as a sort of extension of the party apparatus, extending the institutional ladder on which individuals may pursue their careers (see Hill, 1977, pp. 131–4).

As one would expect, in view of these formal and personnel links between party and Komsomol, the party expresses its concern for the welfare of its junior organization in other ways. The CPSU regularly addresses statements to the Komsomol; as noted, party leaders address Komsomol congresses—this is seen as one of the significant forms of party influence over the activity of all public organizations, including the Komsomol (Petrenko and Shapko, 1977, p. 196)—and the CPSU Central Committee's report to the party congress regularly contains a passage assessing the work of the Komsomol in the process of communist construction (see, for example, *XXV s"ezd*, I, p. 110).

At the level of the enterprise, the Komsomol plays a role in many cases as significant as that of the primary party organization. This is particularly so in those industries, such as clothing and textiles and many branches of light industry, that employ large numbers of workers directly from school or vocational training. There, the Komsomol organization may be significantly larger than the PPO, so that the Komsomol organization secretary occupies an important and responsible position, alongside the trade union branch chairman, the PPO secretary and management, in the administration of the enterprise. In that case, the Komsomol organization secretary has his own office and is fully involved, under party supervision, in negotiating bonuses, welfare facilities, and the like on behalf of workers, and also in stimulating the workforce to greater output and better quality work. To this end, joint party-Komsomol meetings are held, attended by members of both organizations, and joint working groups are sometimes set up. Still at enterprise level, party organization committees regularly receive reports from the Komsomol committee, whose meetings (as well as the general meetings of the Komsomol organization) are often attended by the PPO secretary or committee members (Khaldeev and Krivoshein, 1979, pp. 277–9).

More broadly in political life, Komsomol members are elected as deputies of the soviets and as members of committees of trade unions and all other kinds of society, where they work alongside party members and are effectively under the same party discipline (see Jacobs, 1972, p. 508, with reference to the local soviets): although formally regarded as 'nonparty,' Komsomol members possess the same degree of moral and political commitment as party members; this ensures a communist majority even when party members form a numerical minority.

A final dimension to the relationship deserves comment: the Komsomol's role in Soviet foreign policy, a factor mentioned by Soviet writers (for example, V. I. Bol'shakov, in Paskar' *et al.*, 1977, p. 62). The Komsomol, as the 'official' representative of Soviet youth and students, maintains contacts with 'progressive youth' in 130 or so countries (Paskar' *et al.*, 1977, p. 62) and participates in various international youth organizations, such as the World Federation of Democratic Youth and the International Union of Students; in addition, it 'actively comes out in support of forces fighting against imperialism and colonialism, and for freedom and national independence, and in every way furthers the widening and strengthening of the unity of the world communist and democratic movement of youth' (Petrovichev, 1979, pp. 150–1).

In short, we can see how important the Komsomol is to the party, in view of the significance of socialization for the future of Soviet (or any other) society. Through the Komsomol, the party aims to tap the energy and enthusiasm of youth and channel it into directions deemed appropriate for creating the new society. As Leonid Brezhnev expressed this aim:

> As a mother solicitously cherishes her children, so the party must bring up the younger generation—the hope and future of our great motherland—strong in spirit, steadfast and selfless fighters for our great cause. (Quoted in Khaldeev and Krivoshein, 1979, pp. 283–4)

### The Party and the Unions

In terms of membership numbers, the most massive organizations in the USSR are the trade unions, which embrace virtually the entire workforce, or about 135 million men and women; this includes all employed party members. In view of this near-saturation coverage, the party takes a keen interest in the unions' activities. Indeed, it has always done so, and modern Soviet writers remind us that the Bolsheviks were involved in getting the early trade union movement off the ground at the beginning of the century (Petrovichev *et al.*, 1972, p. 407). Lenin ascribed a particular role to them in raising the level of consciousness of the Soviet worker, for whom they were to serve as 'schools of administration, schools of economic management, schools of communism' (quoted in Petrovichev *et al.*, 1972, p. 408; Chekharin, 1977b, p. 83). The party program repeats this formula and asserts the CPSU's intention to enhance the trade unions' prestige and influence. In the present era of developed socialism, party policy toward them is said to be 'to increase further the trade unions' role and the level of their work, to promote their activity and initiative, building up their personnel and demanding more from the Communists active in the trade unions' (Chekharin, 1977b, p. 85). In short, at the most general level, the party has a *policy* toward the trade unions: it determines their place in the Soviet system, and any developments in their role are at its behest and with its sanction.

In the USSR today, every workplace—with the exception of a large segment of collectivized agriculture—has its union branch, which works under the guidance of the party committee and receives 'recommendatory' decisions from it (Khaldeev and Krivoshein, 1979, p. 269). Its chairman is approved by the party committee and frequently is himself a party member, as are the members of the branch and territorial committees of the various unions, and the officers of the inter-union coordinating councils at the different administrative levels. Whether or not the branch officers are themselves party members, however, the union representatives work alongside the party, the Komsomol, and the management in controlling the work patterns of the enterprise and in negotiating the allocation of bonuses, the holiday rota, the provision of amenities for workers, and so forth. As with the soviets and the Komsomol, the party organizations discuss the work of the unions and provide leadership through placing party members in union positions. At branch level, party organizations make a point of nominating 'good organisers and real enthusiasts' for election to union committees as a form of party assignment and pay attention to their progress as union officers, often putting on training courses and seminars addressed by party and other officials; in addition, party groups are formed within the elected union branch committees, which are directed by the party committee or bureaus and 'help the party members to act within the union organisation with cohesion and effectiveness' (Khaldeev and Krivoshein, 1979, pp. 270–2).

This involvement of the party in staffing the unions' apparatus is a nationwide phenomenon, which attests to the political significance of the unions. For example, the chairman of the All-Union Central Council of Trade Unions is frequently a holder of high political office: Shelepin held that position from 1967 until his disgrace in 1975, and, although his occupancy of that post was interpreted as a demotion (from Central Committee secretary), he nevertheless retained his full membership of the Politburo; at the level of the republic, P. P. Petrik headed the Moldavian council of trade unions from 1972, after serving in several party posts in the republic (see Hill, 1977, p. 162). Administrative positions in the trade union organization are, therefore, part of the general administrative network, embracing party, state, industrial, and other posts; these tend to be staffed from a single pool or reserve, within which appointments are directed by the party through *nomenklatura*.

There are further ways in which the unions are associated with the party. One is through participation in the public enlightenment effort (Chekharin, 1977b, p. 84). The unions run thousands of public lecture centers, clubs, palaces of culture, libraries, and other amenities; alone or in collaboration with state bodies, the unions publish ten national newspapers, including *Trud*, organ of the All-Union Central Council of Trade Unions, with a daily circulation of some 14 million copies. The journalists working on these publications are all party members, and the editorial line is given by the central party authorities (see below): there is no independent 'trade union view' of political issues. In factories, the editors of wall newspapers are jointly nominated by the party bureau and the trade union committee (Khaldeev *et al.*, 1975, p. 369).

Finally, like the Komsomol, the unions pursue the party's and Soviet government's foreign policy goals, 'in order to consolidate peace and improve the international climate.' They maintain contacts with unions in about 130 countries and exchange fraternal visits and send delegations to each other's congresses. In their contact with unions in market economies, the Soviet unions stress working-class solidarity in the struggle for 'their vital rights and social and democratic freedoms' (Chekharin, 1977b, pp. 87–8).

Nevertheless, although the Soviet unions are undoubtedly one of the means through which the CPSU pursues its policies, their political significance is less than that of the soviets or the Komsomol.

### The Party and Special-Interest Associations

The Komsomol and the trade unions are regarded as the most important of the mass public organizations, yet there are scores of others—from sports clubs and societies to political education circles, from the Society of Inventors to the Soviet Political Sciences Association—that coordinate the activities of Soviet citizens, both privately and professionally, and channel them in 'appropriate' directions. The channeling is done by the party. In recent years, increased attention has been paid to these organizations, which 'actively assist the party in resolving a series of problems connected with the further specialization and professionalization of management, raising the level of organization and discipline of the members of society, and the qualitatively better fulfillment by them of assignments of a socio-political significance' (Shapko *et al.*, 1977, p. 266).

At branch level, with societies based mainly on workplaces, the PPO 'co-ordinates and directs the efforts' of the various associations and keeps the higher party organs informed about their activities (Khaldeev *et al.*, 1975, pp. 279, 284). As in the soviets and all other nonparty bodies, the party members within a branch of a society or club form a party group, subordinated to the appropriate party committee, its members bound by party decisions. These include decisions about who is suitable for election as chairman or secretary even of such an innocuous body as a parent-teachers' association, for whom such a position might be a party assignment. Even though in many cases such positions are taken by nonparty individuals, they are effectively chosen by the party group, whose nomination is invariably endorsed: party members, of course, have no option but to vote for the sponsored nominee (Khaldeev *et al.*, 1975, p. 282).

This brings us to a further, and potentially significant, aspect of the public organizations, which is being given some attention in the Soviet Union (see, for example, Shapko *et al.*, 1977, ch. 8): their role in leadership training. As we saw in Chapter 2, the party is cross-pressured in its recruitment policies: it feels a need to have within its ranks people in leadership positions; it also needs to remain a working-class party; and in addition it wishes to advance workers to positions of leadership by giving them the appropriate skills, knowledge and experience. The mass organizations can be used to reduce the conflict of these pressures, by permitting the workers to acquire experience in running organizations and by providing an outlet for the energies of talented people outside the party, through constructive participation in the leadership of organizations that nevertheless remain under party guidance.

It is easy to interpret this party involvement in the work of public organizations as an effort to control activity across the whole spectrum of human interests. When a new society is established—say, the Society for Nature Protection, set up in the mid-1960s—this may be seen as an attempt by the party, through its sponsorship, to control opinion and defuse a developing public pressure before it represents a political challenge. Such associations are then used as a channel for educating ('indoctrinating') the public about the party's own views on particular issues. However, we saw in Chapter 1 that increasing attention has been paid in recent years to the expression of interests in Soviet society and the need to accommodate them in policy making. From this, one can present a different interpretation of the party's attention to the mass organizations: they can be seen as an additional means of acquiring knowledge of the current state of opinion among those sections of the relevant profession or the concerned public who join such associations. On the basis of that knowledge, it can perhaps devise policies that are better informed, more competent, and more acceptable to concerned citizens—in short, better policies—than it otherwise might do; it can also, if it wishes, involve the members of individual societies in the process of educating the public at large in favor of new, 'progressive' policies that might fly in the face of well-entrenched interests.

The case of environmental protection, mentioned above, is illuminating in this respect. Although Western critics charge the Soviet Union with fairly ineffectual efforts in this field (Perry, 1973), nevertheless the question has been on the political agenda for some years now (see Tarschys, 1979, p. 172). The establishment of the Society for Nature Protection might have been a move to prevent the articulation of critical views by the concerned public and associated with the long tradition of priority for heavy industry, efficiency, output at all costs, and other entrenched views. In fact, it has been accompanied by a welter of protective legislation, however moderate its effects in practice, and serious expression of concern in the press and by politicians: the party congress's directives on the Five Year Plan now contain a section on environmental protection. There is little evidence of a direct link between the society and the party's policy outputs in this sphere (see Kelley, 1978; Gustafson, 1981); yet, clearly the society has not been used by the authorities merely to pacify opinion and persuade it to accept the claims of industry; moreover, one Soviet scholar has attributed the environmental legislation to the impact of public opinion (Safarov, 1975, p. 169). It is also perhaps reasonable to assume that the sports societies have some influence in preparing the party's policies toward sports and recreation, and musical and other cultural societies' views may be taken into consideration by those responsible for policy toward the arts. (By contrast, though, it is undoubtedly true that Soviet sports associations reflect the party's policy in dealings with, say, Israel or South Africa; and those entrusted with leadership positions in, say, the Union of Writers tend to be selected for their orthodox views.)

The relationship between the party and the mass organizations is thus a complex one. The party sees its duty toward them as consisting of giving guidance and providing leadership, and this may be seen as using the associations for developing an approved ethos, an approved set of values and opinions; nevertheless it also seems likely that the CPSU in the era of 'developed socialism' sees these organizations as a valuable means of tapping the interests and aspirations of the public, which is more and more said to consist of the 'new Soviet man': educated, sophisticated, with a broad range of intellectual and other needs, interests, and wants. As a recent Soviet writer expressed it: 'The role of the public organizations in government of the state is also raised in connection with the fact that they take an ever more active part in the process of rule-making' (Topornin, 1975, p. 93).

Finally, it should not be forgotten that communists are themselves members of such associations out of interest in the causes that they espouse. A communist joins a sports society, not primarily because the party as an institution wants a communist in a leading position, but because he or she is interested in sport; another joins a theatre club to enjoy amateur theatricals. Although what they aspire to achieve in their chosen field of interest may be guided and limited by what is officially considered appropriate at a given time, the boundaries of what is legitimate nevertheless vary over time and from place to place and are affected by cultural patterns, tradition, and public tastes, and not just by politically inspired values. The party attempts to shape people's interests, aspirations, and tastes but is in turn shaped by them.

We have shown that, in supervising and guiding the mass organizations, the party uses methods similar to those employed in its dealings with the state: it takes the initiative in selecting leaders; it forms party groups within nonparty institutions, whose members are answerable to the party committee; the committee or bureau discusses the work of the mass organizations; and there is interlocking membership among party activists, mass organization activists, and the general membership of the various institutions. As one might expect, the problem of *podmena* arises, and party activists have to be constantly reminded that their task is to ensure that these nonparty bodies themselves display initiative and a high level of responsibility:

> Those party activists are profoundly wrong who, instead of giving help to the mass organizations . . ., suppose that it is simpler to take it all upon themselves, to do it themselves . . .Experience shows that any ordering-about or supplantation [*podmena*] reduces the responsibility and activity of the members of the mass organizations, and adversely affects the training of people, and the development in them of the habits of managing public affairs. (Khaldeev *et al.*, 1975, pp. 279–80)

This kind of statement clearly implies that the problem is a serious one, and demonstrates that *podmena*—an overbearing involvement on the part of the party in its relations with other institutions—extends right through Soviet society.

### The Party and the Press

Although not an institution in the conventional sense, it is convenient to consider here the party's relationship with the Soviet press. Because of its powerful role in circulating information and forming public opinion, the press has always commanded the close attention of the party authorities, who regard it as 'an important means of propagating communist views, and for training the masses ideologically and organising them for the struggle to create the new society' (Petrovichev *et al.*, 1972, p. 348). Significant episodes in the early history of the party concerned Lenin's attempts to establish and control a party organ, first *Iskra* (The Spark), and then *Pravda* (see Schapiro, 1970, chs 2, 3, 7).

The scale of the Soviet publishing operation is vast: more than 8,000 newspapers in 1983, with an annual total of almost 41 billion (41,000 million) copies; more than 5,000 periodicals, with many more than 3 billion (3,000 million) copies annually. Some of these publications are directly owned by the party: the best-known is *Pravda* (*Truth*), official organ of the CPSU Central Committee. The Pravda publishing house is a major concern, publishing also the journal *Kommunist*, which contains authoritative statements on a range of matters, *Partiinaya zhizn'* (*Party Life*), a fortnightly journal for party officials and members, dealing in practical terms with party life, and a number of other periodicals. Figures given to the Twenty-Fifth Congress stated that in 1976, the party published 386 newspapers and 273 journals; one printing of each amounted to 86 million newspaper copies and 81 million journals (*XXV s''ezd*, I, pp. 118–21). The congress of 1986 was told that the party owned 114 publishing houses, with 78 printing plants: profits from these were the second main source of party funds, after membership dues, and their contribution had grown by 80 percent (*Pravda*, February 26, 1986, p. 11). The editors of the major central publications—notably *Pravda, Kommunist,* and *Izvestiya* (*News*—the organ of the government)—are normally members of the party Central Committee and take their editorial policy from the party. At the local level, newspapers are usually the official organ of the appropriate party committee together with the local soviet, and the house journals of factories are sponsored by the party committee, the Komsomol, the trade union, and management. Editors are appointed by party committees, under the *nomenklatura*, and journalists are normally party or Komsomol members; even the appointment of the editorial committees of 'wall newspapers' in factories and institutions is carefully influenced by the party organizations, which nominate 'the most active, politically mature and authoritative comrades.' Once appointed, the editorial board works under the leadership of the party bureau and trade union committee, although it is stressed that this does not preclude criticism of party officials in the wall newspaper (Khaldeev *et al.*, 1975, pp. 317, 369); even so, the editorial content is firmly supervised by the party (Khaldeev and Krivoshein, 1979, p. 354).

On top of that, the party authorities pay particular attention to the training and ideological standards of journalists. For example, the Central Committee issued a statement on June 15, 1983, resolving 'to facilitate an improvement in the training of journalistic personnel and raising their qualifications,' adding that journalists must be 'active and bold seekers-out of what is new, staunch political fighters,' excelling in 'high ideological fiber and competence and an irreproachable journalistic ethic' (*Pravda*, June 16, 1983; see also White, 1985b). At the local level, party committees organize training courses for the part-time correspondents and editors of factory newspapers (Khaldeev *et al.*, 1975, p. 373). This means, of course, that quite apart from formal censorship by Glavlit (Committee for the Preservation of State Secrets in the Press), those engaged in producing the Soviet mass media exercise an effective self-censorship. The boundaries of what may be published are not static and, in fact, are constantly being tested: indeed, occasionally rather remarkable ideas are expressed in print (see Hill, 1980a, for examples).

Yet the fundamental principle still holds: the press is regarded as the servant of the party and the government, its aim being to educate the Soviet public to support their policies. If the press is considered to be failing in this, the party reserves the right to intervene: 'Party committees should in a businesslike way . . . direct the work of the means of mass information and propaganda, raise their fighting capacity and authority, . . . provide support for principled statements, . . . react sharply to cases of inattentive attitudes to problematic and critical materials' (*Pravda*, June 16, 1983); they must regularly review editorial boards' work plans (Petrovichev *et al.*, 1972, p. 350). Indeed, it was stated in the mid-1960s that 'as a rule' party committees review and confirm planned editorial themes, and sometimes production programs, receive editors' reports at meetings of party committee bureaus, and discuss the role and performance of the press at plenums (Vlasov, 1967, pp. 27–8). In addition, party secretaries and other officials regularly contribute articles to the press, and the speeches of Politburo members, especially the General Secretary, are frequently printed in full in all the main newspapers. Furthermore, the party uses the press as a sounding board or listening post, by raising issues and inviting readers' comments: the mid-1960s debate on the discipline of political science is one example (see Hill, 1980a, ch. 1). More generally, the party committees are urged to keep in touch with the contents of the editorial postbag ('Partiinoe rukovodstvo pressoi,' 1979; also *XXV s"ezd*, I, p. 124). In 1985, *Pravda* alone received nearly 1,500 letters a day (*Pravda*, January 1, 1986).

It thus is clear that the Soviet press is very closely associated with the party, which allocates a special role to it in the advance toward communism. As a recent party statement put it: 'Mass political work is called on to strengthen the unity of party and people, to raise the masses' communist conviction and level of political activity, to develop their creative energy. Forming the consciousness of communists and all members of our socialist society is not the task of ideological workers alone. It is the cause of the whole party' (*Pravda*, June 16, 1983).

## The Party and the Outside World

We have stressed that the CPSU sees itself as the vanguard of Soviet society and the nucleus of the USSR's political system. Its claims and the range of its self-imposed responsibility are not, however, limited to that country alone. Indeed, in principle, the communist movement does not recognize nationality as a significant factor in human relations, although in practice the Soviet Union is a nation-state among nation-states in the world community of the present century. Not only that, the CPSU and the Soviet government firmly accept the nation-state as a normal phenomenon and support the efforts of guerilla movements and others engaged in wars of 'national liberation' aimed at creating new states.

The CPSU sees itself as 'an integral part of the international communist movement,' adhering to the principle of 'proletarian and socialist internationalism' and promoting 'the strengthening of co-operation and cohesion of the fraternal socialist countries' (*Rules*, prologue). The Soviet party is supposedly 'an equal among equals, [which], thanks to its enormous revolutionary experience and consistent internationalism, the significance of its contribution to the cause of building a new society, and its selfless struggle for preserving and strengthening the peace, has won universal respect, and, in the estimation of her sister communist parties, "serves as a model for revolutionary movements in the whole world"' (Yudenkov *et al.*, 1979, p. 290, quoting *XXV s"ezd*, II, p. 55). As another Soviet source puts it, 'The organic combination and unity of basic national and international interests is one of the deepest manifestations of the nature and essence of the CPSU' (Petrovichev *et al.*, 1972, p. 48).

This interest declares itself in a number of ways, most eloquently in the participation in CPSU congresses of scores of 'fraternal delegates' from communist parties around the world (see Chapter 3). Moreover, the first major section of the Central Committee's report to congress consists of a survey of the world situation and the CPSU's international activity (for example, *XXVI s"ezd*, I, pp. 21–48). In his report to the Twenty-Fifth

Congress, Leonid Brezhnev declared that the majority of delegates to the congress had been involved in one way or another in the international sphere (*XXV s"ezd*, I, p. 58). He also pointed out that many party members work abroad, in Soviet embassies, consulates and trade missions, as correspondents for the Soviet news media, or as specialists on the Soviet overseas aid program. Clearly, the CPSU's foreign interests are widespread, and there are a number of dimensions to the question.

In the sphere of foreign *policy*, as in other policy areas, the Soviet state is not an independent entity. The broad outlines of Soviet foreign policy are endorsed by the party congress and are said to represent 'an example of the dialectical interrelation of the basic Leninist principles of foreign policy, the analytical generalization of the historical practice and experience of building socialism in the USSR and the formation and development of the world system of socialism, and the peculiarities of the present worldwide revolutionary process' (Yudenkov *et al.*, 1979, p. 274). Although there is a distinct Ministry of Foreign Affairs, and a Ministry of Foreign Trade, and other state-sponsored institutions such as Intourist, which arranges tourism between the USSR and the rest of the world, foreign *policy* is determined by the central party authorities—essentially the Politburo, of which the foreign minister, then Andrei Gromyko, became a full member in 1973, after sixteen years in the post, and the central Secretariat, which was joined in March 1986 by Anatolii Dobrynin, long-serving ambassador to Washington. The Politburo clearly makes use of the state's administrative and diplomatic apparatus, especially the intelligence-gathering apparatus of the KGB (a state committee) for information in formulating its policy (see Shevchenko, 1985, ch. 19 and p. 244); it can also be assumed that the everyday consular, trade and other contacts between Soviet and other foreign representatives are carried on without direct reference to the Politburo. Yet the party as an institution claims credit for any successes in foreign affairs (see Yudenkov *et al.*, 1979, ch. 13). Central Committee secretaries now regularly meet to discuss international affairs and ideological matters (*XXVI s"ezd*, I, p. 22), and in crises the Politburo and the central apparatus take charge. In the words of Georgi Shakhnazarov (1972, pp. 86-7): 'It is fully understood that the ruling party cannot avoid taking the operative decisions necessary on such occasions, and is obliged together with the highest organs of state power to take upon itself the whole responsibility for every political step.'

In addition to making use of the appropriate sections of the state apparatus, the party has its own important international department, with sections dealing with the major geographical areas: Africa, Europe, Britain and the Commonwealth, North America, the Middle East, and so on. Charged with managing the party's relations with the world communist movement, this influential department enjoys a wide range of responsibilities, both external and domestic, linked to its advisory role for the policy makers (see Kitrinos, 1984). In the 1970s and early 1980s, this department was headed by a senior secretary, B. N. Ponomarev, and the department for relations with the socialist countries by K. V. Rusakov. Personnel changes prior to and during the 1986 Congress and apparent restructuring of the central apparatus imply a period of fluidity as the new leadership assesses its relations with the rest of the world.

This brings us to a second major dimension of the CPSU's foreign contacts, which complicates the whole question of Soviet foreign relations. Not only does the Soviet Union, as a state, have diplomatic, trade, and cultural links with other sovereign states, but the CPSU also has direct links with overseas communist parties, ruling and nonruling, for which one of the Central Committee secretaries has general responsibility. Thus, relations between the Soviet Union and, say, Poland consist of interstate relations (including collaboration in Comecon and the Warsaw Pact) and interparty relations. Periodically, the CPSU sponsors international gatherings of communist and workers' parties, as in Berlin in 1976, or the 1973 Moscow congress of peace-loving forces. Summit meetings in the Crimea between the heads of the ruling parties, without the presence of presidents and prime ministers, became traditional in the 1970s (Yudenkov *et al.*, p. 275); these have been supplemented by meetings between party and state delegations (*XXVI s"ezd*, I, p. 22): and, as noted, Communist Party delegations visit one another's congresses.

These different levels of contact between the CPSU and the Soviet state and other states can produce protocol difficulties. Khrushchev, and Stalin before him, combined the posts of party General (or First) Secretary and prime minister, so it was not clear in which capacity the leader was negotiating with foreign heads of government; and in fact the dual position made that question irrelevant. Up until 1977, Brezhnev was head of the party but held no formal state position that was acceptable in protocol terms to Western governments. It was notable that during the 1960s, foreign contacts tended to be made by the prime minister, Aleksei Kosygin, or the titular head of state, Nikolai Podgorny. From the early 1970s, though, it was Brezhnev, the party General Secretary, who increasingly paid official visits abroad and received and negotiated with Western heads of government (including, in 1971, the West German chancellor, Willy Brandt, and subsequently various United States presidents) (Yudenkov *et al.*, 1979, pp. 293, 295). The protocol problem was formally solved by his assumption of the presidency in 1977, underlining the unity of party and state and making it clear that, in both foreign and domestic affairs, the initiator of policy formalized its enactment. Gorbachev rejected recent precedent in July 1985 by elevating the veteran foreign minister, Andrei Gromyko, to the post; but it was he, as party General Secretary, who met the United States president in Geneva in November that year.

# CHAPTER 7

# Some Questions

In the previous chapters of this book, we have been concerned with examining the role, personnel, structures, and functioning of the Communist Party in the Soviet system. We saw that it is a permanently ruling party, with no rivals for power. It sees itself as offering ideological and political leadership to the Soviet people in their striving to attain communism. Such 'striving' is itself a creation of the CPSU, which has determined that it is in the interests of the Soviet people to build such a society. This determination, as we saw, comes from the party's special relationship with the ideology, based on the writings of Marx, Engels, and Lenin. This ideology is said to be scientific: it is universally true, and incorporates the laws of social development. The CPSU uniquely comprehends those laws, which permit it always to adopt the 'correct' policies, appropriate for the present stage of building communism. Moreover, the presence of a communist party armed with such insights is seen as an objective requirement for any society on the road toward communism—a precept that was enforced with well-known consequences in Czechoslovakia in August 1968. Moreover, as society moves toward communism, that role will grow. In the words of a former prime minister of Moldavia (subsequently promoted to work in Gosplan in Moscow):

> It is important . . . to stress that the growth of the party's role in the period of building communism is a general law for all countries in the world. In present conditions it is made manifest only in our country, for the USSR is so far the only country building communism. But as other socialist countries enter the period of communist construction, [this] law will inevitably find its manifestation there as well. (Paskar', 1974, p. 78)

We saw in Chapter 3 that the party possesses a complex institutional structure that penetrates into practically every place of employment in the country. Party members are distributed across virtually all areas of

Soviet life: in industry, agriculture, education, health care, administration, trade, construction, the armed forces, even deep sea fishing and embassies abroad. Primary party organizations, ranging in size from only a handful of members to many hundreds, subdivided by workshop and shift, are formed so that the party shall have a direct influence over citizens in what is regarded as their most significant situation: at work. Party members are selected for their ideological commitment, their political reliability, their performance as workers, and their personal qualities; and extremely high demands are made of them.

In performing its 'leading and guiding' role, the party is engaged in the ideological training of its members and the wider public; it charts the basic political course for Soviet society, deciding fundamental questions of policy, and making use of the state apparatus to give its policies legal force and to implement them. The relationship between the party, the state, and other organizations, as we saw, is complex. We argued that the picture of a party standing, as it were, 'above' the state and society, adopting ideologically derived policies and handing them down for use in 'mobilizing' the masses to carry out the party leaders' schemes and plans is a much-distorted oversimplification, even though evidence in support of such an interpretation is not hard to discover. Increasingly, we argued, the party uses a variety of procedures for consulting the state apparatus and, particularly since the early 1970s, the population.

This analytical description raises a number of problems that need to be considered in summing up the CPSU and its position in the system. In this concluding chapter, we turn our attention to some of these. Is it appropriate to see the CPSU as a 'political party'? Does the concept of 'elite' help us understand the party's nature? Is it in some sense a class? And what of the future: can the CPSU solve the mounting problems for its own identity, created by the economic and social changes in Soviet society?

### Is the CPSU a Political Party?

It has been fashionable to argue that the CPSU is not 'really' a political party (Nagy, 1981, p. 75-9, citing Epstein, 1967, and Sartori, 1976). The most celebrated formulation is Sigmund Neumann's, made in 1956 (in Blondel, 1969a, p. 69):

> the very definition of party presupposes a democratic climate and hence makes it a misnomer in every dictatorship. A one-party system (*le parti unique*) is a contradiction in itself. Only the coexistence of at least one other competitive group makes a political party real.

The theorists of totalitarianism, basing their analysis in large part on the experience of the Soviet Union under Stalin, wrote in a similar vein.

What they called 'a totalitarian leader's following' was, they said, 'decidedly different from the kind of party usually found in constitutional democratic regimes': their structures appeared similar, but their 'inner dynamic' was quite different. Hence, to use the word *party* in such a context is 'a rather bewildering use of the word' (Friedrich and Brzezinski, 1965, p. 45).

The Soviet riposte to such writing is critical, indeed hostile. With a fair degree of accuracy, despite their intemperate language, two Soviet scholars noted in 1967 that 'the apostles of anti-communism pounce with particular fury on the position of the party in the republic of soviets, making it object number one for their slanderous fabrications, their verbal subversions of the foundations of socialist society' (Barabashev and Sheremet, 1967, p. 31). More recently, another Soviet writer, Farukshin (1973, p. 50), has quite rightly pointed out that this approach is essentially semantic (relying on the meaning of the Latin root *pars*), adding his belief that it is both unscientific and deliberately anti-Soviet.

With the development of the comparative study of politics since the 1960s, scholars in the West have tended to expand their theory in order to accommodate single-party systems. Indeed, in view of the emergence of nondictatorial single parties in many countries of the world in the past quarter of a century, not to do so would have excluded from consideration a significant number of the world's political systems, so the qualification proposed by Neumann has been dropped (Merkl, 1970, pp. 271–2). The single-party system is nowadays seen as one of a number of party systems available to political leaders in governing a society, and such a view sidesteps the problems inherent in the earlier approach. The modern approach to political parties is open, rather than restrictive, embracing many organizations that seek to hold political power (Ball, 1977, p. 75), whether or not they exist in competition with rivals. Hence, the CPSU can be included in an analysis that sees parties as organizations that have certain common elements but that show considerable flexibility (Blondel, 1973, pp. 82–3; Nagy, 1981).

Through such an approach, in our opinion, the concept of party is itself enriched and insights can be acquired through comparisons and contrasts between the CPSU and other parties (including, for example, communist parties in competitive systems and in communist party-dominated systems, such as exist in several states in the 'communist' world). To reject, as writers in the 1950s did, all single parties as not 'really' being parties is to follow the road to intellectual bankruptcy.

Nevertheless, as we argued in Chapter 1, the CPSU is not a party in the conventional sense, nor would it wish to be regarded as such. It sees itself as 'a party of a new type,' formed by Lenin as 'a genuinely revolutionary party of the working class of Russia' at a time when no party in Europe could serve as a model: after the death of Engels, reformism had taken over in the movement (Bugaev, 1979, p. 9). A Soviet monograph on the CPSU as a party of a new type argued in particular that one of its characteristic features is its high level of organization, associated with the high level of political consciousness (Bondar', 1982, pp. 95–100). These are, as has been made clear, features toward which the CPSU has aspired since Lenin's day, and they do distinguish the CPSU from the much laxer organizations and rules typical of 'bourgeois' parties aiming essentially to win elections. Western scholars too have identified the party as of a distinctive type, but a party nevertheless. Raymond Aron, for example, characterized it as a 'monopolistic' party, which 'claimed to have a monopoly of political activity or political representation' ('Can the party . . .?', 1967, p. 165), and as such it has served as a model for other parties in other political systems based on the Soviet example. Leonard Schapiro (1970, pp. 621, 625) also employs the term *monopolistic*.

One has to conclude, along with the participants in a discussion of single-party systems held in 1967, under the intriguing title of 'Can the party alone run a one-party state?', that the world has moved on since Neumann expressed his view, and new types of political system, with fresh forms of institution, have come into being. It is the task of political science to accommodate these forms into an enriched theory; the CPSU represents one such example.

### Is the CPSU an Elite?

A more substantial question concerns whether it is appropriate to view the CPSU as an elite, and this question cannot be dismissed so easily. As in the case of the concept of *party*, it is possible to reduce this question to a matter of semantics, saying: 'It all depends on what we mean by elite.' So it does; but to leave it there does not advance our understanding of the party's nature.

Whereas a party possesses an identifiable structure, and certain goals and functions can be ascribed to it, an elite is a much more elusive and less concrete notion. Certainly the word has been applied to the CPSU in one form or another by Western writers. For example, Karel and Irene M. Hulicka (1967, p. 35) referred to it as 'an elitist organization, which is dominated by a few leaders who attempt to exercise complete control over all aspects of Soviet society.' Others apply the term more restrictively, to refer to the staff employees in the apparatus (Armstrong, 1959; Blackwell, 1972); the Central Committee, at either All-Union or republic level (Gehlen and McBride, 1968; Levytsky, 1970; Cleary, 1974); or the Politburo (G. K. Schueller, in Lasswell and Lerner, 1965).

Soviet writers, as one would expect, indignantly reject such notions. Thus, Topornin (1975, p. 51) writes: 'The CPSU's development decisively refutes attempts by bourgeois ideologists to depict it in the form of some ruling "elite," an exclusive organisation, whose members are occupied only with matters connected with the wielding of power.' In a similar vein, Chekharin (1977b, p. 262) replies to the 'slanderers of socialist democracy' by quoting Brezhnev, to the effect that the only privilege enjoyed by communists is that of devoting more effort than others to the common cause, and the only special right is that of being in the forefront where difficulties are the greatest. Topornin (1975, p. 52) also stresses the burdens of membership and elsewhere emphasizes how ordinary the members are (in Tikhomirov, 1975, pp. 99–100).

What seems to worry Soviet writers about the word 'elite' is its connotations of superiority, privilege, extra rights, separation from the masses; and Lenin is frequently cited on the impermissibility of joining the party in order to gain benefits. They also reject the whole concept of elitism and elites, which they caricature as 'a division of society into those who have power (the elite) and those who are subjected to it (the people).' This is seen as 'a complete antidemocratic doctrine,' which is unsustainable on a number of grounds. In the USSR specifically, it is argued, 'Politics and government, i.e. the spheres which previously were the exclusive prerogative of the ruling class, have become a field for the practical activity of all the working people' (Kerimov, 1979a, pp. 106, 107, 116).

While conceding some of the arguments that may be advanced against Western elite theories, this might nevertheless be a concept that can provide insights into Soviet political life.

The fact is that in certain regards the CPSU does possess some of the characteristics of an elite, whether defined as a minority set apart from society (Keller, 1968, p. 26), as a functional group that has high status in society (Bottomore, 1966, p. 14), or as small minorities who appear to play an exceptionally influential part in political and social affairs (Parry, 1969, p. 13). Some of these we have already seen. Its self-image is of a vanguard, distinguished from the class of which it is a part by its higher level of ideological and political consciousness. Its recruitment policies are exclusive: the party openly states that not everyone may join, but only 'the best.' Membership is restricted—although not to a particular size or proportion of the population—and admissions procedures are exacting, complex, and prolonged. The party also insists on the 'purity' of its ranks, and operates a system of 'self-cleansing' (*samoochishchenie*) as a means of maintaining high standards (Turishchev, 1975, p. 187): this involves periodic waves of expulsions, sometimes amounting to a purge. All these features serve to distinguish the party membership from the nonparty masses, who are immune to these negative aspects of involvement in the party. In addition, party members enjoy tremendous prestige, they are regarded as the foremost representatives in their daily life, they enjoy access to privileged information, and they are, above all, members of an institution that wields complete political authority and that has the power to move them into positions of responsibility and trust.

Yet, as both Rigby (1968, p. 412) and Hough (1977, p. 133) have observed, the party is an elite of a rather peculiar kind. In the first place, the boundary between party membership and being a nonparty citizen is blurred, to some extent, even though it obviously exists. For one thing, it is doubtful whether many of the 19 million members of the party enjoy greater power, at any rate, than their workmates or members of their family. A fair proportion of them may be selected to serve as deputies, as trade union secretaries, as Komsomol officers, even as members of lower party organs: but in a political system as centralized as that of the USSR, such participation does not really accord much power to those people involved; in any case, nonparty citizens are also selected for many of these offices. Furthermore, the sheer size of the party—which is to grow still further, according to the official line—again makes one sceptical about applying the concept of *elite* to such a diffuse body of men and women. Party membership, as such, guarantees relatively little. Rigby (1968, p. 453) suggests that the party is a 'representative elite,' which 'links up the various elites of Soviet society . . . by overlapping with them, not by incorporating them.' Hough (1977, p. 139) argues that the party represents a highly active segment of Soviet society that bears up well in comparisons with the West. Clearly, then, in some senses the CPSU can usefully be considered as a type of elite.

To a considerable extent, it appears that whether the CPSU is viewed as a elite depends on one's own position: inside it, or outside. Those outside include both Western observers—most of them, perhaps, hostile—and Soviet citizens, who, despite assertions of their unswerving support, are in many cases apolitical, if not antipathetic to the party and all it stands for (see Tikhomirov, 1975, p. 277). Both groups find little difficulty in convincing themselves that the party is indeed a privileged elite, while nevertheless acknowledging that there are some shining examples of outstanding dedication and devotion to the public good to be found among the party's members at all levels. Those people inside the party may genuinely believe that they are in fact close to the masses, that they constitute 'an inseparable constituent part of the people, devoting all its energies to the good of the people and acting with their full support' (Topornin, 1975, p. 51).

But appointment to practically all positions of authority *is* reserved for party members, and many ordinary Soviet citizens will openly state that party membership is a necessity for career advancement in most fields: that is one of the 'rules of the game.' The question then arises: are the party officials—the full-time officers in the apparatus, the party members in important state and industrial positions—really the elite? Here, one is possibly on safer ground in using the concept, although this too is denied by Soviet commentators (Derbinov *et al.*, 1984, p. 23). The power that accrues to party secretaries, at least from the *raikom* level upward, and workers in the apparatus is considerable, and the Soviet press itself frequently—too frequently, one presumes, for the satisfaction of the top leadership—testifies to the possibilities for misusing power and the ingenuity of its own officers in exploiting their position. Moreover, from a certain level in the structure upward, privileges are widely known to exist: access to consumer goods in short supply; the chance to see Western films that are never put on general release; the use of private hotels, sanatoria, and country dachas; the provision of a car, perhaps with a chauffeur; the possibility of travel abroad; and, near to the summit of political power, special shops that obviate the necessity of coming into contact with the masses (Kaiser, 1977, ch. 4; Matthews, 1978; Voslensky, 1984, ch. 5). Indeed, an astonishingly frank article in the party newspaper *Pravda*, shortly before the 1986 Congress, referred directly to this phenomenon as something that disturbed readers for its obvious exacerbation of inequalities in Soviet society (Samolis, 1986).

But again, the boundaries are hard to determine. The rural *raikom* secretary two thousand miles from Moscow is clearly not in the same league as the Politburo members who have the ultimate power to make or break his career. Soviet writers often point out that a high proportion of leaders are recruited from among workers and peasants (for example, Topornin, 1975, p. 61), adding that the high levels of education among them not so much represent badges of distinction as reflect the achievement of socialism in providing for social advancement (Chekharin, 1977b, pp. 195–6). What is not certain is that a worker or peasant who moves into administration, at whatever level, will retain personal links with his former class or even continue to support its values: indeed, it has been suggested that the party ought to study the effect of individuals' social groups on their performance as party members, since 'objective conditions cannot fail to have an influence on the way of life, social psychology, etc.' (Utenkov *et al.*, 1977, p. 44). Indeed, more broadly, the psychology of public officials is being examined by Soviet social scientists (Obolonsky, 1979).

Neither do we know much for certain about how the Soviet public regards its leaders: whether, for example, Soviet public opinion is generally characterized by 'them and us' attitudes. Officially, it is not, although *émigrés* and dissidents would assert that it exists, and it is by no means difficult to find Soviet citizens who are prepared to run down their government. Stephen White (1979, p. 111) refers in this context to 'considerable cynicism' toward those responsible for managing the Soviet system; Hedrick Smith (1976, pp. 255–6) finds that ordinary Russian tend to refer to the rulers as *vlasti*, 'they' (literally, 'the authorities'; see also Bialer, 1980, p. 182). But such evidence is largely impressionistic and anecdotal; in contrast we can concede one of Chekharin's points: lots of children of workers, and to a lesser extent peasants, do enter the administrative workforce, and we can perhaps assume that this is seen as a desirable social advance (see Bialer, 1980, ch. 8). In this regard, the Soviet Union shares with Western industrial societies a belief that the 'successful' working-class child is the one who manages to escape into a white-collar job. In this situation, the concept of *elite* in relation to the political and administrative stratum shades off into the concepts of *stratification* and *differentiation*, which are perhaps more appropriate to an understanding of Soviet society.

## Is the Party a Class?

Clearly, if the party as a whole can scarcely be referred to as an elite, it is even less appropriate to see it as a class. As we have seen, it draws its members from a wide range of social and occupational groups in society, and they perform diverse social roles. There is no such thing as a distinctive party 'life-style,' except in so far as party members are expected to devote more of their time and energy to political activities. It is hard to envisage a sense of 'class-consciousness' that links the champion milkmaid with the general manager of, say, the Gorky automobile works, although they may both feel that they are doing their bit, as party members, for the cause of building communism. Most significantly, at least from the point of view of the Marxist theoretician, the party possesses no distinctive relationship to the means of production.

Yet the concept of a ruling class is to be found widely scattered in the non-Soviet literature. In one of the best-known studies of the communist form of rule, written with the benefit of insights from within the system, Milovan Djilas (1966, ch. 3) characterized the members of the unified party-state-managerial bureaucracy as 'the new class.' Leon Trotsky (1967, pp. 248–52), while rejecting the concept of *class*, identified the 'bureaucracy' as the 'ruling stratum' of Soviet society. Alec Nove uses the notion of *nomenklatura* to identify the holders of power, arguing (1975, p. 626) that those who attain their ruling positions through that means are 'in command' of the means of production, a point extensively amplified by Voslensky (1984); Nove also suggests (1983, p. 301) that they 'exhibit something close to class consciousness.' Even *Pravda* carried an account of a reader's letter, which expressed the view that the Central Committee was separated from the working class by a 'slow-moving, inert and viscous "party-administrative layer,"' consisting of individuals looking only for privileges (Samolis, 1986).

However, even they do not possess one of the major attributes of a ruling class, in Marxist theory: they may command, but they do not own, the means of production. They are vulnerable; they cannot pass on capital to their heirs, although there is evidence that they enjoy greater access to higher education (see Lane, 1978, pp. 505–7), and this helps to ensure that movement out of the intelligentsia into the proletariat and peasantry is insignificant, if it exists at all. In addition, with the rapid expansion of industry, and the technological revolution that is transforming the occupational balance in favor of the 'white-collar' employee, the class structure of Soviet society is likely to remain relatively fluid for some time to come, further hindering the development of a sense of class-consciousness among that group. Hence, one must conclude that the idea of the CPSU, or even its officers and officials, as a class is inappropriate.

A further consideration has a bearing on this: the general place of the party in Soviet soviety, elaborated in Chapter 1. We have seen in the course of this book that the CPSU has undergone a series of profound changes in its structures, its membership, and its functioning during almost eighty years of its existence. It is, in fact, in many senses at the heart of Soviet society, as well as of the political system. It is not merely a power structure, or an organization through which the top leaders rule: it is now an institution through which many millions of Soviet citizens derive their livelihood, and millions more attain their social status. An organization whose members comprise one in ten of the adult population, it is an employer of scores of thousands: not only *apparatchiki*, but also secretaries, chauffeurs, janitors, receptionists, accountants and—increasingly—computer operators and others possessing the skills of modern office management; its subsidiary enterprises, such as publishing houses, employ more thousands of workers. The Central Committee expends large sums on housing, office accommodation, and recreation facilities for its own employees (*Pravda*, February 26, 1986, p. 11). Through its direction of the *nomenklatura* system, still others are dependent on the party. If to these people are added the spouses and children of members and employees, it can then be seen that a large segment of the total Soviet population relies directly or indirectly on the party for its livelihood, its career development, and its social and political status.

Even so, at the very least, its image has become somewhat tarnished in the light of revelations of corruption, embezzlement, slack discipline, careerism, and a host of other evils that became rampant in the late

Brezhnev years and that were revealed in the speeches of Mikhail Gorbachev and others to the party Congress in February 1986 and in press articles in the period leading up to that event. This explains, to a significant degree, the repeated call under Gorbachev for purity and honesty to be the characteristics of party members.

### The Party's Future

The CPSU, then, is somewhat difficult to characterize, and indeed this conclusion is one that Soviet scholars have reached: for them, 'bourgeois' scholars are engaging in a futile exercise in attempting to categorize the CPSU according to the criteria of their own, class-based theories (see Farukshin, 1973). Robert J. Osborn (1974, p. 237) has similarly argued that 'The qualities of the Party can be judged only in terms of the tasks it is expected to perform. To measure it against external standards of bureaucratization or representativeness is to miss the point that it had to be adapted to the needs of the larger political system of which it formed the core.' Criticism of the CPSU and its role in terms of bourgeois democratic theory has little impact, since the party does not judge itself or the world in such terms. The CPSU exists for a different purpose: its aim is to guide the Soviet Union in the direction of communism, which it understands. All talk of 'pluralism' is at best irrelevant, at worst downright subversive. Such a political model, it is claimed, does not properly account for political processes even in bourgeois countries (Kerimov, 1979a, pp. 117–23), and it is certainly not a model that the CPSU wishes to emulate. Quite apart from the fact that the processes of confrontation politics look unattractive, particularly to a party that has enjoyed unfettered power for more than sixty years, the CPSU believes that its own view of the world enables it to understand the underlying relationships in society. Hostility between groups with separate and conflicting economic interests lies at the basis of bourgeois society. In the Soviet Union, the very possibility of such antagonism has been eliminated, it is argued, by the abolition of the private ownership of capital. There is thus no need for competing political parties, since parties represent the interests of different classes.

Such has been the party's traditional explanation of its monopoly position in Soviet society, in contrast to the competing parties of Western systems. We saw in Chapter 1, however, that the concept of interests has been given fresh scrutiny by Soviet scholars during the past quarter of a century, and, although all sectors of society are said to possess identical *fundamental* interests, the various social groups also have specific, or secondary, interests they have a right to express and that the political authorities have an obligation to take account of in framing policies. The question that arises, therefore, is whether the CPSU as it has developed to date really possesses the capacity to take the secondary interests of all groups into account. It can easily argue that it truly expresses their fundamental interests, since it defines what those interests are; but it is less clear that it is equipped to play the more subtle role of identifying the multiplicity of sectional and individual interests and aggregating them into policies suitable for the whole of society.

If the CPSU were to find itself unable to cope with the range of demands that were being fed into its decision-making organs, there are a number of ways in which it might respond. One might be a return to Stalinist methods: repression of secondary interests, and strict emphasis on the 'common' goal of building communism, along lines defined by the party, basing its justification for policies on appeals to its ideological wisdom. Such a development cannot be ruled out entirely, given the presence within and close to the Soviet leadership of representatives of political trends that would welcome a return to such methods of rule (see Medvedev, 1975, chs. 3, 4). A more positive response might be to permit sectional groups to exist within the CPSU's own structures: a workers' section, a peasants' section, a section for trade employees, and so on. Such a development might be seen by some as infringing the Tenth Congress's ban on fractions in the party; however, something that might conceivably be adduced as a precedent is Khrushchev's splitting of the party apparatus into agricultural and industrial units between November 1962 and November 1964 (see Armstrong, 1966), although the disgrace to which Khrushchev was consigned after his removal from power in 1964 suggests that to be unlikely for the time being. Nevertheless, the party has a range of experience that it could again draw on in the future.

Alternatively, the party might decide to modify the political structures fundamentally, by switching to government by popular front, such as exists in Poland, the GDR, Czechoslovakia, and elsewhere. In that system, several distinct party organizations exist, each drawing its membership from a specific segment of society, and all acting together under the umbrella of the communist-led 'front.' No such suggestion has been made in the Soviet Union, although there are a number of indicators that suggest the idea may not be entirely ruled out.

First, one writer has ruled it out. Farukshin (1973) argued that communist-led multiparty systems were a reflection of a mixed economy, and as the economic institutions were gradually nationalized, so the need for more than one party would disappear. And he added the following (p. 243):

> The specific interests of the different classes, social strata and groups that are preserved under socialism do not necessarily demand for their expression and realization the existence of separate political parties.

They can be taken account of and expressed by the Communist Party as the party of the workers. As socialist society develops, the preconditions are created for the replacement of the multi-party system where it exists by a system with a single Marxist-Leninist party.

Clearly, for Farukshin (and others) a change from the CPSU's monopoly rule would be a retrograde step, although he acknowledged (pp. 106–7) that different parties can represent the interests of a single class.

However, there is also developing in Soviet society, particularly among scholars, a substantial interest in the progress of other communist-led systems. B. A. Strashun, for example (1973, p. 46), has favorably written of the system of partially contested elections in a number of socialist states, a system that depends on the existence of noncommunist parties. Other writers also have pointed to parallels and contrasts between Soviet political practice and legislation and those of other countries in the socialist bloc (see Hill, 1980a, p. 189). In distinction from Farukshin, Shakhnazarov (1974, p. 22–3) has argued that 'The multi-party system in the countries that embarked upon socialist development after the Second World War has stood the test of time.' More recently, it is implied that the Soviet one-party system arose almost accidentally, because the other 'democratic' parties refused to collaborate with the Bolsheviks (Tikhomirov and Chirkin, 1985, p. 149). The author of this idea (Strashun) lists and classifies the range of parties in other socialist states and concludes (p. 150) that 'neither the one-party nor the multi-party system is a natural sign of a socialist political system'; he then examines in some detail the systems of the 'national front' through which communist parties 'lead,' in what Wiatr (1970, p. 1239) has called a 'hegemonic party system.'

The importance of such statements seems to be that the USSR—and specifically the CPSU—acknowledges the legitimacy of other countries' and other communist parties' experience in building socialism and may even be prepared to emulate them on certain specific points where they have led the way. A *noncompetitive* party system is seen as one legitimate organizational form for a socialist system (see Arkhipov, 1980, pp. 124–5), and at least a model exists if the CPSU ever feels a need to expand the political base of the system, by permitting new structures to serve for political participation and interest articulation.

If that is a possibility, what is the likelihood of a system's developing that could even be called 'pluralist'? Might the CPSU eventually—perhaps in a generation, or two, or three—be obliged to dismantle the system that has served its purpose to date? A number of scholars in the West have claimed to identify signs of pluralist tendencies appearing in Soviet politics (see White, 1978, pp. 101–6; Solomon, 1983). Yet one searches in vain for any indication, however slight, of a positive orientation toward pluralism in Soviet writings and speeches. One finds nothing but contemptuous dismissal of the whole idea. Indeed, Soviet scholars seem to regard the term *pluralist* as abusive, along with *totalitarian*: they clearly do not appreciate that those scholars who use the epithet *pluralist* are trying to be generous to the USSR and are in fact aiming their attack, not at the Soviet system, but at the theorists of totalitarianism.

As regards this question, Topornin (1975, p. 91) writes of 'so-called pluralist democracy,' stating also that the concepts of political pluralism and the free play of political forces are 'deeply alien to Soviet people' (p. 48). In the same vein, Marchenko (1973, p. 100) sees pluralist theories as intended to 'mask the class essence of the capitalist system,' a point also made by Farukshin, who says (1973, p. 247) that 'in Soviet society there are no objective reasons for the existence of so-called political pluralism': he adds (p. 248) the assertion that Soviet society is characterized not by pluralism and polycentrism, but by 'political unity and popular power.' The word *futility* has been applied to pluralist analyses of the 'democratic man' (Kerimov, 1979a, p. 121). *Pluralism, the free play of political forces*: such phrases sound too close to anarchy to a party that declaims the need for planning if society is to progress (Kerimov, 1979b, p. 181). So pluralism, we can reliably conclude, is not likely to be on the Soviet political agenda in the foreseeable future.

This means, then, that the CPSU intends to continue its present role in the system: that of guiding Soviet society in the direction of communism, which it will define, elaborating theoretical concepts to explain and justify new developments as they occur. In doing so, it will have to solve two major kinds of question: those concerned with its own internal life; and those that concern its relations with other institutions.

We saw in Chapter 2 that the party faces a severe dilemma over the growth of its numbers and the regulation of its composition. A particular problem here is the need to have within its ranks the 'leaders' of society. As the Soviet economy continues to expand and becomes structurally more complex and technically more sophisticated, the ranks of those engaged in governmental and managerial functions will expand steadily. The time may not be far off when the party will have to entrust positions of responsibility on a significant scale to persons outside its own ranks. If that happens, then the meaning of party membership may undergo a change: it will no longer be a requirement for advancement through the administrative apparatus. Yet such a development might also create crises of authority in the economy if the enormous prestige that accrues, in official eyes, to party members is denied to these managers but is possessed by a substantial proportion of the workforce under them. That is but one angle of the problem.

In addition, as has been increasingly argued since the 1970s, there is an overdue need for intraparty democratization (see Hill, 1980a, ch. 7), a point taken from the 1961 party program and repeated in the 1986 edition. That requires raising the level of political culture of cadres, indeed the application of a more sophisticated personnel policy, after the massive weeding out that has accompanied the change in generations at the very top. The new recruits to positions of authority within the party will have to cease regarding any criticism from below as undermining their own personal authority, so that ordinary party members will feel encouraged to perform the role that is expected of them in pinpointing weaknesses, unmasking inefficiency, revealing incompetence. In general, if the party is to play its self-appointed role effectively, the new techniques for gathering and processing information will have to be welcomed and developed.

As regards the party's relations with other institutions, decisive efforts will have to be taken to eradicate *podmena*, parallelism, and petty tutelage, which simply suffocate the state and other institutions, destroy confidence, and stifle initiative. Given the fact that the leading core in all nonparty bodies consists of party members, what this really means is that the party as an institution will have to develop the confidence to trust itself as a collection of individuals. The party needs to take a fresh view of its own members and recall that it is they who are ultimately the people on whom it must depend.

The CPSU faces a society that is ever growing richer, better educated, more highly skilled, experienced and self-confident, and possessing increasing amounts of leisure time. It faces also a country with a number of difficult problems that will require solution: energy supplies, population dynamics and the distribution of the workforce, industrial growth, inefficient agriculture, ethnic pressures, and foreign relations. Many western observers expected the change in leadership to a younger generation to free the system from the 'partial paralysis' (Gustafson, 1981, p. 143) that overcame it in the late Brezhnev years and permit much-needed policy innovation (see Hough, 1980; Brown and Kaser, 1982, *passim*); even genuine political reform might be contemplated (see Colton, 1984). Whatever the prospects for significant political change under Gorbachev, the existing problems will impinge more pressingly on the capabilities of the political system. In such conditions, the CPSU may find that governing the Soviet Union is even more difficult in the last decade and a half of the twentieth century than it was in earlier periods.

# CPSU Politburo
# at March 6, 1986

| Name | Year of Birth | Age in 1986 | Nationality | Position |
|------|------|------|------|------|
| * Gorbachev, M. S. | 1931 | 55 | Russian | CPSU Central Committee General Secretary |
| Aliev, G. A. | 1923 | 63 | Azerbaidzhani | first deputy prime minister |
| Vorotnikov, V. I. | 1926 | 60 | Russian | prime minister, RSFSR |
| Gromyko, A. A. | 1909 | 77 | Russian | chairman, USSR Supreme Soviet presidium (president) |
| * Zaikov, L. N. | 1923 | 63 | Russian | secretary, CPSU Central Committee (defence industries) |
| Kunaev, D. A. | 1912 | 74 | Kazakh | first secretary, Kazakhstan central committee |
| * Ligachev, Ye. K. | 1920 | 66 | Russian | secretary, CPSU Central Committee (broad responsibilities) |
| Ryzhkov, N. I. | 1929 | 57 | Russian | prime minister |
| Solomentsev, M. S. | 1913 | 73 | Russian | chairman, Party Control Committee |
| Chebrikov, V. M. | 1923 | 63 | Russian | chairman, KGB |
| Shevardnadze, E. A. | 1928 | 58 | Georgian | minister of foreign affairs |
| Shcherbitskii, V. V. | 1918 | 68 | Ukrainian | first secretary, Ukrainian central committee |

### Candidate Members

| Name | Year of Birth | Age in 1986 | Nationality | Position |
|------|------|------|------|------|
| Demichev, P.N. | 1918 | 68 | Russian | minister of culture[1] |
| * Dolgikh, V. I. | 1924 | 62 | Russian | secretary, CPSU Central Committee (heavy industry and energy) |
| Yel'tsin, B. N. | 1931 | 55 | Russian | first secretary, Moscow *gorkom* |
| Slyun'kov, N. N. | 1929 | 57 | Belorussian | first secretary, Belorussian central committee |
| Sokolov, S. L. | 1911 | 75 | Russian | minister of defence |
| Solov'ëv, Yu. F. | 1925 | 61 | Russian | first secretary, Leningrad *obkom* |
| Talyzin, N. V. | 1929 | 57 | Russian | chairman, Gosplan |

155

| Name | Year of Birth | Age in 1986 | Nationality | Position |
|------|------|------|------|------|
| Central Committee Secretariat (in addition to Politburo members marked *) | | | | |
| Biryukova, A. P. | 1929 | 57 | Russian | (consumer goods, social policies) |
| Dobrynin, A. F. | 1919 | 67 | Russian | (foreign relations) |
| Zimyanin, M. V. | 1914 | 72 | Belorussian | (ideology) |
| Medvedev, V. A. | 1929 | 57 | Russian | (scientific and educational institutions) |
| Nikonov, V. P. | 1929 | 57 | Russian | (agriculture) |
| Razumovskii, G. P. | 1936 | 50 | Russian | (party organizational work) |
| Yakovlev, A. N. | 1924 | 62 | Russian | (propaganda) |

1. On June 18, 1986, Demichev was relieved as minister of culture and elected first deputy chairman, USSR Supreme Soviet presidium.

# Key Dates in the Party's History

| | |
|---|---|
| 1898 | Founding Congress in Minsk. |
| 1903 | Second Congress in Brussels and London: party splits into Bolsheviks and Mensheviks. |
| 1906 | Fourth Congress in Stockholm: attempts to reunite the party. |
| 1917 | October 25 (November 7): Bolsheviks seize power in Petrograd; Lenin becomes prime minister. |
| 1921 | Tenth Congress: fractionalism banned; New Economic Policy introduced. |
| 1922 | Union of Soviet Socialist Republics formed. |
| 1924 | January 21: death of Lenin. |
| 1928 | Trotsky exiled; First Five Year Plan begins; collectivization of agriculture inaugurated. |
| 1929 | Trotsky deported. |
| 1934 | Seventeenth Congress—'Congress of the Victors'; new party rules adopted. December 1: Sergei Kirov assassinated; purges begin. |
| 1936 | New Constitution adopted. |
| 1937–38 | Great Purge. |
| 1939 | Eighteenth Congress: formal abandonment of mass purges. |
| 1941 | June 22: German invasion of USSR. |
| 1945 | End of 'Great Patriotic War' (Second World War). |
| 1952 | Nineteenth Congress: new party rules adopted; Politburo renamed Central Committee presidium. |
| 1953 | March 6: death of Stalin; Malenkov named prime minister and senior party Secretary. March 14: Malenkov replaced as senior Secretary by Khrushchev. Early September: Khrushchev becomes First Secretary. |
| 1956 | Twentieth Congress: Khrushchev's 'secret' speech inaugurates de-Stalinization. |

1957    'Anti-party group' crisis ends in victory for Khrushchev.
1959    Twenty-First Congress.
1961    Twenty-Second Congress: Stalin removed from Lenin
        mausoleum; new party program and rules adopted.
1964    October 13: Khrushchev removed from office; Leonid
        Brezhnev named First Secretary.
1966    Twenty-Third Congress: Brezhnev's title changed to General
        Secretary; Central Committee presidium renamed Politburo.
1971    Twenty-Fourth Congress.
        September: death of Khrushchev, in retirement.
1976    Twenty-Fifth Congress.
1977    New Constitution adopted; Brezhnev appointed president, as
        well as CPSU General Secretary.
1981    Twenty-Sixth Congress: revision of 1961 party program
        authorized.
1982    November 10: death of Central Committee General Secretary
        Leonid Brezhnev; replaced in that post by Yuri V.
        Andropov.
1984    February 9: death of Yuri Andropov; replaced as Central
        Committee General Secretary by Konstantin U. Chernenko.
1985    March 10: death of Konstantin Chernenko; replaced as Cen-
        tral Committee General Secretary by Mikhail S. Gorbachev.
1986    February–March: Twenty-Seventh Congress: new draft of
        program and rules adopted; new Politburo and Secretariat
        under Gorbachev elected.

# Bibliography

Aimbetov, A., *et al.* (1967), *Problemy sovershenstvovaniya organizatsii i deyatel'nosti mestnykh Sovetov* (Alma-Ata: Nauka).

Allison, Graham T. (1971), *Essence of Decision: Explaining the Cuban Missile Crisis* (Boston, Mass.: Little, Brown).

Almond, G. A., and Powell, G. Bingham (1966), *Comparative Politics: A Developmental Approach* (Boston, Mass: Little, Brown).

Almond, G. A., and Verba, Sidney (1963), *The Civic Culture: Political Attitudes and Democracy in Five Nations* (Princeton, N.J.: Princeton University Press).

Apollonov, L. A. (1976), *Verkhovnyi organ leninskoi partii* (Moscow: Politizdat).

Arkhipov, B. (1980), 'Mnogopartiinost' v usloviyakh sotsialisticheskogo stroitel'stva,' *Kommunist*, no. 3, pp. 124–8.

Armstrong, John A. (1959), *The Soviet Bureaucratic Elite: A Case Study of the Ukrainian Apparatus* (London: Atlantic Books).

Armstrong, John A. (1961), *The Politics of Totalitarianism: The Communist Party of the Soviet Union from 1934 to the Present* (New York: Random House).

Armstrong, John A. (1966), 'Party bifurcation and elite interests,' *Soviet Studies*, vol. XVII, pp. 417–30.

Armstrong, John A. (1973), *Ideology, Politics, and Government in the Soviet Union: An Introduction,* 3rd ed. (London: Nelson).

Arutyunyan, N. Kh. (1970), *Partiya i Sovety* (Moscow: Izvestiya).

Avtorkhanov, Abdurakhman (1966), *The Communist Party Apparatus* (Chicago: Henry Regnery).

Babii, B. M., *et al.* (eds) (1976), *Politicheskaya organizatsiya razvitogo sotsialisticheskogo obshchestva (pravovye problemy)* (Kiev: Naukova dumka).

Babiy, B., and Zabigailo, V. (1979), 'Popular participation in government as a criterion of democracy,' in Chirkin *et al.* (1979), pp. 31–40.

Ball, Alan R. (1977), *Modern Politics and Government,* 2nd ed. (London: Macmillan).

Barabashev, G. V., and Sheremet, K. F. (1967), 'KPSS i Sovety,' *Sovetskoe gosudarstvo i pravo*, no. 11, pp. 31–41.

Bazin, M. Ya., *et al.* (1968), *Pervichnaya partiinaya organizatsiya—osnova partii* (Kishinev: Kartya Moldovenyaske).

Bezuglov, A. A. (1971), *Sovetskii deputat: gosudarstvennopravovoi status* (Moscow: Yuridicheskaya literatura).

Bialer, Seweryn (1980), *Stalin's Successors: Leadership, Stability, and Change in the Soviet Union* (Cambridge: Cambridge University Press).

Bilinsky, Yaroslav (1967), 'The rulers and the ruled,' *Problems of Communism*, vol. XVI, no. 5, pp. 16–26.

Blackwell, Robert E., Jr. (1972), 'Elite recruitment and functional change: An analysis of the Soviet obkom elite, 1950–1968,' *Journal of Politics*, vol. 34, pp. 124–52.

Blackwell, Robert E., Jr. (1979), 'Cadres policy in the Brezhnev era,' *Problems of Communism*, vol. XXVIII, no. 2, pp. 29–42.

Blondel, Jean (1969a), *An Introduction to Comparative Government* (London: Weidenfeld & Nicolson).

Blondel, Jean (ed) (1969b), *Comparative Government: A Reader* (London: Macmillan).

Blondel, Jean (1973), *Comparing Political Systems* (London: Weidenfeld & Nicolson).

Blyakhman, L., and Shkaratan, O. (1977), *Man at Work: The Scientific and Technological Revolution, the Soviet Working Class and Intelligentsia* (Moscow: Progress).

Bondar', V. Ya. (1982), *Leninskaya partiya—partiya novogo tipa* (Moscow: Politizdat).

Bottomore, T. B. (1966), *Elites and Society* (Harmondsworth: Penguin).

Breslauer, George W. (1982), *Khrushchev and Brezhnev as Leaders: Building Authority in Soviet Politics* (London: Allen & Unwin).

Brezhnev, L. I. (1970), *Leninskim kursom: Rechi i stat'i*, vol. 2 (Moscow: Politizdat).

Brezhnev, L. I. (1977), 'O proekte Konstitutsii Soyuza Sovetskikh Sotsialisticheskikh Respublik' (speech at CPSU Central Committee plenum, May 24, 1977), *Kommunist*, no. 8, pp. 34–44.

Brezhnev, L. I. (1979), speech at CPSU Central Committee plenum, November 1979, *Pravda*, November 28, pp. 1–2.

Brown, A. H. (1974), *Soviet Politics and Political Science* (London: Macmillan).

Brown, Archie (1979), 'Eastern Europe: 1968, 1978, 1998,' *Daedalus*, Winter, pp. 151–74.

Brown, Archie (1980), 'The power of the General Secretary,' in Rigby *et al.* (1980), pp. 135–57.

Brown, Archie, (1982), 'Leadership succession and policy innovation,' in Brown and Kaser (1982), pp. 223–53.

Brown, Archie (ed) (1984), *Political Culture and Communist Studies* (London: Macmillan).

Brown, Archie, and Gray, Jack (eds) (1977), *Political Culture and Political Change in Communist States* (London: Macmillan).

Brown, Archie, and Kaser, Michael (eds) (1978), *The Soviet Union since the Fall of Khrushchev*, 2nd ed. (London: Macmillan).

Brown, Archie, and Kaser, Michael (eds) (1982), *Soviet Policy for the 1980s* (London: Macmillan).

Brumberg, Abraham (ed) (1962), *Russia under Khrushchev* (London: Methuen).

Bugaev, Ye. (1979), 'V. I. Lenin o Kommunisticheskoi partii kak partii novogo tipa, eë ideinykh i organizatsionnykh osnovakh,' *Partiinaya zhizn'*, no. 24, pp. 9–17.

Bulycheva, A. (1980), 'Partiinaya zabota ob ekonomii metalla,' *Partiinaya zhizn'*, no. 8, pp. 40–3.

Bunce, Valerie (1981), *Do New Leaders Make a Difference? Executive Succession and Public Policy under Capitalism and Socialism* (Princeton, N.J.: Princeton University Press).

'Can the party . . .' (1967), 'Can the party alone run a one-party state?', *Government and Opposition*, vol. 2, pp. 165–80.

Carr, E. H. (1966), *The Bolshevik Revolution, 1917–23*, vol. 1 (Harmondsworth: Penguin).

Chekharin, Ye. M. (1977a), *Razvitie politicheskoi sistemy Sovetskogo obshchestva na sovremennom etape (lektsiya)* (Moscow: Mysl').

Chekharin, Ye. M. (E. M.) (1977b), *The Soviet Political System under Developed Socialism* (Moscow: Progress).

Chernenko, K. U. (1975), 'Nekotorye voprosy sovershenstvovaniya partiinogo i gosudarstvennogo apparata,' *Voprosy istorii KPSS,* no. 8, pp. 3–18.

Chernyshev, A. (1978), 'Formulirovka dolzhna byt' tochnoi,' *Partiinaya zhizn'*, no. 13, p. 78.

Chirkin, V., *et al.* (eds) (1979), *Political Systems: Development Trends* (Moscow: 'Social Sciences Today' Editorial Board, USSR Academy of Sciences).

Christman, Henry M. (ed) (1969), *Communism in Action: A Documentary History* (New York: Bantam Books).

Churchward, L. G. (1975), *Contemporary Soviet Government,* 2nd ed (London: Routledge & Kegan Paul).

Clarke, Roger A. (1967), 'The composition of the Supreme Soviet, 1958–66,' *Soviet Studies*, vol. XIX, pp. 53–65.

Cleary, J. W. (1974), 'Elite career patterns in a Soviet republic,' *British Journal of Political Science*, vol. 4, pp. 323–44.

Cocks, Paul (1978), 'Administrative rationality, political change, and the role of the Party,' in Ryavec (1978), pp. 41–59.

Cohen, Stephen F., Rabinowitch, Alexander, and Sharlet, Robert (eds) (1980), *The Soviet Union since Stalin* (London: Macmillan).

Colton, Timothy J. (1984), *The Dilemma of Reform in the Soviet Union* (New York: Council on Foreign Relations).

*Constitution* (1977), *Constitution (Fundamental Law) of the Union of Soviet Socialist Republics* (Moscow: Novosti).

Daniels, Robert V. (1976), 'Office holding and elite status: the Central Committee of the CPSU,' in Paul Cocks, Robert V. Daniels, and Nancy Whittier Heer (eds), *The Dynamics of Soviet Politics* (Cambridge, Mass.: Harvard University Press), pp. 77–95.

Danilova, Y. Z., et al. (1975), Soviet Women: Some Aspects of the Status of Women in the USSR (Moscow: Progress).

'Delo Lenina . . .' (1980), 'Delo Lenina zhivët i pobezhdaet,' Partiinaya zhizn', no. 1, pp. 59–60.

Deputaty (1966), Deputaty Verkhovnogo Soveta SSSR: sed'moi sozyv (Moscow: Izvestiya).

Derbinov, Yu. V., et al. (eds) (1975), Pervichnaya partiinaya organizatsiya—avangard trudovogo kollektiva (Moscow: Mysl').

Derbinov, Yu. V., Yermolaev, V. Ya., and Musaev, A. M. (eds) (1984), Razvitie vnutripartiinykh otnoshenii na sovremennom etape (Moscow: Mysl').

Deutsch, Karl W. (1966), The Nerves of Government: Models of Political Communication and Control (with a New Introduction) (New York: The Free Press).

Djilas, Milovan (1966), The New Class (London: Unwin Books).

Dunmore, Timothy (1980), 'Local party organs in industrial administration: the case of the ob"edinenie reform,' Soviet Studies, vol. XXXII, pp. 195–217.

Easton, David (1953), The Political System (New York: Knopf).

Easton, David (1965), A Systems Analysis of Political Life (New York: Wiley).

Epstein, Leon (1967), Political Parties in Western Democracies (New York: Praeger).

Evans, Alfred B., Jr. (1977), 'Developed socialism in Soviet ideology,' Soviet Studies, vol. XXIX, pp. 409–28.

Fainsod, Merle (1959), Smolensk under Soviet Rule (London: Macmillan).

Farrell, R. Barry (ed) (1970), Political Leadership in Eastern Europe and the Soviet Union (London: Butterworths).

Farukshin, M. Kh. (1973), Partiya v politicheskoi sisteme Sovetskogo obshchestva (protiv konseptsii sovremennogo antikommunizma) (Kazan: Izdatel'stvo Kazan'skogo Universiteta).

Fleron, Frederic J., Jr. (1970), 'Career types in the Soviet political leadership,' in Farrell (1970), pp. 108–39.

Frank, Peter (1971), 'The CPSU obkom first secretary: a profile,' British Journal of Political Science, vol. 1, pp. 173–90.

Frank Peter (1978), 'The changing composition of the Communist Party,' in Brown and Kaser (1978), pp. 96–120.

Frank, Peter (1982), 'What is the relationship between party and state in the USSR?' in Lewis et al. (1982), pp. 47–59.

Frank, Peter (1984), 'Political Succession in the Soviet Union: Building a Power Base' (Colchester: University of Essex, Russian and Soviet Studies Centre, Discussion Paper Series, no. 2).

Friedgut, Theodore H. (1979), Political Participation in the USSR (Princeton, N.J.: Princeton University Press).

Friedrich, Carl J., and Brzezinski, Zbigniew K. (1966), Totalitarian Dictatorship and Autocracy, 2nd ed (New York: Praeger).

Frolic, B. Michael (1972), 'Decision making in Soviet cities,' American Political Science Review, vol. LXVI, pp. 38–52.

Gehlen, Michael P. (1969), The Communist Party of the Soviet Union: A Functional Analysis (Bloomington, Ind., and London: Indiana University Press).

Gehlen, Michael P., and McBride, Michael (1968), 'The Soviet Central Committee: an elite analysis,' *American Political Science Review*, vol. LXII, pp. 1232–41.

Gilison, Jerome M. (1968), 'Soviet elections as a measure of dissent: the missing one percent,' *American Political Science Review*, vol. LXII, pp. 814–26.

Gill, Graeme (1980), 'The Soviet leader cult: reflections on the structure of leadership in the Soviet Union,' *British Journal of Political Science*, vol. 10, pp. 167–86.

Glezerman, G., and Iovchuk, M. (1978), 'Sovetskii obraz zhizni i formirovanie novogo cheloveka,' *Kommunist*, no. 4, pp. 119–25.

Gogichaishvili, M. A. (1969), *Partiinoe sobranie—shkola ideinogo vospitaniya kommunistov* (Moscow: Politizdat).

Golyshev, P. (1975), 'Odinnadtsatoe poruchenie,' *Partiinaya zhizn', no. 1, pp. 67–8.*

Gorbachëv, M. S. (1985a), 'O sozyve ocherednogo XXVII s''ezda KPSS i zadachakh, svyazannykh s ego podgotovkoi i provedeniem' (speech at CPSU Central Committee plenum, April 23, 1985), *Kommunist*, no. 7, pp. 4–20.

Gorbachëv, M. S. (1985b), 'Vystuplenie deputata M. S. Gorbachëva,' *Sovety narodnykh deputatov*, no. 8, pp 5–6.

Gorshenev, V. M., and Kozlov, B. Ye. (eds) (1976), *Zakon o statuse deputatov na praktike (Materialy nauchno-prakticheskoi konferentsii)* (Yaroslavl: Verkhne-Volzhskoe knizhnoe izdatel'stvo).

Gromyko, A. A. (1985), Speech at CPSU Central Committee plenum, March 11, 1985, *Kommunist*, no. 5, pp. 6–7.

Gustafson, Thane (1981), *Reform in Soviet Politics: Lessons of Recent Policies on Land and Water* (Cambridge: Cambridge University Press).

Hammer, Darrell P. (1971), 'The dilemma of party growth,' *Problems of Communism*, vol. XX, pp. 16–21.

Harasymiw, Bohdan (1969), *'Nomenklatura:* the Soviet Communist Party's leadership recruitment system,' *Canadian Journal of Political Science*, vol. 2, pp. 493–512.

Harasymiw, Bohdan (1971), 'The qualifications of local party and government leaders in the Soviet Union and the development of pluralism,' *Canadian Slavonic Papers*, vol. 13, pp. 314–42.

Harasymiw, Bohdan (1984), *Political Elite Recruitment in the Soviet Union* (London: Macmillan).

Harding, Neil (ed) (1984), *The State in Socialist Society* (London: Macmillan).

Hill, Ronald J. (1969), 'Participation in the Central Committee plenums in Moldavia,' *Soviet Studies*, vol. XXI, pp. 193–207.

Hill, Ronald J. (1973), 'Patterns of deputy selection to local soviets,' *Soviet Studies*, vol. XXV, pp. 196–212.

Hill, Ronald J. (1976), 'The CPSU in a Soviet election campaign,' *Soviet Studies*, vol. XXVIII, pp. 590–8.

Hill Ronald J. (1977), *Soviet Political Elites: The Case of Tiraspol* (London: Martin Robertson).

Hill, Ronald J. (1980a), *Soviet Politics, Political Science and Reform* (Oxford: Martin Robertson).

Hill, Ronald J. (1980b), 'Party-state relations and Soviet political development,' *British Journal of Political Science*, vol. 10, pp. 149-65.

Hill, Ronald J. (1980c), 'Party linkage in a communist one-party state: the case of the CPSU,' in Kay Lawson (ed), *Political Parties and Linkage: A Comparative Perspective* (New Haven, Conn.: Yale University Press), pp. 345-69.

Hoffmann, Erik P. (1978), 'Information processing in the party: recent theory and experience,' in Ryavec (1978), pp. 63-87.

Hoffmann, Erik P. (1980), 'Changing Soviet perspectives on leadership and administration,' in Cohen *et al.* (1980), pp. 71-92.

Hough, Jerry F. (1969), *The Soviet Prefects: The Local Party Organs in Industrial Decision-Making* (Cambridge, Mass.: Harvard University Press).

Hough, Jerry F. (1976), 'The Brezhnev era: the man and the system,' *Problems of Communism*, vol. XXV, no. 2, pp. 1-17.

Hough, Jerry F. (1977), *The Soviet Union and Social Science Theory* (Cambridge, Mass.: Harvard University Press).

Hough, Jerry F. (1979), 'The generation gap and the Brezhnev succession,' *Problems of Communism*, vol. XXVIII, no. 4, pp. 1-16.

Hough, Jerry F. (1980), *Soviet Leadership in Transition* (Washington, D.C.: The Brookings Institution).

Hough, Jerry F., and Fainsod, Merle (1979), *How the Soviet Union Is Governed* (Cambridge, Mass.: Harvard University Press).

Hulicka, Karel, and Hulicka, Irene M. (1967), *Soviet Institutions, the Individual and Society* (Boston, Mass.: Christopher Publishing House).

Jacobs, Everett M. (1970), 'Soviet local elections: what they are, and what they are not,' *Soviet Studies*, vol. XXII, pp. 61-76.

Jacobs, Everett M. (1972), 'The composition of local soviets, 1959-1969,' *Government and Opposition*, vol. 7, pp. 503-19.

Jacobs, Everett M. (1976), 'A note on Jewish membership of the Soviet Communist Party,' *Soviet Jewish Affairs*, vol. 6, pp. 114-15.

Jacobs, Everett M. (ed) (1983), *Soviet Local Politics and Government* (London: Allen & Unwin).

Kadeikin, V. A., *et al.* (eds) (1974), *Voprosy vnutripartiinoi zhizni i rukovod-yashchei deyatel'nosti KPSS na sovremennom etape* (Moscow: Mysl').

Kaiser, Robert G. (1977), *Russia: The People and the Power,* revised ed (Harmondsworth: Penguin).

Kanet, Roger E. (1968), 'The rise and fall of the All-People's State: recent changes in the Soviet theory of the state,' *Soviet Studies,* vol. XX, pp. 81-93.

Kassof, Allen (ed) (1968), *Prospects for Soviet Society* (London: Pall Mall).

Keep, J. L. H. (1963), *The Rise of Social Democracy in Russia* (Oxford: Clarendon Press).

Keizerov, N. M. (1983), *Politicheskaya i pravovaya kul'tura: metodologi-cheskie problemy* (Moscow: Yuridicheskaya literatura).

Keller, Suzanne (1968), 'Elites,' in David L. Sills (ed), *The International Encyclopedia of the Social Sciences*, Vol. 5 (New York: Macmillan and The Free Press), pp. 26-9.

Kelley, Donald R. (1978), 'Environmental problems as a new policy issue,' in Ryavec (1978), pp. 88-107.

Kerimov, D. A. (ed) (1979a), *Soviet Democracy in the Period of Developed Socialism* (Moscow: Progress).

Kerimov, D. A. (ed) (1979b), *Sovetskaya demokratiya v period razvitogo sotsializma*, 2nd ed. (Moscow: Mysl').

Khaldeev, M. I., *et al.* (compilers) (1975), *Pervichnaya partiinaya organizatsiya: opyt, formy i metody raboty* (Moscow: Politizdat).

Khaldeev, M. I., and Krivoshein, G. I. (eds) (1979), *Pervichnaya partiinaya organizatsiya: opyt, formy i metody raboty*, 2nd ed (Moscow: Politizdat).

Kharchev, A. G., *et al.* (eds) (1976), *Moral' razvitogo sotsializma (Aktual'nye problemy teorii)* (Moscow: Mysl').

Khrushchev, Nikita (1971), *Khrushchev Remembers* (London: Deutsch).

Kirchheimer, Otto (1966), 'The transformation of Western European party systems,' in Joseph La Palombara and Myron Weiner (eds), *Political Parties and Political Development* (Princeton, N.J.: Princeton University Press), pp. 177–97.

'K itogam otchëtov i vyborov' (1980), 'K itogam otchëtov i vyborov v partiinykh organizatsiyakh,' *Partiinaya zhizn'*, no. 3, pp. 24–8.

Kitrinos, Robert W. (1984), 'International Department of the CPSU,' *Problems of Communism*, vol. XXXIII, no. 5, pp. 47–67.

*Knizhka* (1974), *Knizhka partiinogo aktivista 1975* (Moscow: Politizdat).

Korolëv, A. M. (1967), *Partiya i Komsomol* (Moscow: Mysl').

*KPSS: Naglyadnoe posobie* (1973), *Kommunisticheskaya partiya Sovetskogo Soyuza: Naglyadnoe posobie po partiinomu stroitel'stvu* (Moscow: Politizdat).

*KPSS v rez.* (1971–8), *KPSS v rezolyutsiyakh i resheniyakh s''ezdov, konferentsii i Plenumov TsK*, 12 vols (Moscow: Politizdat); Vol. 7 (1971); Vol. 8 (1972); Vol. 9 (1972); Vol. 11 (1978).

'KPSS v tsifrakh' (1977), 'KPSS v tsifrakh (K 60-i godovshchine Velikoi Oktyabr'skoi Sotsialisticheskoi Revolyutsii),' *Partiinaya zhizn', no. 21, pp. 20–43*.

'KPSS v tsifrakh' (1981), 'KPSS v tsifrakh: nekotorye dannye o razvitii partii v period mezhdu XXV i XXVI s''ezdami KPSS,' *Partiinaya zhizn'*, no. 14, pp. 13–26.

'KPSS v tsifrakh' (1983), 'KPSS v tsifrakh (K 80-letiyu Vtorogo s''ezda RSDRP),' *Partiinaya zhizn'*, no. 15, pp. 14–32.

'KPSS v tsifrakh' (1986), 'KPSS v tsifrakh: nekotorye dannye o razvitii partii v period mezhdu XXVI i XXVII s''ezdami KPSS,' *Partiinaya zhizn'*, no. 14, pp. 19–32.

Kravchuk, S. S. (ed) (1967), *Gosudarstvennoe pravo SSSR* (Moscow: Yuridicheskaya literatura).

'Kto prikhodit' (1983), 'Kto prikhodit v partiyu,' *Pravda*, September 26, 1983.

Kuftyrev, A. I. (1981), *Politicheskaya organizatsiya sotsialisticheskogo obshchestva* (Moscow: Izd. Moskovskogo Universiteta).

Kulinchenko, B. A., *et al.* (eds) (1978), *Voprosy povysheniya urovnya partiinoi raboty na sovremennom etape* (Moscow: Mysl').

Lane, David (1976), *The Socialist Industrial State: Towards a Political Sociology of State Socialism* (London: Allen & Unwin).

Lane, David (1978), *Politics and Society in the USSR*, 2nd ed (London: Martin Robertson).

Lasswell, Harold D., and Lerner, Daniel (eds) (1965), *World Revolutionary Elites: Studies in Coercive Ideological Movements* (Cambridge, Mass.: MIT Press).

Lesnyi, V. M., and Chernogolovkin, N. V. (eds) (1976), *Politicheskaya organizatsiya razvitogo sotsialisticheskogo obshchestva: struktura i funktsii* (Moscow: Izdatel'stvo Moskovskogo Universiteta).

Levytsky, Borys (1970), *The Soviet Political Elite*, xeroxed manuscript distributed by the Hoover Institution on War, Revolution and Peace (Stanford, Calif.: Stanford University Press).

Lewin, Moshe (1985), *The Making of the Soviet System: Essays in the Social History of Interwar Russia* (London: Methuen).

Lewis, Paul G., Clifton, Robert A., and Frank, Peter (1982), *The Machinery of Rule*, prepared for the Open University 'Soviet Politics' course (Milton Keynes: The Open University Press).

Linden, Carl A. (1966), *Khrushchev and the Soviet Leadership, 1957–1964* (Baltimore, Md.: Johns Hopkins University Press).

Löwenhardt, John (1982), *The Soviet Politburo* (Edinburgh: Canongate).

Luk'yanov, A. (1980), 'Zhiznennost' idei Lenina o Sovetakh,' *Kommunist*, no. 1, pp. 28–40.

Lyaporov, N. D. (compiler) (1979), *Sputnik partgruporga 1980* (Moscow: Politizdat).

Makarov, V. (1980), 'Proshli mimo prostupka kommunista,' *Partiinaya zhizn'*, no. 3, p. 77.

Manyakin, S. (1985), 'Ustav KPSS—zakon partiinoi zhizni,' *Partiinaya zhizn'*, no. 24, pp. 42–6.

Marchenko, M. N. (1973), *Politicheskaya organizatsiya Sovetskogo obshchestva i eë burzhuaznye fal'sifikatory* (Moscow: Izdatel'stvo Moskovskogo Universiteta).

Matthews, Mervyn (1972), *Class and Society in Soviet Russia* (London: Allen Lane/The Penguin Press).

Matthews, Mervyn (1978), *Privilege in the Soviet Union: A Study of Elite Life-Styles under Communism* (London: Allen & Unwin).

McAuley, Mary (1969), *Labour Disputes in Soviet Russia, 1957–1965* (London: Oxford University Press).

McAuley, Mary (1977) *Politics and the Soviet Union* (Harmondsworth: Penguin).

McAuley, Mary (1980), 'Party recruitment and the nationalities in the USSR: a study in centre-republican relationships,' *British Journal of Political Science*, vol. 10, pp. 461–87.

Medvedev, Roy A. (1975), *On Socialist Democracy* (London: Macmillan).

Merkl, Peter H. (1970), *Modern Comparative Politics* (New York: Holt, Rinehart & Winston).

Miller, J. D. B. (1965), *The Nature of Politics* (Harmondsworth: Penguin).

Miller, John H. (1977), 'Cadres policy in nationality areas: recruitment of first and second secretaries in non-Russian republics of the USSR,' *Soviet Studies*, vol. XXIX, pp. 3–36.

Miller, John H. (1982), 'The communist party: trends and problems,' in Brown and Kaser (1982), pp. 1–34.

Mills, Richard M. (1981), 'The Soviet leadership problem,' *World Politics*, vol. XXXIII, no. 4, pp. 590–613.

'Mnenie kommunista' (1980), *Pravda,* May 21, p. 1.

Moses, Joel C. (1981), 'The impact of *nomenklatura* in Soviet regional elite recruitment', *Soviet Union/Union Soviétique*, vol. 8, part 1, pp. 62–102.

'Mozhno li . . .' (1978), 'Mozhno li bespartiinogo izbrat' v sostav komissii po vyrabotke proekta resheniya otkrytogo partsobraniya?' *Partiinaya zhizn'*, no. 13, pp. 77–8.

Nagy, Charles J. (1981), *Political Parties and System Flexibility* (Washington, D.C.: University Press of America).

Naida, S. F., *et al.* (eds) (1967), *Sovety za 50 let* (Moscow: Mysl').

'Nekotorye dannye' (1982), 'Nekotorye dannye po rostu partiinykh ryadov i seti partiinykh organizatsii (na 1 yanvarya 1982 goda),' *Partiinaya zhizn'*, no. 10, pp. 36–7.

Nove, Alec (1975), 'Is there a ruling class in the USSR?' *Soviet Studies*, vol. XXVII, pp. 615–38.

Nove, Alec (1977), *The Soviet Economic System* (London: Allen & Unwin).

Nove, Alec (1983), 'The class nature of the USSR revisited,' *Soviet Studies*, vol. XXXV, no. 3, pp. 298–312.

Obolonsky, Alexander (1979), 'The public employee as an object of socio-psychological analysis,' in Semyonov *et al.* (1979), pp. 207–14.

'Ob otkrytom partiinom sobranii' (1980), *Partiinaya zhizn'*, no. 4, p. 66.

O'Dell, Felicity Ann (1978), *Socialisation through Children's Literature: The Soviet Example* (Cambridge: Cambridge University Press).

*Organizatsionno-partiinaya rabota* (1974), *Organizatsionno-partiinaya rabota: Problemy i opyt* (Moscow: Moskovskii rabochii).

*Organizatsionno-ustavnye voprosy* (1973, 1978), *Organizatsionno-ustavnye voprosy KPSS: spravochnik v voprosakh i otvetakh* (Moscow: Politizdat).

Osborn, Robert J. (1974), *The Evolution of Soviet Politics* (Homewood, Ill.: Dorsey Press).

Paputin, V. (1970), 'Partiinoe rukovodstvo Sovetami,' in *Sovershenstvovat' rabotu Sovetov deputatov trudyashchikhsya* (Moscow: Izvestiya), pp. 202–18.

Parry, Geraint (1969), *Political Elites* (London: Allen & Unwin).

*Partgruporg* (1968), *Partgruporg: Zapisnaya knizhka 1969* (Moscow: Politizdat).

*Partiinaya organizatsiya v usloviyakh proizvodstvennogo ob"edineniya (po materialam Vsesoyuznogo seminara sekretarei partiinykh organizatsii promyshlennykh predpriyatii, Gorkii, aprel' 1977 g.)* (1977) (Moscow: Politizdat).

*Partiinaya zhizn'* (1980), no. 7.

'Partiinoe rukovodstvo pressoi' (1979), *Pravda,* June 12, p. 1.

'Partiinye komitety i pis'ma trudyashchikhsya' (1975), *Moskovskaya pravda,* June 11, p. 1.

Paskar', P. N. (1974), *Sovety deputatov trudyashchikhsya v sisteme politicheskoi organizatsii obshchestva (na materialakh Moldavskoi SSR)* (Kishinev: Shtiintsa).

Paskar', P. N., *et al.* (eds) (1977), *Sotsial'no-klassovaya i politicheskaya struktura sotsialisticheskogo obshchestva (voprosy nauchnogo kommunizma)* (Kishinev: Shtiintsa).

Perry, Jack (1973), 'The USSR and the environment,' *Problems of Communism*, vol. XXII, no. 3, pp. 52–4.

Petrenko, F. F., and Shapko, B. M. (1977), *Partiinoe stroitel'stvo na sovremennom etape* (Moscow: Mysl').

Petrovichev, N. A. (1979), *Vazhnyi faktor vozrastaniya rukovodyashchei roli KPSS* (Moscow: Politizdat).

Petrovichev, N. A., *et al.* (1972), *Partiinoe stroitel'stvo: uchebnoe posobie,* 3rd ed (Moscow: Politizdat).

Poladich, P. (1978), 'Kak byli vosprinyaty kriticheskie zamechaniya,' *Partiinaya zhizn'*, no. 11, p. 68.

Ponomarëv, B. N. (1979a), 'Real'nyi sotsializm i ego mezhdunarodnoe znachenie,' *Kommunist*, no. 2, pp. 17–36.

Ponomarëv, B. N. (1979b), *Existing Socialism and Its International Significance*, translation of Ponomarëv (1979a) (Moscow: Novosti).

*Pravda*, November 28, 1979 (report of CPSU Central Committee plenum); December 1, 1979 (report of USSR Supreme Soviet session); March 10, 1980 (reports of Party Control Committee investigations).

*Pravda*, May 19, 1982 (speech by B. N. Pastukhov at Nineteenth Komsomol Congress).

Pravdin, A. (1974), 'Inside the CPSU Central Committee (an interview with Mervyn Matthews),' *Survey*, vol. 20, no. 4, pp. 94–104.

*Programme* (1961), *Programma KPSS* (CPSU Program, adopted at XXII CPSU Congress, 1961): repr. in *KPSS v rez.*, Vol. 8, pp. 196–305.

Pye, Lucian W. (1966), *Aspects of Political Development* (Boston, Mass.: Little, Brown).

*Raionnyi komitet partii* (1974), 2nd ed (Moscow: Politizdat).

Razumov, Ye. Z. (1983), *Problemy kadrovoi politiki KPSS* (Moscow: Politizdat).

Reshetar, John S., Jr. (1972), *The Soviet Polity: Government and Politics in the USSR* (New York: Dodd, Mead).

Reutskii, I., and Yevdokimov, D. (1974), *Informatsiya—instrument partiinogo rukovodstva* (Moscow: Moskovskii rabochii).

Rigby, T. H. (1968), *Communist Party Membership in the USSR, 1917–1967* (Princeton, N.J.: Princeton University Press).

Rigby, T. H. (1970), 'The Soviet leadership: towards a self-stabilizing oligarchy?' *Soviet Studies*, vol. XXII, pp. 167–91.

Rigby, T. H. (1976), 'Soviet Communist Party membership under Brezhnev,' *Soviet Studies*, vol. XXVIII, pp. 317–37.

Rigby, T. H. (1977), 'Soviet Communist Party membership under Brezhnev: a rejoinder,' *Soviet Studies*, vol. XXIX, pp. 452–3.

Rigby, T. H. (1980), 'A conceptual approach to authority, power and policy in the Soviet Union,' in Rigby *et al.* (1980), pp. 9–31.

Rigby, T. H. (1985), 'The CPSU from Stalin to Cernenko: Membership and Leadership,' in Georg Brunner *et al.* (eds), *Sowjetsystem und Ostrecht: Festschrift für Boris Meissner zum 70. Geburtstag* (Berlin: Duncher & Humblot), pp. 143–58.

Rigby, T. H., Brown, Archie, and Reddaway, Peter (1980), *Authority, Power and Policy in the USSR: Essays dedicated to Leonard Schapiro* (London: Macmillan).

Rodionov, P. A. (1967), *Kollektivnost'—vysshii printsip partiinogo rukovodstva* (Moscow: Politizdat).

*Rules* (1977), *Rules of the Communist Party of the Soviet Union* (Moscow: Progress).

Rush, Myron (1968), *Political Succession in the USSR*, 2nd ed (New York: Columbia University Press).

Ryavec, Karl W. (ed) (1978), *Soviet Society and the Communist Party* (Amherst: University of Massachusetts Press).

Safarov, R. A. (1975), *Obshchestvennoe mnenie i gosudarstvennoe upravlenie* (Moscow: Yuridicheskaya literatura).

Samolis, T. (1986), 'Ochishchenie: otkrovennyi razgovor,' *Pravda*, February 13.

Sartori, Giovanni (1976), *Parties and Party Systems: A Framework for Analysis* (Cambridge: Cambridge University Press).

Schapiro, Leonard (1961), 'The party and the state,' *Survey*, no. 38, pp. 111–16.

Schapiro, Leonard (ed) (1963), *The USSR and the Future: An Analysis of the New Program of the CPSU* (New York: Praeger).

Schapiro, Leonard (1970), *The Communist Party of the Soviet Union*, 2nd ed (London: Methuen).

Schapiro, Leonard (1971), 'Keynote—compromise,' *Problems of Communism*, vol. XX, no. 4, pp. 2–8.

Scott, Derek J. R. (1969), *Russian Political Institutions*, 4th ed (London: Allen & Unwin).

Semyonov, V., *et al.* (eds) (1979), *Political Theory and Political Practice* (Moscow: 'Social Sciences Today' Editorial Board, USSR Academy of Sciences).

Shabanov, Yu. V. (1969a), *Problemy Sovetskoi sotsialisticheskoi demokratii v period stroitel'stva kommunizma* (Minsk: Nauka i tekhnika).

Shabanov, Yu. V. (1969b), *Partiinoe rukovodstvo Sovetami deputatov trudyashchikhsya* (Minsk: Belarus').

Shakhnazarov, G. Kh. (1972), *Sotsialisticheskaya demokratiya: nekotorye voprosy teorii* (Moscow: Politizdat).

Shakhnazarov, Georgi (1974), *The Role of the Communist Party in Socialist Society* (Moscow: Novosti).

Shapko, V. M., *et al.* (eds) (1977), *KPSS—rukovodyashchee yadro politicheskoi sistemy sovetskogo obshchestva* (Moscow: Mysl').

Shapko, V. M., *et al.* (eds) (1979), *Voprosy vnutripartiinoi zhizni i rukovodyashchei deyatel'nosti KPSS na sovremennom etape*, 2nd ed (Moscow: Mysl').

Sherrill, Kenneth S. (1969), 'The attitudes of modernity,' *Comparative Politics*, vol. 1, pp. 184–210.

Shevchenko, Arkady N. (1985), *Breaking with Moscow* (London: Cape).

Shevtsov, V. S. (1978), *The CPSU and the Soviet State in Developed Socialist Society* (Moscow: Progress).

Shumakov, A. V., and Zudin, V. V. (eds) (1973), *Knizhka partiinogo aktivista 1974* (Moscow: Politizdat).

Smirnov, S. A., *et al.* (eds) (1973), *Khrestomatie po partiinomu stroitel'stvu* 2nd ed (Moscow: Politizdat).

Smith, Hedrick (1976), *The Russians* (London: Time Books).

Solomon, Susan Gross (ed) (1983), *Pluralism in the Soviet Union: Essays in honour of H. Gordon Skilling* (London: Macmillan).

'Soobshchenie' (1985), 'Soobshchenie ob itogakh vyborov v Verkhovnye Sovety soyuznykh, avtonomnykh respublik i v mestnye Sovety narodnykh deputatov,' *Sovety narodnykh deputatov*, no. 4, pp. 28-32.

Sorlin, Pierre (1969), *The Soviet People and Their Society: From 1917 to the Present* (New York: Praeger).

*Spravochnik sekretarya* (1967), *Spravochnik sekretarya pervichnoi partiinoi organizatsii*, 2nd ed (Moscow: Politizdat).

Stepanyan, Ts. A., and Frish, A. S. (eds) (1979), *Razvitoi sotsializm i aktual'nye problemy nauchnogo kommunizma* (Moscow: Nauka).

Stepanyan, Ts. A., *et al.* (eds) (1968), *Klassy, sotsial'nye sloi i gruppy v SSSR* (Moscow: Nauka).

Stewart, Philip D. (1968), *Political Power in the Soviet Union: A Study of Decision-Making in Stalingrad* (Indianapolis, Ind., and New York: Bobbs-Merrill).

Strashun, B. A. (1973), 'Razvitie izbiratel'nogo prava sotsialisticheskikh stran,' *Sovetskoe gosudarstvo i pravo*, no. 7, pp. 42-9.

Strashun, B. A. (1976), *Sotsializm i demokratiya (sotsialisticheskoe narodnoe predstavitel'stvo)* (Moscow: Mezhdunarodnye otnosheniya).

Suslov, M. A. (1977), *Na putyakh stroitel'stva kommunizma: rechi i stat'i*, vol. 2 (Moscow: Politizdat).

Taagepera, Rein, and Chapman, Robert Dale (1977), 'A note on the ageing of the Politburo,' *Soviet Studies*, vol. XXIX, pp. 296-305.

Tarschys, Daniel (1979), *The Soviet Political Agenda: Problems and Priorities, 1950-1970* (London: Macmillan).

Taubman, William (1973), *Governing Soviet Cities: Bureaucratic Politics and Urban Development in the USSR* (New York: Praeger).

Tikhomirov, Yu. A. (ed) (1975), *Demokratiya razvitogo sotsialisticheskogo obshchestva* (Moscow: Nauka).

Tikhomirov, Yu. A. (ed) (1978), *Sovetskoe gosudarstvo v usloviyakh razvitogo sotsialisticheskogo obshchestva* (Moscow: Nauka).

Tikhomirov, Yu. A., and Chirkin, V. Ye. (eds) (1985), *Osnovy teorii politicheskoi sistemy* (Moscow: Nauka).

Topornin, B. N. (1975), *Sovetskaya politicheskaya sistema* (Moscow: Politizdat).

Trotsky, Leon (1967), *The Revolution Betrayed: What Is the Soviet Union and Where Is It Going?* (London: New Park Publications).

Truman, David (1951), *The Governmental Process* (New York: Knopf).

Tucker, Robert C. (1973), 'Culture, political culture, and communist society,' *Political Science Quarterly*, vol. 88, pp. 173-90.

Turishchev, Yu. G. (1975), *KPSS—zhivoi, razvivayushchiisya politicheskii organizm* (Moscow: Politizdat).

Ukrainets, P. P. (1976), *Partiinoe rukovodstvo i gosudarstvennoe upravlenie* (Minsk: Belarus').

Unger, Aryeh, L. (1977), 'Soviet Communist Party Membership under Brezhnev: a comment,' *Soviet Studies*, vol. XXIX, pp. 306–16.

*Ustav VLKSM* (1985), *Ustav Vsesoyuznogo Leninskogo Kommunisticheskogo Soyuza Molodëzhi*, adopted by the Fourteenth Congress, with amendments adopted by the XV, XVII, XVIII, and XIX Congresses (Moscow: Molodaya Gvardiya).

Utenkov, A. Ya., *et al.* (eds), *Vnutripartiinaya demokratiya i povyshenie aktivnosti kommunistov* (Moscow: Mysl').

Veselov, N. (1973), *The Communist Party and Mass Organisations in the USSR* (Moscow: Novosti).

Vinogradov, N. N. (1980), *Partiinoe rukovodstvo Sovetami v usloviyakh razvitogo sotsializma* (Moscow: Mysl').

Vlasov, V. I. (1967), *Partiinoe rukovodstvo pechat'yu* (Moscow: Mysl').

Volkov, Genrikh (1985), 'The Party's Theoretical Banner,' *Moscow News*, no. 44 (November 3), pp. 3, 12.

Voronovskii, N. A. (1967), *Leninskie printsipy podbora, rasstanovki i vospitaniya kadrov* (Moscow: Mysl').

Voslensky, Michael (1984), *Nomenklatura: Anatomy of the Soviet Ruling Class* (London: Bodley Head).

'V Tsentral'nom Komitete KPSS' (1979), *Pravda*, May 6, p. 1.

'Vybornyi aktiv' (1980), *Pravda*, May 24, p. 1.

'Vysokoe zvanie' (1976), 'Vysokoe zvanie kommunista,' *Pravda*, February 17, p. 1.

Waller, Michael (1981), *Democratic Centralism: An Historical Commentary* (Manchester: Manchester University Press).

White, Stephen (1977), 'Political socialization in the USSR: a study in failure?' *Studies in Comparative Communism*, vol. X, pp. 328–42.

White, Stephen (1978), 'Communist systems and the "iron law of pluralism,"' *British Journal of Political Science*, vol. 8, pp. 101–17.

White, Stephen (1979), *Political Culture and Soviet Politics* (London: Macmillan).

White, Stephen (1985a), 'Propagating Communist Values in the USSR,' *Problems of Communism*, vol. XXXIV, no. 6, pp. 1–17.

White, Stephen (1985b), 'Non-competitive elections and national politics: the USSR Supreme Soviet Elections of 1984,' *Electoral Studies*, vol. 4, no. 3, pp. 215–29.

Wiatr, Jerzy J. (1970), 'Political Parties, Interest Representation and Economic Development in Poland,' *American Political Science Review*, vol. LXIV, pp. 1239–45.

Wiatr, Jerzy (1982), 'To make agreement real—the Party must renounce the monopoly of power . . .,' translated in *Communist Affairs*, vol 1, no. 3, pp. 679–88.

Wolfe, Bertram D. (1966), *Three Who Made a Revolution* (Harmondsworth: Penguin).

Wolfe, Bertram D. (1969), *An Ideology in Power: Reflections on the Russian Revolution* (London: Allen & Unwin).

*XXII s"ezd Kommunisticheskoi partii Sovetskogo Soyuza: Stenograficheskii otchët* (1962), 2 vols (Moscow: Politizdat).

*XXIII s''ezd Kommunisticheskoi partii Sovetskogo Soyuza: Stenograficheskii otchët,* (1966) 2 vols (Moscow: Politizdat).

*XXIV s''ezd Kommunisticheskoi partii Sovetskogo Soyuza: Stenograficheskii otchët* (1971), 2 vols (Moscow: Politizdat).

*XXV s''ezd Kommunisticheskoi partii Sovetskogo Soyuza: Stenograficheskii otchët* (1976), 3 vols (Moscow: Politizdat).

*XXVI s''ezd Kommunisticheskoi partii Sovetskogo Soyuza: Stenograficheskii otchët* (1981), 3 vols (Moscow: Politizdat).

*Yezhegodnik* (1978), *Yezhegodnik Bol'shoi Sovetskoi Entsiklopedii, 1978* (Moscow: Sovetskaya entsiklopediya).

Yudenkov, A. F., *et al.* (eds) (1979), *Rukovodyashchaya rol' KPSS v usloviyakh razvitogo sotsializma* (Moscow: Mysl').

Yudin, I. N. (1973), *Sotsial'naya baza rosta KPSS* (Moscow: Politizdat).

Yudin, I. N., *et al.* (1973), *Nekotorye voprosy organizatsionno-partiinoi raboty* (Moscow: Politizdat).

Yudin, I. N., *et al.* (1975), *Internatsional'nyi printsip v stroitel'stve i deyatel'nosti KPSS* (Moscow: Politizdat).

Zabulis, G. (1980), 'Otbor i vybor,' *Pravda*, January 5, p. 3.

# Index

173